ADMINISTERING SPECIAL EDUCATION: IN PURSUIT OF DIGNITY AND AUTONOMY

ADVANCES IN EDUCATIONAL ADMINISTRATION

Series Editor: Richard C. Hunter

Volume 1–5:   Series Editor Paul W. Thurston
Volume 6:   Series Editor Richard C. Hunter

ADVANCES IN EDUCATIONAL ADMINISTRATION
VOLUME 7

ADMINISTERING SPECIAL EDUCATION: IN PURSUIT OF DIGNITY AND AUTONOMY

EDITED BY

KERN ALEXANDER

College of Education, University of Illinois at Urbana-Champaign, USA

RICHARD C. HUNTER

College of Education, University of Illinois at Urbana-Champaign, USA

2004

ELSEVIER
JAI

Amsterdam – Boston – Heidelberg – London – New York – Oxford
Paris – San Diego – San Francisco – Singapore – Sydney – Tokyo

ELSEVIER B.V.	ELSEVIER Inc.	**ELSEVIER Ltd**	ELSEVIER Ltd
Radarweg 29	525 B Street, Suite 1900	**The Boulevard, Langford**	84 Theobalds Road
P.O. Box 211	San Diego	**Lane, Kidlington**	London
1000 AE Amsterdam	CA 92101-4495	**Oxford OX5 1GB**	WC1X 8RR
The Netherlands	USA	**UK**	UK

First edition 2004

British Library Cataloguing in Publication Data
A catalogue record is available from the British Library.

ISBN: 0-7623-1145-2
ISSN: 1479-3660 (Series)

⊗ The paper used in this publication meets the requirements of ANSI/NISO Z39.48-1992 (Permanence of Paper).
Printed in The Netherlands.

Working together to grow
libraries in developing countries

www.elsevier.com | www.bookaid.org | www.sabre.org

CONTENTS

LIST OF CONTRIBUTORS

Kern Alexander	Educational Organization & Leadership, Champaign, IL, USA
Warren J. Blumenfeld	Department of Curriculum and Instruction, Iowa State University, Ames, IA, USA
Bettie Posey Bullard	Department of Special Education, University of South Alabama, Mobile, AL, USA
Richard England	Freed-Hardeman University, Henderson, TN, USA
Moira A. Fallon	Department of Education and Human Development, State University of New York College at Brockport, Brockport, NY, USA
Wendy A. Harriott	School of Education, Monmouth University, West Long Branch, NJ, USA
Verle Headings	Department of Pediatrics & Child Health, Division of Medical Genetics, Howard University, College of Medicine, Washington, DC, USA
Richard C. Hunter	Educational Organization & Leadership, Champaign, IL, USA
K. G. Jan Pillai	School of Law, Temple University, Pennsylvania, Philadelphia, PA, USA
Karen Rabren	Auburn Transition Leadership Institute, Rehabilitation & Special Education Department, College of Education, Auburn University, Alabama, USA
Donna Power Rogers	Department of Special Education, University of South Alabama, Mobile AL, USA

Andrea L. Rotzien   Psychology Department, Grand Valley State University, Allendale, MI, USA

George H. S. Singer   Department of Education. University of California at Santa Barbara, Santa Barbara, CA, USA

PREFACE

Public school educators are confronted daily with myriad issues that demand unique knowledge of not only educational processes, but of political and financial ones as well. Among the most important of these issues are the social and moral responsibilities to educate children with disabilities. During the late 1960s and 1970s, the nation experienced a new sensitivity to human rights as well as an increased awareness of the indignities suffered as a result of discrimination and the denial of rights of persons with disabilities. Of late, the mood of the people and the national leadership has appeared to turn somewhat away from the abiding interest in human rights; nonetheless, the recognition of rights continues, as they have emanated from federal Constitutional interpretations and statutes. Both sources of rights constitute a persistent reflection of civil and cultural advancements of significant proportions. Thus, rights have become vested by action of government, and the public schools have been, in large part, the vehicle for ensuring the realization of these rights. School administrators, by virtue of their public responsibilities, have been the advance guard in effectively achieving and implementing these rights. Children with disabilities have posed a particular educational challenge because remediation of disabilities was intensely personal and many times unique to the individual child. Thus, of necessity, the educational responses and procedures were correspondingly singular and in most cases very complex, requiring a substantial commitment of public school financial resources. It goes without saying that the right to an appropriate education remains a hollow promise without provision of adequate and continuing public support.

Beyond the necessity of the state to recognize and finance rights for individual freedoms and liberties, there also issues forth the less visible but equally important professional education process to efficiently provide the required appropriate education. This responsibility requires not only the well-trained professional eye to identify the disabilities of children, but also the ability to know and understand what educational measures are best applied to remediate the situation.

This book seeks to provide some insight for the assistance of public school administrators who work daily with children with disabilities. Chapters contained herein deal with issues pertaining to the identification of disabilities, the public obligation to provide the education necessary to honor the rights of children with disabilities, and the educational strategies needed to respond to individual needs.

We are much indebted to the authors who have contributed to this volume and we are further indebted to them for their assistance in and understanding of the long process to publication. We are most appreciative of the good work of Bruce Roberts of Elsevier, in the United Kingdom, who was helpful beyond measure throughout the entire project.

Kern Alexander
Richard C. Hunter
Editors

INTRODUCTION AND OUTLINE OF THE BOOK

Since November 29, 1975, when President Gerald Ford signed the original bill entitled the Education for All Handicapped Children Act (EAHCA), school services for disabled children have been a major component of public school administration in America. The ethical awareness and the legal complexities engendered by this legislation have required school superintendents nationwide to develop expertise, provide leadership, and wrestle with budgetary issues in accommodating and providing equal opportunity for these children. Subsequent amendments to the federal legislation, coupled with state initiatives expanding opportunity, have created an endless array of conditions requiring pervasive knowledge of special education and sharply honed administrative skills. In particular, the 1997 amendments to the IDEA expanded the law beyond merely requiring access; it furthered an emphasis on outcomes and educational performance, and helped clarify the concept of inclusion.

This book encompasses several of the critical issues that face school administrators in implementing programs for children with disabilities, including discussions of social discrimination and disabilities, disproportionate discriminatory effects on African American children and other minorities, appropriate assessments of disabilities, use of diagnostic data, disabilities in transition, provision of inclusion in general classrooms, outcome-altering interventions, and defensible methods assessment and evaluation.

The Chapters are as follows:

Chapter 1 *Rights Compromised: Special Education, Costs, and Residual Funding*, by Kern Alexander, Professor, University of Illinois at Urbana-Champaign, who served on one of the original implementation task forces of the Education of All Handicapped Children Act (EAHCA) for the U.S. Office of Education, and Richard C. Hunter, Professor, University of Illinois, Urbana-Champaign, Illinois, formerly an urban school superintendent in Richmond, Virginia and Baltimore, Maryland. This chapter describes the problem of the lack of adequate funding and the inherent restraints that affect the lives of children with disabilities.

Chapter 2 *Equal Protection, Disabilities, and other Forms of Discrimination*, by K. G. Jan Pillai, I. Herman Stern Professor of Law, School of Law, Temple

University, Pennsylvania. This chapter sets the context of the discussion of disability and school administration and discusses the limitations of the Equal Protection Clause and the necessity for the Americans with Disabilities Act (ADA). Parallel issues in context of redress of other social discrimination in school segregation are set forth and related to equal access for children with disabilities.

Chapter 3 *Disproportionality of African Americans in Special Education Programs: A Form of Resegregation*, by Warren J. Blumenfeld, Assistant Professor, Department of Curriculum and Instruction, Iowa State University, Ames, Iowa. This chapter presents and explains school administrators' dilemma in meeting the needs of children in special education while guarding against categorizations that would resegregate the school along racial lines. The discussion covers recent studies that have shown that African American children may be misidentified as disabled and set aside in special and different instructional arrangements.

Chapter 4 *Youth With Disabilities in Transition: Strategies for Positive Change*, by Karen Rabren, Associate Professor, Auburn University, Alabama. The 1997 amendments to the EAHCA require school districts and states to document outcomes and provide assessments of progress for students with disabilities. Moreover, the legislation requires that schools provide evidence of positive transition of students with disabilities into employment and other post-school environments. This chapter pursues those issues and suggests strategies that can be used by school administrators to effectuate such transition.

Chapter 5 *Rethinking the Assessment of Maladaptive Behavior*, by Richard England, Associate Professor of Special Education, Freed-Hardeman University, Tennessee. An essential aspect in the determination of need for special education is the early and proper assessment of maladaptive behavior of children. The degree to which individuals will ultimately be able to function and maintain themselves independently in society is an essential concern of educators. Learning disabilities may not be readily discernable to parents and even to disability education specialists. This chapter discusses this important and difficult aspect of assessment and identification.

Chapter 6 *Risk Screening Strategies for Protecting the Well-Being of the Child*, by Verle Headings, Professor, Department of Pediatrics & Child Health Division of Medical Genetics, Howard University College of Medicine, Washington, D.C. At critical junctures in child assessment and evaluation, professional educators must rely on the medical profession for at-risk effects, even as early as prenatal causation. Screening strategies that identify prenatal exposures which can result in disabilities is a concern of both educators and physicians. This chapter discusses applications of risk screening that can permit more timely interventions for the most vulnerable children.

Chapter 7 *Inclusion of Children with Disabilities in General Education Classrooms*, by Wendy A. Harriott, Assistant Professor, Monmouth University, New Jersey. Inclusion or mainstreaming of children with disabilities is one of the most contentious and perplexing issues confronting school superintendents and special education specialists. A considered and balanced view of what constitutes an appropriate, least restrictive environment is essential to properly addressing the needs of children with disabilities, as is, of course, accommodation and adherence to legal requirements. This chapter provides guidance in this important realm for school administrators.

Chapter 8 *International Attitudes Toward Children with Disabilities: Identifying Risk Factors for Maltreatment*, by Andrea L. Rotzien, Assistant Professor, Grand Valley State University, Michigan. In order to better understand the educational necessities of public and private schools for children with disabilities, school leaders must be sensitive to the societal attitudes that shape institutional responses. This chapter reviews literature from several countries, including the United States, and describes cultural mores and societal practices that affect children with disabilities. From this broad perspective, informative observations and conclusions are drawn regarding addressing the educational needs of children with disabilities.

Chapter 9 *A Meta-Analysis of Comparative Studies of Depressive Symptoms in Mothers of Children with and Without Disabilities*, by George H. S. Singer, Professor, University of California at Santa Barbara. The ability of school administrators to deal with issues concerning special education can be greatly enhanced if they understand the dilemma borne by parents of children with disabilities. This chapter provides a unique approach, giving school leaders insights into the effects of children with disabilities upon their parents, the emotional stress that often results, and the implicit impact that can be visited upon the parent-school relationship.

Chapter 10 *Teacher-Observed Behaviors of Post-Traumatic Stress Symptoms of Students in General, Gifted, and Special Education*, by Bettie Posey Bullard, Assistant Professor and Director of the Gifted Program, University of South Alabama and Donna Power Rogers, Undergraduate Program Coordinator, University of South Alabama. Shocking incidences such those occurring in Colombine, Paducah, and of course, New York on September 11 undoubtedly have marked effects on everyone, but may be most deleterious to sensitive youth of school age. School administrators, teachers and guidance counselors, by virtue of their *in loco parentis* responsibilities, must respond when school children are affected. This chapter seeks to provide useful information gained from research after September 11 that may better inform educators about post-traumatic syndrome.

Chapter 11 *Preparing Inclusive Special Educators: Policy Implications for Partnerships Among Public Schools, Colleges and Universities*, by Moira A. Fallon, Associate Professor, State University of New York, College at Brockport, New York. The field of special education is facing a critical shortage of qualified and certified educators who are prepared to teach all learners. In order to meet these ever increasing demands of standards based education, K-12 public schools, colleges, and universities must collectively examine the changing context of teacher recruitment, preparation, and retention. The purpose of this chapter is to review the research literature on the recruitment, retention, and recognition of high quality inclusive educators. From this review, the implications are drawn for new policy development that will improve the outcomes for all learners.

1. RIGHTS COMPROMISED: SPECIAL EDUCATION, COSTS AND RESIDUAL FUNDING

Kern Alexander and Richard C. Hunter[*]

INTRODUCTION

In the United States, a child with a disability is vested with the statutory right to a free appropriate public education. Public school districts fulfill this right with an individualized education program designed to address the educational needs of the child. As with all governmental programs designed to extend positive benefits, statutory rights to a free appropriate public education come with attendant and commensurate costs that must be paid by the taxpayer. Rights have costs, and while the rights may be absolute, the remedy to a rights deficiency is subject to political processes. To borrow from Ronald Dworkin's famous aphorism, costs and politics ultimately trump the right to a free appropriate public education.

PUBLIC SCHOOLS AND INDIVIDUAL AUTONOMY

In all societies, persons with disabilities have suffered from prejudice and exclusion. Such discrimination is so endemic to most societies and cultures in private interactions, that the device of government must be employed to remedy

*Kern Alexander and Richard C. Hunter are Professors of Educational Administration at the University of Illinois, Urbana-Champaign.

Administering Special Education: In Pursuit of Dignity and Autonomy
Advances in Educational Administration, Volume 7, 1–12
Copyright © 2004 by Elsevier Ltd.
All rights of reproduction in any form reserved
ISSN: 1479-3660/doi:10.1016/S1479-3660(04)07001-5

and repair the wrongs visited upon persons with disabilities. Indeed, it is the mark of a more advanced society where the government, through its various mechanisms, acts to affirmatively remove the barriers erected by private insensitivity and discrimination. The public schools are foremost among these mechanisms of government that have been responsive to the needs of persons with disabilities.

It is the public school, therefore, that is the principle instrument in American society whose purpose it is to vest the individual with the capacity to, as fully as possible, obtain autonomy and acquire freedom of thought and action. Public schools are a necessary counterweight against the inevitable restraints and limitations that individuals, by either omission or commission, place upon each other if left to their own volition and devices. Public schools, by virtue of their communal nature, have a normative structure that provides common ground for toleration and mutual respect. In such a setting, children are part of a plural community that more readily lends itself to fostering their autonomy, whether or not they have disabilities.

Education gives children with disabilities a chance to acquire independence and autonomy. Autonomy of the individual has two aspects. The *first* is the right of liberty from governmental restraint. *Liberty* is a cardinal right; a natural right that can be conceived of as a "negative right," as government "shall not" deny a liberty right without a compelling reason. It is this aspect of fundamental rights that the U.S. Supreme Court has enforced through numerous decisions having to do with education, most of which find textual basis in the First Amendment's religion, speech and assembly provisions; the Fourth Amendment's search and seizure restraints; the Fifth Amendment's mandate that no person shall be deprived of life, liberty or property without due process of law; and the Fourteenth Amendment's Equal Protection and Due Process Clauses, that have been instrumental in the protection of fundamental rights. All of these impact education policy. All children, including those with disabilities, are entitled to constitutional protection of their liberties and freedoms, which bestow autonomy on each individual.

The *second* aspect of autonomy is what has become known as *dignity* rights (Alexander & Alexander, 2005, p. 87). Dignity, or the right to be respected by others regardless of disability, is of basic human interest and worth. The right of dignity is usually thought to include personal security, work and means of earning a reasonable wage – an adequate standard of living, including shelter, food, clothing, healthcare and of course, education. The idea that the state must help provide for the essentials of human existence is not fully developed even today, but we know that, as a matter of morality and ethics, human worth and dignity are implicit in the social contract. For example, a basic moral imperative is that a person with a disability must not be denied the opportunity to succeed in life simply because the state will not provide sufficient resources to permit assistance in overcoming a disability. The social contract between a disabled individual and the state requires positive state action to provide programs and services to improve the human condition. Jeremy Waldron clearly explained the economic and social aspects of this fundamental right when he wrote:

> It is no longer widely assumed that human rights must be pinned down to the protection of individual *freedom*. Humans have other needs as well, related to health, survival, culture, *education*, and ability to work. We all know from our own case how important these needs are ... It is how widely (though not universally) accepted that material needs generate moral imperatives which are as compelling as those related to democracy and civil liberty. If we want a catalogue of what people owe each other as a matter of moral priority, we should look not only to liberty, but also to the elementary conditions of material well being ... Everyone has a right to a standard of living adequate for health and well being of himself and his family [emphasis added] (Waldron, 1993, in Henkin et al., pp.157–159).

Thus, according to Waldron, the state has an obligation to the individual with a disability to provide the positive support necessary to mitigate incapacities that may be a limitation on his or her liberty and autonomy.

Failure of government to act to remedy such incapacities may be justified as far too cumbersome, too administratively difficult, or too costly. These arguments were used initially where states failed to provide appropriate education for children with disabilities. To provide for the redress of a handicap that limits liberty may therefore have a price tag that the government is unwilling to bear. This is particularly true in the case of *dignity* rights related to economic well being, because large governmental programs, such as those needed for individuals with disabilities, constitute major budget items. In this regard, Ronald Dworkin writes:

> So if rights make sense at all, then invasion of a relatively important right must be a very serious matter. It means treating a man as less than a man, or as less worthy of concern than other men. The institution of rights rests on the conviction that this is a grave injustice, and that it is worth paying the incremental cost in social policy or efficiency that is necessary to prevent it (Dworkin, 1997, p. 199).

THE COSTS OF RIGHTS

In their book *The Cost of Rights: Why Liberty Depends on Taxes*, Stephen Holmes and Cass Sunstein have pointed out that rights are costly because remedies are costly, and government must be willing to bear the financial consequences of guaranteeing rights. Holmes and Sunstein hold that "All rights are claims to an affirmative government response," and furthermore, "a disabled state cannot protect personal liberties" (2001, p. 44) of persons with disabilities within that state. Children with disabilities have a claim on public financial resources because moral and ethical values so dictate if government is to ensure the rights of liberty and dignity.

With regard to morality and ethics and their interface with the law, in the watershed cases of *PARC v. Commonwealth* 1971 and *Mills v. Board of Education of District of Columbia* 1972, the federal courts held that in spite of argument by the defense that to educate children with disabilities would cause great financial burden for which there was not adequate funding, such children must be provided a free appropriate public education. The courts concluded that if children without disabilities are given a free appropriate public education, children with disabilities have a right to attend public schools, regardless of the costs involved.[1]

In answer to the financial concerns of the defendant, the District of Columbia schools, the *Mills* court bluntly stated:

> If sufficient funds are not available to finance all of the services and programs that are needed and desirable in the system, then the available funds must be expended equitably in such a manner that no child is entirely excluded from a publicly supported education consistent with his needs and ability to benefit there from. The inadequacies of the District of Columbia Public School System, whether occasioned by insufficient funding or administrative inefficiency, certainly cannot be permitted to bear more heavily on the "exceptional" or handicapped child than on the normal child (Mills, 1972).

It is on this reasoning of rights and costs in which the rationale of the Individuals with Disabilities Education Act (IDEA) is couched. By virtue of the IDEA, a child with a disability has a right to an education and does not need to show that he or she would benefit from an education in order to attend public school. Rather, the inherent dignity of the individual entitles the child with a disability to obtain an education. Whether such a right exists was one of the primary issues emerging from the enactment of the IDEA. The issue was whether the severity of the handicap could be so great as to render the child incapable of benefiting from education. The theory in question was that if a child could not benefit from the educational process, then the state would not be required to provide the educational service. Indeed, the question as to whether a showing of benefit is required at all was the subject of litigation of primary importance for education of children with disabilities. In the case of *Timothy W. v. Rochester School District* 1989, the federal court addressed this precise question and held that the IDEA does not require a child to demonstrate a benefit from education as a condition precedent to participation.

Of course, the right to liberty and autonomy as a matter of due process is not predicated upon showing that one actually benefits from the liberty. Neither is the right of dignity contingent upon some evidentiary proof that a benefit is derived from the dignity gained. The entitlement of dignity through the opportunity for an education is self-evident and sufficiently compelling to justify the costs incurred in public funding.

RIGHTS AND THE PUBLIC TREASURY

The entitlement to a free appropriate public education (FAPE) for children with disabilities is guaranteed by statutes at both the federal and state levels. This guarantee, however, has substantial cost implications for all levels of government. The operative word in FAPE is "public," meaning that a child with a disability must look to the public and not to the private sector for relief. Private schools have no obligation and exercise no responsibility to provide special education for children with disabilities. The statutes obligating public schools to provide a free appropriate public education commit the taxpayer to provide sufficient financial resources to fulfill the public responsibility. Holmes and Sunstein explain that public finance is an "ethical science" (p. 98) because "it forces us to provide public accounting for the sacrifices that we, as a community, decide to make"(p. 98). However, rights have costs, and the draw on the public treasury limits the scope of the rights. According to Holmes and Sunstein, such rights are not absolute, but must be relative, as "nothing that costs money can be an absolute" (p. 97). Provision of a free appropriate public education, therefore, ultimately depends on the extent to which the taxpayer will pay for the costs of providing the appropriate special education at public expense. While Congress and state legislatures have statutorily created the right to special education for children with disabilities; Congress however, admittedly, by its failure to appropriate sufficient funds – financing only a minor portion of the actual costs, has thereby shifted the major share of costs to the respective states. States may, in turn, shift the funding responsibility to the local school districts. Thus, the level of government that, by statute, creates the right may avoid financial responsibility by shifting the burden downward. Therefore, when courts invoke the right to a free appropriate public education, the fiscal burden may fall largely on the property tax resources of the local school district budget. Thus, the cost of the education rights of children with disabilities may largely be absorbed by taxpayers in each community.

The onus of fiscal responsibility becomes an implicit responsibility of the local school administrator who is charged, by the nature of his or her employment, with convincing the public to pay in adequate provision for both special education and regular public school programs. As courts enforce the rights of children with disabilities, the fiscal choices of the local school administrators become more attenuated. The options ultimately become limited and are decided by whether the local school district itself can provide the appropriate education or whether the service should be outsourced to some private institution, usually at a high cost. It is this narrow choice that has created considerable litigation as parents of children with disabilities generally, quite naturally, seek the most exclusive and expensive educational choices if they are assured that the public will bear the full costs, and that they themselves will not be liable for contingent or supplemental costs.

It is precisely the issue of who finally makes the educational determination of what choice is to be made and the amount of public money to be expended that is perhaps the most litigious issue in special education. A plethora of case law exists where parents have unilaterally decided to choose very expensive private special education for their children. (See *Florence County School District Four v. Carter*, 510 U.S. 7, 114 S. Ct. 361 (1993).) In *Carter*, the U.S. Supreme Court said:

> There is no doubt that Congress has imposed a significant financial burden on states and school districts that participate in the IDEA. Yet public educational authorities who want to avoid reimbursing parents for the private education of a disabled child can do one of two things: give the child a free appropriate public education in a public setting, or place the child in an appropriate private setting of the state's choice (Carter, 1993).

Therefore, when the public school does not provide the appropriate education to meet the child's individualized education program (IEP), the parent can enroll the child in a private school, even though the costs are high, and the local public school district in which the child with a disability resides must pay the full tariff as determined by the private school. Yet the situation may be modified where the local public school provides the service and the parents choose to go outside anyway. Then the primary issue becomes whether the local school administrators or the parents have the legal and final authority in deciding where the child is to be educated. The uncertainty of the law as to such final authority became so litigious that in 1997, Congress clarified the IDEA, requiring that the cost of special education, including related services, of a child with a disability at a private school be paid by public school only if the public school does not provide the service. (20 U.S.C. §1412(a)). Therefore, the cost of the right obtained by the child, to be paid for by the taxpayer, has a built-in check that a representative of the public – the public school administrator, preventing the exploitation of the public treasury by the parents' individual interest and the entrepreneurial interests of the private school. This, of course, may be interpreted as a limitation on rights necessitated by the cost restraints of the public treasury.

WHAT ARE THE COSTS?

In large part, the issue that swirls about the ideal of the free appropriate public education is the determination of actual costs. What do rights cost? In the case of the IDEA, the Congress has been, of necessity and to a substantial degree, compelled to rely on the judgment of public school administrators to expound a reasonable position among the parent of the child, the private institution and the taxpayer. In this regard, as Holmes and Sunstein make clear, "Rights must be subject to restrictions in order to prevent their exploitation for wrongful ends" (p.103). Public school administrators become the front line in attempting to meet children's needs while defending public parsimony.

Public school administrators continuously lobby state legislators and Congress, seeking adequate funding of both special education and regular public school programs. However, as with all other public services, the qualification and justification of actual costs are difficult to determine. How much should be the taxpayer provide from local state and federal resources to adequately fund special education is the basic macroeconomic question.

In its simplest form, the equation has two aspects: the number of children requiring a specified educational service per the IEP, and the unit cost of the service – in short, educational need times costs. As Jordan and Stultz pointed out, since the beginning of the 20th century, educational finance theorists have expressed the need for objective measures of educational needs (1976, pp. 164–168). The principle in American educational philosophy that schools should provide equal opportunity to all youths, regardless of social or economic background, was firmly established by the early part of the twentieth century. Equality of educational opportunity has more recently come to mean that every person should have the opportunity to obtain the kind and quality of education that will best meet his or her educational needs and the needs of society. This is, in fact, the definition of an IEP.

The implementation of educational programs based on the needs of students requires the development of objective measures. Johns and Morphet stated that the allocation dimension of school finance models should use a single measure of need that relates programmatic costs to the needs of the target population being served. Establishment of an objective single measure of educational need that is equitable, practical, and relevant has been a primary goal of educational theorists in the pursuit of a state school support program to maximize educational opportunity (1969, p. 289).

More recently, Alexander and Salmon have explained that the costs of rights to special education can best be interpreted in terms of vertical equity, or the unequal treatment of unequals. Needs of children vary widely, the accommodation of which may require widely differing educational solutions, with costs commensurate with the detriment of the disability. In this light, three fundamental policy questions are derived for state education policymakers (1995, p. 212). First, who should be educated? That is, what client population should be served? More specifically, what are the special categories of exceptionality to be served? Second, what educational goals and objectives should be established for children of each exceptionality? Third, what kinds of educational programs are needed for those different children?

Following these initial steps, state and local school administrators must estimate the relative costs for each of the special needs categories. Those children with greater needs, of course, call for programs more costly than those children in regular school programs. Cost analyses may be conducted to disaggregate costs by the type of disability by school-district-wide basis, or state level. Special programs for children with disabilities that are unique or individual-specific must be calculated at actual costs for budgetary purposes.

Aggregation of these costs at the state and local levels requires that the number or percentage of students in each category be estimated by category and program provided. These basic considerations in establishing the state and local funding obligation apply to all programs, whether the student IEPs call for inclusion, individualized instructional settings, or modified resource rooms. Thus, different relative costs may be found in: (1) self-contained classrooms; (2) resource rooms; and (3) inclusion in regular classrooms. The objective and responsibility of the school administrator is to adequately and efficiently address costs that are related to the most effective mode of instruction.

EXTENUATING VARIABLES IN COSTS

The costs of the right to a special education is a highly individualistic determination. The aforementioned steps that may be utilized to quantify costs for budgetary purposes at the state or local school district level may vary depending on the incidence of the number and percentage of children with certain types of disabilities requiring high-cost programs.

There are, however, certain foundational considerations that are implicit in any determination of costs. Such considerations emanate from three aspects of the individualized education program (IEP). They are: (1) determination of least restrictive environment; (2) related services; and (3) separate school placement. Of course, the IEP procedure itself is a highly cost-intensive requirement of the local school district that must be fulfilled for each child in order to comport with the requirements of the IDEA. Beyond the overall recurring costs of the IDEA, the direct programmatic costs associated with the actual instructional program are most pervasive.

Costs associated with the least restrictive environment are particularly difficult to capture. Separating the mixture of costs of special education with regular education in the same classroom leaves wide margins for error in cost analysis. In defining the least restrictive environment, the terms "inclusion," "full-inclusion," and "integrated services" are important, but are not found in Public Law 94-142 (EAHCA, 1975) or Public Law 101-476 (IDEA, 1991) or regulations for these acts. The inclusion rationale came out of the U.S. Department of Education in the early 1980s under the "regular education initiative." Although not set forth in statute, the courts now use these terms when addressing the child's "least restrictive environment."

Thus, even though the terminology continues to evolve, there appears to be sustaining general agreement that children with disabilities should be placed in regular classrooms whenever possible. The desire of Congress for children with disabilities to attend school in regular classrooms was given substantial new support in the 1997 amendments to the IDEA. The statutory language requires that the IEP include "an explanation of the extent, if any, to which the child with not participate with nondisabled children in the regular class. . . ." This expands on earlier IDEA regulations which required the child's IEP to state "the extent that the child will be able to participate in regular educational programs," thus effectively shifting the burden to the school district to show why the student with a disability should *not* participate in a regular classroom. Implicit in this placement objective is the overriding and most important concern that all children benefit from the socialization processes that are inherent in being educated with one's peers. It is this attribute of commonality and mutual participation, so important to the learning process, that advances the time-honored ideal of public schools – all should attend school in common. Yet, cost implications of inclusion are far more elusive in mainstreamed situations than where separation of services is definitive.

A second and highly nebulous cost item in the provision of a free appropriate public education is related services. The IDEA requires that school districts provide children with disabilities with supportive services that will meet their educational needs as prescribed by the Individualized Education Program (IEP). A school district is required to provide "related services" but not "medical services" to children with disabilities. The courts tend to give broad meaning to related services. The Act defines related services as:

> transportation and such developmental, corrective, and other supportive services (including speech pathology and occupational therapy, recreation, and medical counseling services, except that such medical services shall be for diagnostic and evaluative purposes only) as may be required to assist a handicapped child to benefit form special education . . . (20 U.S.C.A. §1401 (17)).

The cost implications for such broad and varied services are obviously pervasive and difficult to quantify for budgetary purposes.

The upshot of the cost issue is that the nature of the "individualized" education program fashioned for each student makes accurate projection of costs for a large school unit, such as a state and certainly the federal government, impossible to precisely determine. Without the ability to budget accordingly for the accurate estimates of numbers of children requiring special education services, and without the ability to determine the aggregate costs of the individualized educational programs on a macro-scale, neither the state not federal governments can provide accurate budgetary projections. Without the capacity to predict costs, both state and federal governments will inevitably underestimate and underfund special education programs. Shortfalls of revenues from the upper levels of government force the responsibility for residual funding downward, onto the shoulders of local school districts and to the principal source of local revenue, the property tax.

EFFECTS OF RESIDUAL FUNDING

Residual funding of the IDEA, leaving local school districts to bear the balance, has at least four negative effects. First, without appropriate funding of the IDEA, it is highly doubtful that full enforcement is possible. The National Council on Disability has recommended that Congress tie full funding of the IDEA to full enforcement of the IDEA (p. 6). Second, the authorization of the IDEA set the federal goal of funding the IDEA at 40% of costs (p. 6). Presently, it is estimated that the federal government appropriates only 18% of the costs, or 18% of the *estimated* costs, for as explained earlier, there is no truly accurate method of determining the actual aggregate costs of special education at the state or federal levels of government. Thus, there is a great likelihood that special education will remain chronically under-funded. Third, by forcing the residual funding of special education downward to the local level, the federal government not only creates conditions of inadequate funding, but conditions of inequitable funding as well. To a substantial degree, this failure subjects children with the same or similar IEPs to widely variant educational conditions because of variations in state and local fiscal capacity. For example, two children residing in different school districts in Ohio may have very different opportunities, as local school district wealth patterns favor one over the other (DeRolph, 1997). In states with a high percentage of local funding and wide discrepancies in per-student property tax bases, equally circumstanced children are treated unequally. This problem is moderated by more adequate state funding and better estimates of actual costs, and is yet further significantly ameliorated by increased federal funding. A fourth negative effect of the present inadequate pattern of federal funding is that residual funding is unfair, forcing the burden to the lowest level of government where the tax system is the most regressive. Where regressive taxes are employed to greater extent, the antipathy for high-cost educational programs becomes more concentrated and intense.

The combination of these negative effects of residual funding may be further illustrated by a situation in Ohio, where two children with the same disability reside in two different school districts where one district significantly more affluent in property tax wealth than the other. The local property tax bears the major part of the public school funding in Ohio. On the average, the local property tax funds a large percentage of school budgets. With the federal government providing only a relatively minor part of funding and the state school fund being inadequate to overcome the disparities created by wide differences in local funding, the two children are funded at much different levels. The limitation on fiscal resources in the poor school district bears down heavily on the ability of the school to fulfill its obligation as required by the IEPs of all the children with disabilities in that school district. Thus, fulfillment of the right of a child with a disability to a free appropriate public education is severely compromise by the funding structure for public schools, and is further exacerbated by the failure of the federal government to appropriate sufficient funds to carry a reasonable part of the costs for special education.

RIGHTS COMPROMISED

From the above discussion, it becomes quite obvious that a child's right to access a free appropriate public education is not absolute, but rather very much dependent on the structure and adequacy of the funding of public education. In the abstract, the right may be absolute, but the funding is relative. As observed at the outset of this chapter, rights have costs, and the realization of rights depends on the commitment of government to enforce those rights. The prospects in life for autonomy and liberty of access to society's benefits are secured by the willingness of government to fund the costs of a remedy (Holmes & Sunstein, p. 120). As Holmes and Sunstein observe, "All rights are protected only to a degree, and this degree depends partly on budgetary decisions about how to allocate public resources" (Holmes & Sunstein, p. 121). When the federal government, on one hand, enacts legislation establishing free appropriate public education as a right, and then only minimally funds the costs, it effectively sanctions a policy of limiting those rights. For children with disabilities, "politics is trumps." With special education, budgetary choices and the exigencies of politics at the federal level trump the ideal of a free appropriate public education (Holmes & Sunstein, p. 121).

NOTE

1. Of course the argument may change considerably if the government did not provide schools for mass, public, universal education.

REFERENCES

20 U.S.C.A. §1401 (17).

20 U.S.C. §1412 (a).

Alexander, K., & Alexander, M. D. (2005). *American public school law* (6th ed.). Belmont, CA: Wadsworth/Thomson Learning.

Alexander, K., & Salmon, R. G. (1995). *Public school finance*. Boston: Allyn and Bacon.

Dworkin, R. (1997). *Taking rights seriously*. Cambridge, MA: Harvard University Press.

Florence County School District Four v. Carter, 510 U.S. 7, 114 S. Ct. 361 (1993).

Holmes, S., & Sunstein, C.R. (2001). *The cost of rights: Why liberty depends on taxes*. New York: W. W. Norton.

Johns, R. L., & Morphet, E. L. (1969). *The economics and financing of education: A systems approach*. Englewood Cliffs, NJ: Prentice-Hall.

Jordan, K. F., & Stultz, J. R. (1976). Projecting the educational needs and costs of elementary and secondary education. In: K. Alexander & K. F. Jordan (Eds), *Educational Need in the Public Economy*. Gainesville, FL: University Press of Florida.

Mills v. Board of Education of District of Columbia, 348 F.Supp. 866 (1972).

Pennsylvania Association of Retarded Children v. Commonwealth, 334 F.Supp. 1257 (E.D. Pa., 1971), 343 F.Supp. 279 (E.D. Pa. 1972).

Public Law 94-142 (EAHCA, 1975).

Public Law 101-476 (IDEA, 1991)

Timothy W. v. Rochester School District, 875 F.2d 954 (1989).

Waldron, J. (1993). Nonsense on stilts. In: Henkin et al. (Eds), *Liberal Rights: Collected Papers, 1981–1991* (pp. 157–159) cited in *Human Rights* (pp. 83–84). New York: Foundation Press, 1999.

2. EQUAL PROTECTION, DISABILITIES, AND OTHER FORMS OF DISCRIMINATION

K. G. Jan Pillai[*]

INTRODUCTION

The tremendous relevance of societal discrimination to special education of the learning disabled cannot be gainsaid. Mistreatment of disabled children in public and private educational institutions is a bad reflection on the moral and egalitarian values of the society at large. "Many students, regardless of race, who are deemed eligible to receive special education services [mandated by federal laws] are unnecessarily isolated, stigmatized, and confronted with fear and prejudice" (Losen & Welner, 2001, p. 407). According to the U.S. Congress, "poor African-American children are 2.3 times more likely to be identified by their teacher as having mental retardation than their white counterpart" (20 U.S.C. §1400 (8)(c) Individuals with Disabilities Education Act (IDEA)). Congress has also found that a highly disproportionate number of elementary and secondary special education students are African-Americans (IDEA §1400 (8)(D)) and their social disadvantage stems from "lack of opportunities in training and educational programs, undergirded by the practices in the private sector that impede their full participation in the mainstream society" (IDEA §1400 (10)).

At the dawn of the twenty-first century, it appears that societal discrimination – discrimination not traceable to identified government action – is beyond the

[*]K. G. Jan Pillai is I. Herman Stern Professor of Law, School of Law, Temple University, Pennsylvania.

Administering Special Education: In Pursuit of Dignity and Autonomy
Advances in Educational Administration, Volume 7, 13–40
Copyright © 2004 by Elsevier Ltd.
ISSN: 1479-3660/doi:10.1016/S1479-3660(04)07002-7

reach of the Equal Protection Clause[1] or any other provision of the United States Constitution. Under the prevailing equality jurisprudence of the Supreme Court, societal discrimination is an amorphous and over-expansive concept that is insufficient justification for public remedial action, such as race-based affirmative action. The Court is concerned that, in the absence of particularized judicial or administrative findings of discrimination by a government actor, a court inclined to proceed on the basis of societal discrimination "could uphold remedies that are ageless in their reach into the past, and timeless in their ability to affect the future"(*Wygant v. Jackson Board of Education*, 1986 and *City of Richmond v. J. A. Croson Co.*, 1989).

The Court's cavalier approach to remediation cannot be attributed to a lack of awareness of the existence or extent of societal discrimination in America. The Court has readily acknowledged that "[t]he unhappy persistence of both the practice and the lingering effects of racial discrimination against minority groups in this country is an unfortunate reality" (*Adarand Constructors, Inc. v. Pena*, 1995, holding that courts must analyze all racial classifications imposed by federal, state, or local governmental actors under strict scrutiny). But the Court has become increasingly hesitant to let the elected representatives of the people enact the measures they think appropriate to alleviate the problem. Declaring its dedication to a "color-blind constitution,"[2] a bare majority of the Court, using a variety of arbitrary review standards, has effectively barred federal, state, and local governments from establishing programs designed to remedy public and private discrimination against racial minorities. Among the minorities hit hardest by the Court's new crusade against race-based remedies are African Americans, who "have suffered discrimination immeasurably greater than any directed at other racial groups" (*J. A. Croson Co.*, 1989, 488 U.S. at 527, Scalia, J., concurring, stating that the fact "is plainly true").

The Court's 1989 decision in *City of Richmond v. J. A. Croson Company*, (488 U.S. at 469, majority opinion) sent shock waves through state and local governments, striking down a program which required prime contractors awarded city construction contracts to set aside at least 30% of their subcontracts to businesses owned by minorities, primarily Blacks. The population of Richmond, the former capital of the Confederate States of America, was 50% Black, but less than 1% of the city's prime construction contracts had been awarded to minorities during the five-year period preceding the establishment of the program (*City of Richmond v. J. A. Croson Company*, 488 U.S. at 479–480). The city argued that its program was necessary to remedy the effects of decades of societal discrimination and discrimination in the construction industry (*City of Richmond v. J. A. Croson Company*, 488 U.S. at 486).[3] However, the Court ruled that the program was not narrowly tailored to further a compelling governmental interest as required by

"strict scrutiny" (*City of Richmond v. J. A. Croson Company*, 488 U.S. at 505)
– a review standard that a majority of Justices agreed to apply to benign racial
classifications for the first time in the Court's history (*City of Richmond v. J. A.
Croson Company*, 488 U.S. at 551, Marshall, J., dissenting).

In order to demonstrate a compelling interest under strict scrutiny, Richmond
was required to provide evidence of "identified discrimination" constituting a
"prima facie case of a constitutional or statutory violation by anyone in the
Richmond construction industry" (*City of Richmond v. J. A. Croson Company*,
488 U.S. at 500). Strict scrutiny's requirement of discriminator-victim specificity
naturally disqualified societal discrimination as a constitutionally acceptable
ground for remedial or prophylactic action. Making clear that the city's gripping
legacy of racial discrimination had no effect on its strict-scrutiny analysis, the
Court declared that, "[w]hile there is no doubt that the sorry history of both private
and public discrimination in this country has contributed to a lack of opportunities
for black entrepreneurs, this observation, standing alone, cannot justify a rigid
racial quota in the awarding of public contracts in Richmond, Virginia" (*City of
Richmond v. J. A. Croson Company*, 488 U.S. at 499).

The practically insurmountable evidentiary requirements of strict scrutiny have
forced state and local governments across the country to dismantle the race-
based remedial programs which had helped minorities in gaining equal access
to education,[4] employment[5] (*Wygant v. Jackson Board of Education*, 1986), and
public contracting[6] (*Contractors Association of E. Pa. v. City of Philadelphia*,
1996). In 1995, a narrow majority of the Court decided to expand application of
strict scrutiny to federal programs benefiting minorities (*Adarand Constructors,
Inc. v. Pena*, 1995). Now that societal discrimination may no longer serve to
justify race-based remedial measures at any level of government, who in the
country is responsible and competent to provide relief to minorities facing
society-wide racial and ethnic discrimination? The obvious answer is nobody
(*see generally* Casebeer, 2000). In effect, the Supreme Court's prevailing equal
protection jurisprudence lets societal discrimination languish ad infinitum, and
restricts judicial remedies to those rare instances in which fragments of societal
discrimination manifest themselves as government action capable of being clearly
identified as discrimination.

The constitutional line separating private discrimination from public
accountability was drawn by the Supreme Court in two cases decided twelve
decades ago. In *United States v. Harris* (1883)[7] the Court struck down part of the
Ku Klux Klan Act of 1871, which made criminal private conspiracies to "deprive
any one of the equal protection of the laws enacted by the State" (*Harris*, 106
U.S. at 639) on the ground that Congress lacked the power under the Fourteenth
Amendment to punish "the action of private persons, without reference to the laws

of the States or their administration by the officers of the State" (*Harris*, 106 U.S. at 640). In the *Civil Rights Cases* (109 U.S. 3, 1883) the Court again reinforced its state-action doctrine by holding that sections of the Civil Rights Act of 1875, which mandated equal treatment of all persons at inns, theaters, and other places of public amusement, transgressed the power of Congress because the provisions sought to punish "[i]ndividual invasion of individual rights" (*Civil Rights Cases*, 109 U.S. at 11).

More recently, the Supreme Court had seemed to veer away from the rigid state-action rule of the *Civil Rights Cases*. In *United States v. Guest*, decided in 1966, six Justices held that Congress has the power to punish private conspiracies that interfere with Fourteenth Amendment rights.[8] Three of the Justices also expressed the view that the *Civil Rights Cases* were wrongly decided insofar as they prohibited Congress from punishing the actions of private individuals[9] (*Id.* at 783). However, in 2000, five Justices of the Rehnquist Court commented on the "enduring vitality of the *Civil Rights Cases* and *Harris*" and dismissed the holding of six Justices in *Guest* as "naked dicta" (*United States v. Morrison*, 2000, Rehnquist, C. J., joined by O'Connor, Scalia, Kennedy, and Thomas, J. J.). In *United States v. Morrison*, the Rehnquist majority invalidated the Violence Against Women Act (*United States v. Morrison*, 529 U.S. at 598)[10] in part because "it is directed not at any state or state actor, but at individuals who have committed criminal acts motivated by gender bias" (*United States v. Morrison*, 529 U.S. at 626).[11]

If one were to characterize the history of equal protection jurisprudence as involving cycles of judicial expansion and contraction of the state-action doctrine, the current trend would be one of contraction. As Justice O'Connor has stated: "[u]nfortunately, [the Court's] cases deciding when private action might be deemed that of the state have not been a model of consistency" (*Edmondson* v. Leesville Concrete Co., 1991, O'Connor, J., dissenting). Nevertheless, any impartial observer can easily discern an unmistakable trend toward shrinking the established boundaries of state action and insulating private discrimination from constitutional scrutiny.

This article argues that, in spite of evidence of the continuing problem of societal discrimination, the Rehnquist Court has been unwilling to allow government to take preventative or remedial measures needed to correct the problem. Part II of this article details the legal techniques the Court has used to view discrimination from the "perpetrator's perspective," thereby exonerating discriminatory state action. Part III highlights how the federal judiciary has restrained state and local governments from abating or ameliorating societal discrimination with legislation. Part IV addresses the doctrine of negative responsibilities, by which the Court has excused government from an equal protection-generated obligation to apply social-welfare legislation in a non-discriminatory manner. Finally, Part V concludes that the Equal Protection Clause should be realigned to meet the original vision of its framers.

INCREASING THE CATEGORIES OF INCONSEQUENTIAL STATE DISCRIMINATION

The Supreme Court has immunized significant portions of discriminatory state action from constitutional scrutiny by using a variety of "unwarranted limiting technicalities" (Black, 1967, 69).[12] These limiting devices, in effect, permit the courts to view the desirability and legitimacy of discrimination from the "perpetrator's perspective" (Freeman, 1978, pp. 1049, 1052) and enable courts to declare "that not everything that looks like discrimination is discrimination" (*Washington v. Davis*, 426 U.S. at 245) (Lawrence, 1983, pp. 831, 845).

The Doctrine of Intent

The most demanding device that operates as a substantive limitation on the Equal Protection Clause is the doctrine of intent. It mandates that, absent convincing proof of discriminatory intent or motive, a law or government policy that demonstrably produces discriminatory impact on any particular group or class will not violate the Constitution (*Id.* at 245).[13] The victims of such discrimination are required to prove that the impugned law or policy was adopted or pursued "because of" – not just "in spite of" – discriminatory intent (*Pers. Adm'r of Mass. v. Feeney*, 1979, citing *Arlington Heights v. Metropolitan Housing Dev. Corp.*, 1977). The intent or motivation requirement completely disregards the question as to what extent "the equal protection doctrine must address the unconscious racism that underlies much of the racially disproportionate impact of governmental policy" (Lawrence, 1987, pp. 317, 355). The effect of the intent doctrine on the victims of disparate impact discrimination has been devastating. The Supreme Court's 1981 decision in *City of Memphis v. Greene* is a telling illustration.

 Greene involved a constitutional challenge to the city's decision, at the behest of the citizens of a white residential community, Hein Park, to close the city's main thoroughfare used primarily by the African American residents of the adjoining neighborhood to traverse Hein Park (*Greene*, 451 U.S. at 102–103). The Court dismissed the challenge, holding that "[t]he city's decision to close [the street] was motivated by its interest in protecting the safety and tranquility of a residential neighborhood" (*Greene*, 451 U.S. at 119). The majority reached this conclusion despite being convinced "that the adverse impact [of the closing] on blacks was greater than on whites" (*Greene*, 451 U.S. at 138, Marshall, J., dissenting). Had the Court been inclined to assess the facts of the case objectively, it could easily have characterized the city's action as "nothing more than 'one more of the many humiliations which society has historically visited' on Negro citizens" (*Greene*, 451 U.S. at 147, Marshall, J., dissenting, quoting *Greene v. City of Memphis*, 610 F.2d 395, 404 (6th Cir. 1979)).

The Court's justification for the intent rule is the apprehension that without the rule there could be a deluge of constitutional challenges to generally applicable revenue, tax, and regulatory laws that disproportionally impact certain segments of the population – an apprehension never substantiated by contemporary or historical evidence (*Washington v. Davis*, 1976, relying on speculative literature).[14] On the contrary, the Court has historically rejected illicit motivation as predicate of unconstitutionality (*see, e.g. United States v. O'Brien*, 1968, rejecting an argument that a federal law banning draft card burning was enacted with the alleged motive of stifling dissent) and instead has accepted fictional justifications to sanitize state action actually motivated by discriminatory intent (*see Palmer v. Thompson*, 1971).[15]

Exculpatory Review Standards

The Supreme Court's most time-honored device for exonerating otherwise discriminatory state action is the lenient standard of judicial review. While the Court reviews racial classification under "strict scrutiny" (*see, e.g. Adarand Constructors, Inc. v. Pena*, 1995)[16] it uses a less demanding "intermediate scrutiny" to review gender classification (*see, e.g. Miss. Univ. for Women v. Hogan*, 1982).[17] However, the Court has permitted states to discriminate against persons on the basis of age or disability without having to offer any convincing legal or moral reason.

The Court has repeatedly declared that "States may discriminate on the basis of age without offending the Fourteenth Amendment if the age classification in question is rationally related to a legitimate state interest" (*Kimel v. Florida Board of Regents*, 2000).[18] States may rely on age as a proxy for other qualities, abilities, or characteristics that are relevant to the states' asserted interests, even if such generalizations are proved to be inaccurate in any individual case (*Kimel*, 528 U.S. at 84). Since age discrimination is presumptively rational under this standard of review, its victims bear the burden of proving that the state action is irrational or that the supporting facts proffered "could not reasonably be conceived to be true by the government decisionmaker" (*Vance v. Bradley*, 1979).

The Court's treatment of disability discrimination is even more disheartening. In *City of Cleburne v. Cleburne Living Center* (1985), the Court reversed the Fifth

Circuit's decision to treat mental retardation as a "quasi-suspect" classification deserving close scrutiny under equal protection jurisprudence (*City of Cleburne v. Cleburne Living Center*, 473 U.S. at 442). Instead, the Court held that legislation discriminating against disabled persons "incurs only the minimum 'rational basis' review applicable to general social and economic legislation" (*Board of Trustees of University of Alabama v. Garrett*, 2001, citing *City of Cleburne*, 473 U.S. at 446).

The Court utilized the same minimum-rationality review in *University of Alabama v. Garrett* (531 U.S. at 366) to minimize the extent and severity of state discrimination against the disabled, thereby prohibiting the application of the Americans with Disabilities Act to discriminatory state government employers. The Court claimed Congress failed to identify a pattern of "irrational" state discrimination in employment against the disabled and, therefore, the states "could quite hardheadedly – and perhaps hardheartedly – hold to job qualification requirements which do not make allowance for the disabled" (*Garrett*, 531 U.S. at 367–368) as mandated by the Act.

Proportionality and Congruence

Even under the lenient rationality review, the states would be vulnerable to liability for age or disability-based discrimination that is irrational and arbitrary (*see, e.g. City of Cleburne*, 473 U.S. at 446, "[t]he State may not rely on a classification whose relationship to an asserted goal is so attenuated as to render the distinction arbitrary or irrational"). Congress has enacted two enforcement statutes – the Age Discrimination in Employment Act (ADEA) (29 U.S.C. §§621–634, 1967) and the Americans with Disabilities Act (ADA) (42 U.S.C. §§12101–12213, 1994) – to provide federal remedies to victims of such discrimination. However, the Supreme Court has come up with an innovative rule – "congruence and proportionality" – to prohibit the enforcement of both statutes against the states. The rule mandates that no remedial legislation of Congress, enacted by virtue of its enforcement powers under the Fourteenth Amendment (U.S. Const. amend. XIV, §5),[19] is "appropriate" unless there is "a congruence and proportionality between the injury to be prevented or remedied and the means adopted to that end" (*City of Boerne v. Flores*, 1997, holding that the Religious Freedom Restoration Act of 1993 exceeds Congress' power under section 5 of the Fourteenth Amendment). Only by "appropriate" remedial legislation can Congress abrogate the states' Eleventh Amendment immunity from private suits (*Kimel v. Florida Board of Regents*, 2000).[20] Both the ADEA and the ADA have failed to pass the test of congruence and proportionality to qualify as appropriate remedial legislation.

The Court has not clearly explained exactly what the "congruence and proportionality" rule means; consequently Congress has never been able to understand or comply with it. In *Kimel v. Florida Board of Regents* (2000), the Court barred the application of the ADEA to states because of Congress' failure to identify or "uncover any significant pattern of unconstitutional [age] discrimination" (*Kimel* 528 U.S. at 90) by the states. Disregarding the conclusion of Congress to the contrary, the Court ruled that Congress had "no reason to believe" broad remedial legislation was necessary and that the legislative determination to apply "the Act to the States was an unwarranted response to a perhaps inconsequential problem" (528 U.S. at 89).

The Court used the same congruence and proportionality rule, with the "pattern of significant unconstitutional discrimination" as its benchmark, to protect states from liability for employment discrimination prohibited by the ADA (*Board of Trustees of University of Alabama v. Garrett*, 2001). Even though the ADA was enacted by an overwhelming majority of both chambers of Congress, after almost a decade of debates and deliberation (*see* Wong, 1990, at E1.), the Court held, in *University of Alabama v. Garrett* (2001), that the ADA did not measure up to the congruence and proportionality test (*Garrett*, 531 U.S. at 372) because it failed to "identify a pattern of irrational state discrimination in employment against the disabled" (*Garrett*, 531 U.S. at 368).[21]

The "congruence and proportionality" rule is the most arbitrary test the Court has ever used to measure the constitutionality of enforcement legislation passed by Congress (*see* Pillai, 2003, p. 645). The Court has never articulated the parameters of the test, including what constitutes an acceptable "pattern" of unconstitutional discrimination (*see* Pillai, 2003, p. 645). The only pattern that emerges from the Court's decisions is the boilerplate application of the test to invalidate federal antidiscrimination laws. It is also now clear that the states are free to discriminate on the basis of age, disability, or gender (*see United States v. Morrison*, 2000)[22] until the discrimination becomes so widespread and numerous as to form the necessary "pattern."

Outsourcing State Action

Both federal and state governments have become quite adept at avoiding the thorny problem of liability for unconstitutional state action by simply contracting out some of their functions to private operators. Five Justices of the Supreme Court currently are inclined to condone the practice. The Court's decision, in *Correctional Services Corporation v. Malesko* (2001), not to recognize a private action for damages against a private corporation operating a halfway house under contract with the federal Bureau of Prisons, is an appropriate illustration. The Court held that the so-called "*Bivens* remedy" (*Bivens v. Six Unknown Named Agents of Fed. Bureau of Narcotics*, 1971)[23] – which allows damages actions against government officers for deprivation of constitutional rights – was not applicable to a private corporation (*Malesko*, 534 U.S. at 63). The Court reasoned that the *Bivens* remedy is "concerned solely with deterring the unconstitutional acts of individual officers" (*Malesko*, 534 U.S. at 71, citing *FDIC v. Meyer*, 510 U.S. 471, 473–474 (1994)) and, therefore, to allow a *Bivens*-type action against government agencies "would mean the evisceration of the *Bivens* remedy, rather than its extension" (*Malesko*, 534 U.S. at 69–70, quoting *Meyer*, 510 U.S. at 485). The Court also noted its hesitation to extend the *Bivens* remedy to government agencies was based in part on its concern that such an extension might entail a "potentially enormous financial burden" to the agency, (*Malesko*, 534 U.S. at 70, quoting *Meyer*, 510 U.S. at 486) and that the question of "[w]hether it makes sense to 'impose asymmetrical liability costs on private prison facilities' " (*Malesko*, 534 U.S. at 72)[24] is for Congress, not the Court, to decide (*Malesko*, 534 U.S. at 72). In this way, the Court bypassed the state-action problem entirely.

　　Four dissenting Justices were not persuaded by the majority's reasoning in *Malesko* (534 U.S. at 75, Stevens, J., dissenting, joined by Souter et al.). They asserted that the plaintiff's Eighth Amendment rights were violated "by a federal agent – a private corporation employed by the Bureau of Prisons to perform functions that would otherwise be performed by individual employees of the Federal Government" (*Malesko*, 534 U.S. at 76). The dissenting Justices agreed with half-a-dozen courts of appeals "that corporate agents performing federal functions, like human agents doing so, were proper defendants in *Bivens* actions" (*Malesko*, 534 U.S. at 77 n. 3, Stevens, J., dissenting, citing decisions from the First, Second, Fifth, Sixth, Ninth and D.C. Circuit courts). The dissenters detected in the Court's decision a "predisposition" against the holding in *Bivens* itself, and predicted that the "tragic consequence" of the decision will be to give incentives "to corporate managers of privately operated custodial institutions to adopt cost-saving policies that jeopardize the constitutional rights of tens of thousands of inmates in their custody" (*Malesko*, 534 U.S. at 81).[25]

Collaborative State Action

The Supreme Court has a long and convoluted history of providing constitutional accommodation to private parties causing deprivations of constitutional rights by actions "having the cast of law" (*Monroe v. Pope*, 1961). Liability for such actions depends on whether they can be fairly ascribable or attributable to the state (*see Lugar v. Edmondson Oil Co.*, 1982).[26] The Court resolves the issue after a two-prong inquiry: first, whether the alleged "deprivation has resulted from the exercise of a right or privilege having its source in state authority," (*Lugar v. Edmondson Oil Co.*, 457 U.S. at 939) and second, whether the private parties "may be appropriately characterized as a 'state actors' " (*Lugar v. Edmondson Oil Co.*, 457 U.S. at 939). The outcome of this inquiry can be quite unpredictable. Consider the Court's creditor repossession cases.

In several creditor self-help cases, the Court held that when the state collaborates with, or its agents aid, a creditor in securing disputed property, the debtor is entitled to the protection of constitutional due process.[27] However, in *Flagg Brothers v. Brooks* (1978) the Court found no constitutional violation when a warehouseman, acting pursuant to the New York Uniform Commercial Code, seized and sold the bailor's (debtor's) property without any hearing (*Flagg Brothers*, 436 U.S. at 166). Since the Code was enacted by the state legislature, and the state's law of conversion gave an exception to the warehouseman to pass good title to the purchasers of the debtor's goods, in fact "the Court was in error" not to recognize state action (Alexander, 1993, pp. 361, 363). However, Justice Rehnquist's majority opinion dismissed the bailor's challenge based on the equal protection and due process clauses of the Fourteenth Amendment (*Flagg Brothers*, 436 U.S. at 166). It did so primarily on the rationale that "the State of New York has not *compelled* the sale of a bailor's goods, but has merely announced the circumstances under which its courts will not interfere with a private sale" (*Flagg Brothers*, 436 U.S. at 166, emphasis added). The opinion made clear that private action cannot be brought within the ambit of the Fourteenth Amendment "by the simple device of characterizing the State's inaction as 'authorization' or 'encouragement,' " and that "[i]t is quite immaterial that the State has embodied its decision not to act in statutory form" (*Flagg Brothers*, 436 U.S. at 165–166). The Court deliberately left undecided the troubling question of the extent to which a city or state may delegate its functions in the areas of education, tax, and fire or police protection to private parties "and thereby avoid the strictures of the Fourteenth Amendment" (*Flagg Brothers*, 436 U.S. at 163–164).

Despite the Supreme Court's decades of effort to confine state action within definite and ascertainable boundaries, the concept remains as volatile and open-ended as ever, susceptible to arbitrary reconfiguration. If a deliberate state decision to refrain from using its collective authority to prevent a private assault on citizens' constitutional rights does not constitute state action, then the concept cannot contribute much to the society's quest for equality.

PASSIVE JUDICIAL PARTICIPATION

The Supreme Court permits societal discrimination to exist by means other than shrinking the domain of state action. The federal judiciary has become a passive participant in the maintenance and fostering of societal discrimination in several discrete areas, including hate crimes, public school desegregation, and higher education contexts.

Hate Crimes

The federal judiciary is unabashedly complicit in providing the mantle of constitutional legitimacy to societal discrimination by restraining state and local governments from abating or ameliorating it with legislation. Ironically, at times the Supreme Court derives its inspiration from outside the Fourteenth Amendment, as it did in 1992 in *R.A.V. v. City of St. Paul*. The case involved the constitutionality of the conviction of a teenager who, in violation of a city ordinance, burned a crudely-made wooden cross in the fenced yard of his across-the-street neighbors, a black family (*R.A.V. v. City of St. Paul*, 1992).[28] The ordinance made it a misdemeanor to place or burn on public or private property symbols, such as a cross or Nazi swastika, "which one knows or has reasonable grounds to know arouses anger, alarm or resentment in others on the basis of race, color, creed, religion or gender" (*R.A.V.*, 505 U.S. at 380). The ordinance was interpreted to prohibit "only those expressions that constitute 'fighting words' " (*R.A.V.*, 505 U.S. at 381).[29]

The Supreme Court unanimously struck down the ordinance as violative of the First Amendment (*R.A.V.*, 505 U.S. at 377–378) but the Justices offered divergent rationales for the decision. In an opinion for the Court, Justice Scalia, joined by Chief Justice Rehnquist and Justices Kennedy, Souter, and Thomas, held that the ordinance impermissibly singled out certain disfavored racially, religiously or sexually offensive fighting words solely on the basis of their expressive content, while leaving expressions vilifying other groups or causes outside the prohibitions of the ordinance (*R.A.V.*, 505 U.S. at 391). According to the majority opinion, the government must prohibit all fighting words or no fighting words at all; selective prohibitions by subject matter are impermissible (*R.A.V.*, 505 U.S. at 419, Stevens, J., joined by White & Blackmun, J. J., concurring in the judgment).

The majority deviated from the Court's long-standing view that fighting words are not within the area of constitutionally protected speech[30] "because their expressive content is devoid of social value and any benefit derived from them is outweighed by the social interest in order and morality" (*Chaplinsky v. New Hampshire*, 1942, holding that the First Amendment does not protect fighting words). The Court's assertion that constitutionally unprotected categories of speech cannot be selectively regulated was easily refuted by Justice Stevens, who cited precedents allowing selective regulation in areas such as obscenity and commercial advertising.[31] Justice Stevens correctly observed that the Court's holding perversely gives "fighting words *greater* protection than is afforded commercial speech" (*R.A.V.*, 505 U.S. at 423).

States should be free to regulate fighting words selectively and unevenly for the simple reason that "[s]ome fighting words are more dangerous or more hurtful than others" (Hylton, 1996, pp. 35, 52). *City of St. Paul* established a First Amendment rule that mandates equal treatment of all fighting words, regardless of their content or their users' point of view. By doing so, the Court created a hierarchy of constitutional values that relegated the value of equality embodied in the Fourteenth Amendment subordinate to values protected by the First Amendment. Significantly, the majority opinion disregarded the city's argument that the ordinance was not intended "to impact on the right of free expression of the accused" but rather to "protect against the victimization of a person or persons who are particularly vulnerable because of their membership in a group that historically has been discriminated against" (*R.A.V.*, 505 U.S. at 394). Had the majority evaluated the constitutionality of the ordinance under the Equal Protection Clause instead of the First Amendment, Justice Scalia would have been compelled to give the same equal protection of the law to the terrorized black family as he gave to the racially bigoted intimidator.

School Desegregation

After the Supreme Court's unequivocal declaration in 1955 that "separate educational facilities are inherently unequal," (*Brown v. Board of Education*, 1954)[32] the constitutional obligation of states to desegregate public schools has never been in doubt. Indeed, the Court has imposed on the states an "affirmative duty to take whatever steps" (*Green v. County School Board*, 1968)[33] are necessary to eliminate the traces and remnants of segregation "root and branch" (*Green*, 391 U.S. at 438). School districts which failed to desegregate "with deliberate speed" (*Brown v. Board of Education (Brown II)*, 1955) were subjected to federal court orders establishing remedial plans and definitive guidelines to achieve desegregation goals "at the earliest practicable date" (*Green*, 391 U.S. at 438–439).

Dozens of school districts across the country have operated under court-supervised desegregation plans for almost three decades with varying degrees of success.[34] However, a recent study conducted by the Harvard Civil Rights Project found that the average white student now attends a public school that is

80% white, while the average black student attends a school that is about one-third white (Frankenburg et al., 2003). The conclusion arrived at by the Project is that the nation's public schools have been undergoing a "process of continuous resegregation" (Frankenburg et al., 2003). According to some, "Much of the blame goes to the court's increased hostility to desegregation suits" (*Fighting School Resegregation*, N. Y. Times, Jan. 27, 2003, at A24 (editorial)).

In the 1990s, the Supreme Court established a new standard of good-faith compliance to decide whether schools subject to desegregation orders should be released from court supervision. In *Board of Education of Oklahoma City v. Dowell* (1991), the Court held that the test for terminating judicial oversight is whether a school district has implemented the original desegregation decree "in good faith" and whether the "vestiges of past discrimination had been eliminated *to the extent practicable*" (*Dowell*, 498 U.S. at 249–250, emphasis added). In effect, public schools are no longer required to eliminate the vestiges of discrimination "root and branch." The Court reiterated the *Dowell* good-faith standard in two successive cases, *Freeman v. Pitts* (1992)[35] and *Missouri v. Jenkins* (1994).[36] This desegregation trilogy "evinced a clear hostility to the continuation of court-ordered desegregation remedies" (Hyytinen, 2001, pp. 661, 669), and not only paved the way for resegregation, but helped perpetuate and reinforce segregated housing patterns in and around the resegregated school districts.

The Supreme Court has long been aware of the inextricable link between school desegregation and neighborhood housing patterns. In *Swann v. Charlotte-Mecklenberg Bd. of Education* (1971), the Court observed that "[p]eople gravitate toward school facilities, just as schools are located in response to the needs of the people. The location of the schools may thus influence the patterns of residential developments of a metropolitan area and have important impact on composition of inner-city neighborhoods" (*Swann*, 402 U.S. at 20–21). Racial composition of schools will have "a profound reciprocal effect on the racial composition of residential neighborhoods which, in turn, may cause further racial concentration within the schools" (*Keyes v. School District No. 1*, 1973).[37] Therefore, in 1971 the *Swann* Court instructed federal district courts to consider segregated residential patterns when fashioning remedies in desegregation cases (*Swann*, 402 U.S. at 21).

The Court no longer considers segregated residential neighborhoods adjoining segregated schools a factor to be taken into account in desegregation cases. Since *Swann* was decided, the Court has rejected interdistrict desegregation remedies, holding that a white suburban school district cannot be required to participate in regional desegregation plans unless it can be demonstrated that official actions of the suburban district contributed to segregation of the affected schools (*Milliken v. Bradley*, 1974, rejecting the Fourteenth Amendment claim of parents of black schoolchildren in the Detroit, Michigan public school system). Despite overwhelming evidence of "white flight" by families from inner cities to suburbs to avoid attending desegregated schools, the Court held in *Freeman v. Pitts* (1992) that the adverse impact of segregated housing patterns on school desegregation efforts has no "constitutional implications" in instances "[w]here resegregation is a product not of state action but of private choices" (*Freeman v. Pitts*, 503 U.S. at 495, 1992).

In the desegregation trilogy, the Court found no constitutional objection against single-race or predominantly segregated schools caused by segregated housing patterns (*Board of Education of Oklahoma City v. Dowell*, 1992; *Freeman*, 503 U.S. at 489; *Missouri v. Jenkins*, 1994). The mutual reinforcement of segregation in schools and housing which the Court constitutionalized in the desegregation trilogy is bound to validate and nurture societal discrimination against minorities.

Desegregation of Higher Education

As noted above, the Supreme Court's use of strict scrutiny categorically bars state and local governments from considering societal discrimination in fashioning remedies for their own past racial discrimination and its lingering effects (*see* Part II.B *supra*.). In *Wygant v. Jackson Board of Education* (1986) and *Richmond v. J. A. Croson Company* (1989), the Court ruled that societal discrimination is an amorphous and insufficient basis for race-based remedies because recognition of such discrimination may call upon courts to "uphold remedies that are ageless in their reach into the past, and timeless in their ability to affect the future" (*Wygant*, 476 U.S. at 276). In *Adarand Constructors, Inc. v. Pena* (1995, holding that any distinction between state and federal racial classification is "untenable"). The Court extended the prohibition to the federal government.

Some conservative federal courts of appeals have taken the Supreme Court standard to its illogical extreme. In *Podberesky v. Kirwan* (1994, *Podberesky II, cert. denied*, 1995), the Fourth Circuit invalidated the University of Maryland's Banneker Scholarship program, a merit-based program reserved for African American students. The program was established to avoid administrative sanctions from the U.S. Department of Education, which had been investigating the university's ignominious discriminatory practices (*Podberesky v. Kirwan*, 1992; *Podberesky I*). One of the grounds for invalidating the program was that it had been designed to remedy the current effect of societal discrimination as reflected by the hostile campus environment for minorities (*Podberesky* II, 1995). The University sought to justify the program because "the atmosphere on campus [was] perceived as being hostile to African American students."

The Fifth Circuit took the Supreme Court's rulings even farther. In *Hopwood v. University of Texas* (1996) the circuit court struck down the University of Texas Law School's special admissions program that gave preference to African Americans and other designated minorities (*Hopwood*, 78 F.3d at 934). The law school had a shameful history of racial discrimination, as evidenced by the famous case of *Sweatt v. Painter* (1950)[38] in which the Supreme Court forced the law school to admit its first African American law student in 1950. Until 1969, the Texas Constitution mandated a dual system of education and the state practiced racial discrimination at all levels of its educational system, from the formative elementary school years to graduate-level study (Holley & Spencer, 1999, pp. 245, 247). The law school argued that its special admission program, instituted under threat of administrative and judicial sanctions, was necessary to achieve a diverse and representative student body (*Hopwood v. Texas*, 1994). However, the Fifth Circuit held that the school's race-conscious admissions policy could not be sustained under the Supreme Court's prevailing strict-scrutiny jurisprudence (*Hopwood*, 78 F.3d at 940–952, 955).[39]

Particularly noteworthy is the relative ease with which the Fifth Circuit dismissed the law school's argument that the admissions program was essential to remedy the continuing effect of the University's past discrimination (*Hopwood*, 78 F.3d at 949–952). To demonstrate the effect, the law school presented at trial evidence of its "lingering reputation in the minority community, particularly with the prospective students, as a 'white school'" and the "perception that the law school is a hostile environment for minorities" (*Hopwood*, 861 F. Supp. at 572). The circuit court rejected the evidence with a tint of cynicism, stating that reputation is mere "knowledge of historical fact" (*Hopwood*, 78 F.3d at 952–953) and "[a]ny racial tension at the law school is most certainly the result of present societal discrimination" (*Hopwood*, 78 F.3d at 953). The court admonished the law school not to reach outside its boundaries to assess past discrimination or its present effects (*Hopwood*, 78 F.3d at 953). It concluded that "the University of Texas System is itself too expansive an entity to scrutinize for past discrimination" and that the law school is the only "appropriate governmental unit for measuring a constitutional remedy" (*Hopwood*, 78 F.3d at 951). If, out of all the educational institutions with a checkered past, the University of Texas is not permitted to consider societal discrimination in its quest for atonement, then no other institution can. This strange predicament is created by the Supreme Court's strict-scrutiny standard.

THE DOCTRINE OF NEGATIVE RESPONSIBILITIES

Shortly after the adoption of the Fourteenth Amendment, the Supreme Court declared that the "[d]uty of protecting all its citizens in the enjoyment of an equality of rights was originally assumed by the States, and it remains there. The only obligation resting upon the United States is to see that the States do not deny the right" (*United States v. Harris*, 1883).[40] In the same term, the Court ruled that the enforcement clause of the Amendment does not authorize Congress to adopt "general legislation upon the rights of citizens, but [only] corrective legislation, that is, such as may be necessary and proper for counteracting such laws as the States . . . are prohibited from making or enforcing."[41] Thus the Court has made it absolutely clear that the states are the sole repositories of the constitutional power required to enact social-welfare legislation. The question is whether the states have an equal protection-generated obligation to exercise that power to protect their citizens from the consequences of societal discrimination.

The Rehnquist Court is quite certain of the answer. In the seminal case of *DeShaney v. Winnebago County Department of Social Services* (1989, holding that the State has no constitutional duty to protect a child from his father after receiving reports of possible abuse) the Court, in an opinion authored by the Chief Justice, declared that the Constitution's "Due Process Clauses generally confer no affirmative right to governmental aid, even where such aid may be necessary to secure life, liberty, or property interests of which the government itself may not deprive the individual" (*DeShaney*, 489 U.S. at 196).[42] The due process claim in the case was based on the government's failure to respond to a request for intervention to prevent a father's repeated child abuse – abuse which ultimately left the child mentally retarded (*DeShaney*, 489 U.S. at 193). Despite undisputed evidence that the government was intimately aware of the continuous abuse, the Court relieved the government from any liability by stating that "[t]he most that can be said of the state functionaries in this case is that they stood by and did nothing when suspicious circumstances dictated a more active role for them" (*DeShaney*, 489 U.S. at 203).

DeShaney likely would have come out the same even if the claim against the government had been made under the Equal Protection Clause because the Court's decision was based on the dogmatic premise that the Constitution is a "charter of negative rather than positive liberties" (*Jackson v. City of Joliet*, 1983, citing *Harris v. McRae*, 448 U.S. 297, 318 (1980), and *Bowers v. DeVito*, 686 F.2d 616, 618 (7th Cir. 1982), *cert. denied*, 465 U.S. 1049 (1984)). Under the concept of negative liberties, the Constitution *does* protect the people from certain state actions, but it *does not* impose on the states "an affirmative duty to take basic care of their citizens" (*DeShaney*, 489 U.S. at 204, Brennan, J., dissenting). Not only does the Constitution cast no blame on states' inaction, it does not even obligate the states to protect the people "from each other" (*DeShaney*, 489 U.S. at 196).

It is not difficult to see the facial absurdity of this theory of legitimized inaction. Its logic will permit, for example, a group of homophobes to practice their faith under the gaze of a permissive government and instill fear in homosexuals in ways subtle enough to evade the grip of existing criminal laws. It is inconceivable that such a flagrant failure of the government to protect homosexuals is condoned by the Equal Protection Clause. If it is, then any level of government can neutralize the Clause or keep its command in abeyance by the simple expedient of deliberate inaction.

Clearly, the idea of negative liberties does not comport with the history and rationale of the Equal Protection Clause. The Clause was designed to protect citizens from both affirmative and negative abuses of power by their government. What prompted the 39th Congress to adopt both the Civil Rights Act of 1866 and the Fourteenth Amendment was the unwavering conviction that the states could not be relied upon to protect the rights of all persons. . . ."A central purpose of both measures was to incorporate the right to protection into the Federal Constitution, and thereby to empower the national government to compel the states to fulfill their duty of protection"(Heyman, 1991, pp. 507, 571. *See also* Bandes, 1990, p. 2271).

The 42nd Congress reiterated the convictions of its predecessor by enacting the Ku Klux Klan Act (Civil Rights Act, ch. 22, §2, 17 Stat. 13 (1871), current version at 42 U.S.C. §1985(3)) which "provided a cause of action for those who are deprived of their civil rights by private parties acting in the absence of state intervention" (Dolan, 1986, pp. 1271, 1291).[43]

Even the Rehnquist Court occasionally intimates that state inaction could sometimes verge on unconstitutional state participation in private discrimination. In the plurality opinion in *City of Richmond v. J. A. Croson Co.*, Justice O'Connor stated that "if the city could show that it had essentially become a 'passive participant' in a system of racial exclusion practiced by elements of the local construction industry, we think it clear that the city could take affirmative steps to dismantle such a system" (*City of Richmond v. J. A. Croson Co.*, 1989, plurality opinion of O'Connor, J., joined by Rehnquist, C. J., White, J.) Even though this statement is couched in permissive language, it has been interpreted as meaning that "the government would be a 'passive participant' in private discrimination whenever its inaction left intact the effects of identifiable private discrimination" (Ayres & Vars, pp. 1610–1611).

The Rehnquist Court's "failure to see that [state] inaction can be every bit as abusive of power as action" (*DeShaney*, 1989) makes the operation and availability of the Equal Protection Clause contingent upon the discretionary choice of the state to act or not to act. The doctrine of negative liberties that underpins the action-inaction dichotomy is a negation of the guaranty of individual safety and security enshrined in the Fourteenth Amendment. When put to the test of the European Court of Human Rights, the doctrine may be roundly condemned as a device that denies the basic human rights and dignity of individuals who are victimized by private discrimination.[44]

SEEPING NEGATIVITY INTO SPECIAL EDUCATION

Ever since the Supreme Court decision in *Brown v. Board of Education* (1954),[45] the states' obligation to assure equality in public education has never been in doubt. But the kind and quality of education the states were obligated to provide learning disabled children remained uncertain and controversial until the federal judiciary stepped in to articulate them. In *Pennsylvania Association for Retarded Children v. Pennsylvania (PARC)* (1972), a federal court ordered the state to provide every retarded person between the ages of six and twenty-one "access to a free public program of education and training appropriate to his learning capabilities" (*PARC*, 343 F. Supp. at 302). Similarly, in *Mills v. Board of Education of the District of Columbia* (1972) the district court ordered the school board to "provide to each child of school age a suitable, publicly supported education regardless of the degree of the child's mental, physical or emotional disability or impairment."[46] Both the *PARC* and *Mills* courts indicated that the disabled children's right to equal education can be derived from the federal constitution.[47]

Spurred by the judicial initiative[48] or imbued with a belated sense of justice, the United States Congress took up the cause of the disabled first by enacting the Rehabilitation Act of 1973 (29 U.S.C. S.701. Section 504 of the Act (29 U.S.C. §794) prohibits discrimination based on disability in any program or activity receiving federal funds) and then the Education for All Handicapped Children Act of 1975 (EAHCA), later amended and renamed the Individuals with Disabilities Education Act (IDEA) (P. L. No. 94–142, 89 stat. 773 (1975), amended by Pub. L. No. 101–476, 104 stat. 1141 (1992) and codified 20 U.S.C. §§1400–1487). Congress sought to enforce the provisions of the statutes through state and local agencies that receive federal funds. The EAHCA specifically requires the recipient of federal assistance to demonstrate that it " has in effect a policy that assures all handicapped children the right to a free appropriate public education" (20 U.S.C. §1412 (1)). The term, "free appropriate public education" is defined as "special education and related services" provided at public expense and without charge in conformity with an individualized educational program (20 U.S.C. §1401 (18)) "specifically designed to meet the unique needs of a handicapped child" (20 U.S.C. §1401 (16)). The statute emphasized the need to mainstream the disabled by educating them in classrooms with children who are not disabled, and in the least restrictive environment."[49] Even though Congress, by enacting EAHCA, determined to "take a more active role under its responsibility for equal protection of the laws to guarantee that handicapped children are provided equal educational opportunity," (S. Rep. No. 94–168, P.9 (1975), U.S. Code Cong. & Admin. News 1975, p. 1433) the Supreme Court has been unwilling to share the congressional resolve. The Court in *Board of Education v. Rowley* maintained that the "intent of the Act was more to open the door of public education to handicapped children on appropriate terms than to guarantee any particular level of education once inside" (*Rowley*, 1982). With such a narrow reading of the Act, the Court rejected the holding of the lower courts that the Act required the state to "maximize the potential of each handicapped child commensurate with the opportunity provided nonhandicapped children" (*Board of Education v. Rowley*, 458 U.S. at 200).

The Supreme Court's interpretation of the Act was stunningly unfair to Amy Rowley, the plaintiff in the case. Amy was a deaf elementary school student who, mostly by virtue of her intelligence and lipreading skills, managed to perform better than the average child in her class and passed from grade to grade (483 F. Supp. 528, 531 (1980). However, Amy's parents believed that she could have done better with the aid of a sign-language interpreter. When the school and the state commissioner of education declined to appoint such an interpreter for Amy, the parents sought relief from federal courts. Both the district court and the court of appeals ruled in Amy's favor. But the Supreme Court reversed the lower courts and held that the Act's mandate for "free appropriate public education" imposed on the states "no clear obligation . . . beyond the requirement that handicapped children receive some form of specialized education," (*Rowley*, 458 U.S. at 195) which need not include the service requested by Amy.

Writing for the majority, then Justice Rehnquist readily acknowledged the truth that by enacting the EAHCA "Congress sought 'to provide assistance to the States in carrying out their responsibilities under . . . the Constitution of the United States to provide equal protection of the law' " (*Rowley*, 458 U.S. at 198, accepting the argument of the United States and Respondent Rowley, and citing the passage from the Senate Report). Nevertheless, he could not come to "think that such statements imply a congressional intent to achieve *strict equality* of opportunity or services" (*Rowley*, emphasis added). He simply imputed to Congress an understanding that equal protection required nothing more than equal access (*Rowley*, 458 U.S. at 200), something "significantly different from any notion of absolute equality of opportunity regardless of capacity" (*Rowley*, 458 U.S. at 199). Intimating complete harmony with the congressional understanding, the Justice designed the Court's attenuated conception of Equal Protection Clause that "does not require States to expend equal financial resources on the education of each child."[50]

Even as he conceded that the EAHCA contemplated a "basic floor of opportunity" for the handicapped, Justice Rehnquist's truncated vision of equal protection reduced the opportunity to "access" to specialized instruction that is "sufficient to confer *some* benefit upon the handicapped child" (*Rowley*, 458 U.S. 200–201). This legal rhetoric did not help Amy Rowley who, without the aid of a sign-language interpreter, could comprehend only "less than half of what is said in the classroom – less than half of what normal children comprehend" (*Rowley*, 458

U.S. at 215). As the three dissenting Justices correctly observed, "[t]his is hardly an equal opportunity to learn, even if Amy makes passing grades" (*Rowley*, 458 U.S. at 215, Justice White, with whom Justice Brennan and Justice Marshall join, dissenting). But Justice Rehnquist was unwilling to read the statute broadly, "*even in furtherance of equality*," as "imposing any particular substantive educational standard upon the States" (*Rowley*, 458 U.S. at 200, emphasis added) or permitting "courts to substitute their own notions of sound educational policy for those of the school authorities which they review" (*Rowley*, 458 U.S. at 206). Thus he relieved the States from what Congress believed to be their constitutional obligation to provide equal educational opportunity to handicapped children. Justice Rehnquist's interpretation of the States' obligation under EAHCA represents another imprudent manifestation of his favorite doctrine of negative responsibilities.

CONCLUSION

The Rehnquist Court readily recognizes that societal discrimination remains an "unfortunate reality" in America (*Adarand Constructors, Inc. v. Pena*, 1995). Nevertheless, the Court is unwilling to permit the federal government or require state governments to take the needed prophylactic and remedial measures to cure these ills. The Equal Protection Clause, which is custom-made to deal with the problems of discrimination and inequality, is trapped in a web of judicially crafted technicalities, standards, and doctrines, all of which are designed to deny, rather than provide, protection to victims of discrimination. The key to finding a legal solution to the problem of societal discrimination is to free the beleaguered Equal Protection Clause from the shackles of the federal judiciary and restore it to the original condition contemplated by its visionary framers.

More than three decades ago, Professor Charles Black of Yale observed that the " 'state action' problem is the most important problem in American law" (Black, Jr., 1967, at 69). Today, the problem has been rendered a complicated jumble by the Supreme Court. In a society saturated with government grants, subsidies, tax exemptions, and an interest group-dominated political process, the line that once separated the public from the private has become increasingly indistinct. Therefore, "it is time to begin rethinking state action" (Chemerinsky, 1985, pp. 503, 505) and the other judicial technicalities that currently cripple the effectiveness of the Equal Protection Clause.

NOTES

1. The Fourteenth Amendment states that "[n]o State shall. . .deny to any person within its jurisdiction the equal protection of the laws." U.S. Const. amend. XIV, §1. For a discussion

of how the Fourteenth Amendment applies the Fifth Amendment to the states, see *Benton v. Maryland*, 395 U.S. 784, 794 (1969), holding that the Fifth Amendment's prohibition on double jeopardy applies to the states through the Fourteenth Amendment, and *Malloy v. Hogan*, 378 U.S. 1, 6 (1964), holding that the Fifth Amendment's prohibition on self-incrimination applies to the states through the Fourteenth Amendment.

2. For a comprehensive exposition of the color-blind Constitution doctrine, see *Andrew Kull, The Color-Blind Constitution* (Harvard University Press ed., 1992). For insightful discussions of equal protection cases in which the Rehnquist Court has adopted that approach, see Keith E. Sealing, *The Myth of a Color-blind Constitution*, 54 Wash U. J. Urb. & Contemp. L. 157 (1998), and Melissa Cole, *The Color-blind Constitution, Civil Rights-Talk, and a Multicultural Discourse for a Post-Reparations World*, 25 N.Y.U. Rev. L. & Soc. Change 127 (1999).

3. Richmond City Counselperson Marsh, stated that "the general conduct of the construction industry in this area, and the State, and around the nation, is one in which race discrimination and exclusion on the basis of race is widespread." *City of Richmond v. J. A. Croson Company*, 488 U.S. at 480.

4. *Regents of the Univ. of Cal. v. Bakke*, 438 U.S. 265 (1978), (special admissions program reserving medical school class positions to minority students held illegal); *Hopwood v. Univ. of Tex.*, 236 F.3d 256 (5th Cir. 2000), public law school could not consider race as factor in its admission policy to remedy present effects of past discrimination.

5. Preferential protection extended to minority employees of school held invalid as violation of Fourteenth Amendment.

6. Permanently enjoining set-asides for black subcontractors on city public works contracts where no firm basis existed that would justify race-based discrimination on part of contractors or of local trade associations.

7. Prior to *Harris*, the Court invalidated §6 of the Civil Rights Act of 1870 and dismissed indictments against private citizens charged with violations of S.6 holding that rights under the Fourteenth Amendment could not be violated by private citizens. *See United States v. Cruikshank*, 92 U.S. 542 (1876).

8. Justice Clark, joined by Justices Black and Fortas, stated that it was "both appropriate and necessary under the circumstances here to say that there now can be no doubt that the specific language of §5 [of the Fourteenth Amendment] empowers the Congress to enact laws punishing all conspiracies – with or without state action – that interfere with Fourteenth Amendment rights." *Id.* at 762. In a separate opinion, Justice Brennan (joined by the Chief Justice and Justice Douglas) stated that "[a] majority of the members of the Court expresses the view today that §5 empowers Congress to enact laws punishing *all* conspiracies . . . whether or not state officers or others acting under the color of state laws are implicated in the conspiracy." *Id.* at 774 (emphasis in original).

9. Justice Brennan, specifically referring to the rule of the *Civil Rights Cases*, added: "I do not accept – and a majority of the Court today rejects – this interpretation of §5."

10. The Act provided a federal civil remedy for the victims of gender-motivated violence.

11. Congress enacted the statute on the strength of a voluminous record demonstrating that state law enforcement was generally biased against women and that the state-court system was inadequate to stop gender-biased violence. *Id.* at 653 (Souter, J., dissenting) "The National Association of Attorneys General supported the statute unanimously," and "Attorneys General from 38 states urged Congress to enact the Civil Rights remedy."

12. Stating that "to be slow to recognize state action, to complicate the concept with unwarranted limiting technicalities, is to confirm racism pro tanto."

13. The intent requirement was formally established in *Washington v. Davis*, 426 U.S. 229 (1976). There the Court brushed aside a challenge to the use of a written test for selecting trainees to the D.C. police force that disqualified a disproportionate number of African American candidates, stating that "we have difficulty understanding how a law establishing a racially neutral qualification for employment is nevertheless racially discriminatory and denies 'any person . . . equal protection of the laws' simply because a greater portion of Negroes fail to qualify than members of other racial or ethnic groups."

14. Contrast with the cases actually brought and listed in *Id.* at 244 n.12.

15. In *Palmer*, the city of Jackson, Mississippi, faced with a court order to desegregate the city's public recreational facilities, decided to close its public swimming pools – a decision that facilitated private owners of some of these pools to operate them on a segregated basis. *Id.* at 218–222. The city argued that "the pools were closed because the city council felt they could not be operated safely and economically on an integrated basis." *Id.* at 225. There was evidence on the record that the mayor of Jackson publicly declared "his dedication to maintaining segregated facilities." *Id.* at 250. "Almost everyone in Jackson, Mississippi, knew that the city closed its public swimming pools solely to avoid integration." Paul Brest, Palmer v. Thompson: *An Approach to the Problem of Unconstitutional Legislative Motive*, 1971 Sup. Ct. Rev. 95, 95 (1971). The Court held that the city could close its swimming pools to all its citizens "for any reason, sound or unsound" without violating the Constitution, and that the city's alleged motivation is constitutionally irrelevant. *Palmer*, 403 U.S. at 226.

16. Holding that racial "classifications are constitutional only if they are narrowly tailored measures that further compelling governmental interests."

17. Holding that gender classifications are constitutional only if they serve "important governmental objectives and that the discriminatory means employed are substantially related to the achievement of those objectives;" *United States v. Virginia*, 518 U.S. 515, 523 (1996).

18. *See also Gregory v. Ashcroft*, 501 U.S. 452, 470 (1991), holding the Missouri Constitution's mandatory retirement provision does not violate equal protection; *Mass. Bd. of Retirement v. Murgia*, 427 U.S. 307, 312–316 (1976), holding that the Massachusetts statute setting a mandatory retirement age for police officers does not violate equal protection.

19. "The Congress shall have power to enforce, by appropriate legislation, the provisions of this article."

20. Interpreting the Eleventh Amendment, the Supreme Court has consistently ruled that "the Constitution does not provide for federal jurisdiction over suits against non-consenting States." *Kimel v. Forida Board of Regents*, 2000); *see also College Sav. Bank v. Florida Prepaid Postsecondary Educ. Expense Board*, 527 U.S. 666, 669–670 (1999); *Seminole Tribe of Florida v. Florida*, 517 U.S. 44, 54 (1996). However, the Court recognized that "the Eleventh Amendment . . . [is] necessarily limited by the enforcement provisions of §5 of the Fourteenth Amendment." *Fitzpatrick v. Bitzer*, 427 U.S. 445, 456 (1976).

21. Countering the Court's snap judgment concerning the lack of evidence of unconstitutional discrimination in the legislative record, Justice Breyer catalogued dozens of congressional hearings, reports, and studies that abundantly demonstrate pervasive state and local government discrimination against the disabled. *See Id.* apps. A, B, and C at 389–424 (Breyer, J., dissenting).

22. *See United States v. Morrison*, 529 U.S. 598, 625–626 (2000). "Or, as we have phrased it in more recent cases, prophylactic legislation under §5 must have a 'congruence and proportionality between the injury to be prevented or remedied and the means adopted

to that end.' " *Id.* (quoting *College Savings Bank v. Florida Prepaid Expense Board*, 527 U.S. 627 (1999), and *City of Boerne v. Flores*, 521 U.S. 507 (1997)).

23. In *Bivens v. Six Unknown Named Agents of Fed. Bureau of Narcotics*, the Court recognized an implied private right of action for damages against federal officers alleged to have violated a citizen's Fourth Amendment rights against unreasonable searches and seizures.

24. The Court also noted that remedies under state laws may be available to the plaintiffs in the case. *Malesko*, 534 U.S. at 73–74.

25. Citing the amicus brief of the Legal Aid Society of New York, which explained that "private prisons are exempt from much of the oversight and public accountability faced by the Bureau of Prisons" and that a private prison corporation whose first loyalty is to its stockholders, not the public interest, will be tempted to take cost-cutting measures at the expense of prison inmates.

26. Holding that conduct causing the deprivation of a constitutional right protected against infringement by a State must be fairly attributable to the State and laying out a two-part test for attribution.

27. *See, e.g., North Georgia Fishing, Inc. v. Di-Chew, Inc.*, 419 U.S. 601 (1975), writ of garnishment issued by court clerk on affidavit of creditor; *Sniadach v. Family Fin. Corp.*, 395 U.S. 337 (1969), court clerk issued summons for garnishment at request of creditor; *Fuentes v. Shevin*, 407 U.S. 67 (1972), writ of replevin required only that private applicant file a complaint and a bond; *Lugar v. Edmondson Oil Co.*, 457 U.S. 922 (1982), creditor utilized procedures in a state statute authorizing prejudgment attachment.

28. A similar statute sought to challenge the constitutionality of a Virginia statute which banned cross burning with the intent to intimidate a person or group. The Court, in *Virginia v. Black*, struck down a provision of the same statute that treated "any cross burning as prima facie evidence of intent to intimidate." 123 S.Ct. 1536, 1541 (2003). This rebuttable presumption was considered crucial to the enforcement of the statute because of the inherent difficulty in establishing intent in most cases. Moreover, as Justice Thomas stated in his solitary dissent, "[i]n our culture, cross burning has almost invariably meant lawlessness and understandably instills in its victims well-grounded fear of physical violence." 123 S.Ct. at 1564 (Thomas, J., dissenting). He regretted that the "plurality laments the fate of an innocent cross-burner who burns a cross, but does so without an intent to intimidate." 123 S.Ct. at 1568. The very events that triggered the prosecution in the case, including an attempted cross burning in the yard of an African American family, abundantly substantiated the arguments of Justice Thomas and highlighted the significance of the presumption created by the Virginia statute.

29. The United States Supreme Court accepted this as the "authoritative" interpretation of the Minnesota Supreme Court.

30. *See, e.g., Roth v. United States*, 354 U.S. 476, 483 (1957), holding "libelous utterances are not within the area of constitutionally protected speech;" *Sable Communications of Cal., Inc. v. FCC*, 492 U.S. 115, 124 (1989), holding "the protection of the First Amendment does not extend to obscene speech."

31. Justice Stevens noted, for instance, that the Court allowed the federal government to prohibit false advertising directed at airline passengers, while leaving other commercial advertisements unregulated. *See R.A.V.*, 505 U.S. at 422.

32. *See also Swann v. Charlotte-Mecklenburg Board of Education*, 402 U.S. 1, 15 (1971), citing *Green v. County School Board*, 391 U.S. 430, 437–438 (1968), stating that the

"objective today remains to eliminate from the public schools all vestiges of state-imposed segregation."

33. *Green v. County School Board*, holding that a school district in which not a single white student had elected to attend a former African American school, and 85 percent of the African American students still attended that school, the school board had not achieved adequate compliance with their duty to create a system in which admission to schools is not determined based on race.

34. Two of the best examples of successful desegregation are Charlotte-Mecklenburg, North Carolina, and Wilmington-New Castle, Delaware. *See* David J. Armor, *The End of School Desegregation and the Achievement Gap*, 28 Hastings Const. L. Q. 629, 639–642 (2001).

35. 503 U.S. 467, 492 (1992), holding that A court's discretion to order the incremental withdrawal of its supervision in a school desegregation case must be exercised in a manner consistent with the purposes and objectives of its equitable power.

36. 515 U.S. 70, 89 (1994), noting that "[t]he ultimate inquiry is whether the constitutional violator has complied in good faith with the desegregation decree since it was entered, and whether the vestiges of past discrimination have been eliminated to the extent practicable." (internal citations omitted).

37. *Keyes v. School Dist. No. 1*, 413 U.S. 189, 202 (1973), holding that a finding of intentionally segregative school board actions in a meaningful portion of a school system created a presumption that other segregated schooling within the system was not adventitious.

38. In *Sweatt*, the Supreme Court held that a state law denying African Americans entry into the University of Texas Law School prevented affected students from receiving an education "substantially equal" to the education received by white students. 339 U.S. at 634 n.1. The Court reasoned that this amounted to a violation of the Equal Protection Clause of the Fourteenth Amendment and, consequently, ordered the African American petitioner admitted to the Law School. 339 U.S. at 636.

39. The Fifth Circuit concluded that "[t]he law school has presented no compelling justification, under the Fourteenth Amendment or Supreme Court precedent, that allows it to continue to elevate some races over others . . . " *Hopwood*, 78 F.3d at 934.

40. The *Harris* Court quoted *United States v. Cruikshank*, 92 U.S. 542 (1876), which held that the Constitution of the United States must grant Congress the power to pass a law in order for that law to be valid.

41. The Civil Rights Cases, 109 U.S. 3, 13–14 (1883), *reconfirmed in City of Boerne v. Flores*, 521 U.S. 507, 524–525 (1997), holding that the Freedom Restoration Act exceeds Congress' §5 enforcement powers.

42. *Repeated in Webster v. Reproductive Health Services*, 492 U.S. 490, 507 (1989), holding that the Court need not pass on the constitutionality of a statute's preamble; that the statutory ban on use of public employees and facilities for performance or assistance of nontherapeutic abortions did not contravene the Constitution; and the issue of constitutionality of the statute's prohibition on use of public funds to encourage or counsel women to have nontherapeutic abortions was moot.

43. Representative Garfield stated that "States shall not deny the equal protection of the laws implies that they shall afford equal protection." *Id.* (citing Cong. Globe, 42nd Cong., 1st Sess. 153 app. (April 4, 1871). *See also* Justice Blackmun's dissenting opinion in *Brotherhood of Carpenter v. Scott*, 463 U.S. 825, 839 (1983).

44. The European Court will judge the validity of the doctrine under the provisions of the European Convention on Human Rights which require that contracting state parties "agree not only to refrain from conduct interfering with citizens' rights, but also agree to 'secure to everyone within their jurisdiction the rights and freedoms defined in Section I of this Convention'" Tania Schriver, *Establishing an Affirmative Governmental Duty to Protect Children's Rights: The European Court of Human Rights as a Model for the United States Supreme Court*, 34 U.S. F. L. Rev. 379, 383 (2000).

45. 347 U.S. 483, 493 (1954). Educational opportunity "where the state has undertaken to provide it, is a right which must be made available to all on equal terms."

46. Id. at 878. The Court also enjoined the defendant from excluding "any child from such publicly supported education on the basis of a claim of insufficient resources." (id).

47. The *PARC* court found that the state law that prohibited educational opportunity to the disabled violated the Due Process Clause. The also observed that the Equal Protection Clause may be implicated "because the premise of the [state] statute which necessarily assumes that certain retarded children are uneducable and untrainable lacks a rational basis in fact." (343 F. Supp. at 283). The *Mills* court exclusively relied on the Due Process Clause to support its holding.

48. A congressional report indicated that the PARC and Mills decisions influenced the enactment of the EAHCA in 1975 (see H.R. Rep. No. 94-332 at 3–4 (1975).

49. For a description of the principles of "mainstreaming" and "the" least restrictive environment, see Mei-lan E. Wong, *The Implications of School Choice for Children with Disabilities*, 103 Yale L. J. 827 (1993).

50. Justice Rehnquist claimed that the Court had held the same view about the Equal Protection Clause in two prior cases – *San Antonio Independent School District v. Rodrigues*, 411 U.S. 1 (1973); and *McInnis v. Ogilvie*, 394 U.S. 322 (1969) both involving no issue of education of the handicapped.

REFERENCES

20 U.S.C. §1400 (8)(c) (1975) Individuals with Disabilities Education Act.

29 U.S.C. §§621–634 (1967) Age Discrimination in Employment Act.

29 U.S.C. §701Rehabilitation Act of 1973.

42 U.S.C. §§12101–12213 (1994) Americans with Disabilities Act.

42 U.S.C. §1985(3) Civil Rights Act. *See also*, Civil Rights Act, ch. 22, §2, 17 Stat. 13 (1871).

Alexander, L. (1993). *The public private distinction and constitutional limits on private power*, 10 Const. Comment 361, 363.

Armor, D. J. (2001). *The end of school desegregation and the achievement gap*, 28 Hastings Const. L. Q. 629, 639–642.

Bandes, S. (1990). *The negative constitution: A critique*, 88 Mich. L. Rev. 2271.

Black, C. L., Jr. (1967). *The supreme court: 1966 term, foreword: "state action," equal protection, and California's proposition 14*, 81 Harv. L. Rev. 69, 107.

Brest, P. (1971). Palmer v. Thompson: *An approach to the problem of unconstitutional legislative motive*, 1971 Sup. Ct. Rev. 95, 95.

Casebeer, K. M. (2000). *The empty state and nobody's market: The political economy of non-responsibility and the judicial disappearing of the civil rights movement*, 54 U. Miami L. Rev. 247.

Chemerinsky, C. (1985). *Rethinking state action*, 80 Nw. U. L. Rev. 503, 505.

Cole, M. (1999). *The color-blind constitution, civil rights-talk, and a multicultural discourse for a post-reparations world*, 25 N. Y. U. Rev. L. & Soc. Change 127.

Dolan, M. (1986). *State inaction and section 1985(3): United brotherhood of carpenters and joiners of America v. Scott*, 71 Iowa L. Rev. 1271, 1291. Representative Garfield stated that "States shall not deny the equal protection of the laws implies that they shall afford equal protection." *Id.* (citing Cong. Globe, 42nd Cong., 1st Sess. 153 app. (April 4, 1871)).

Fighting School Resegregation, N. Y. Times, Jan. 27, 2003, at A24 (editorial).

Frankenburg, E. et al. (2003). A multiracial society with segregated schools: Are we losing the dream? The civil rights project: Harvard Univ. 4 (January 2003), *available at* http://www.civilrightsproject.harvard.edu (last visited Nov. 30, 2003).

Freeman, A. D. (1978). *legitimizing racial discrimination through antidiscrimination law: A critical review of supreme court doctrine*, 62 Minn. L. Rev. 1049, 1052.

Heyman, S. J. (1991). *The first duty of government: Protection, liberty and the fourteenth amendment*, 41 Duke L. J. 507, 571.

Holley, D., & Spencer, D. (1999). *The Texas ten percent plan*, 34 Harv. C.R.-C.L. L. Rev. 245, 247.

Hylton, K. N. (1996). *Implications of Mill's theory of liberty for the regulation of hate speech and hate crimes*, 3 U. Chi. L. Sch. Roundtable 35, 52.

Hyytinen, N. S. (2001). *Proposition 209 and school desegregation programs in California*, 38 San Diego L. Rev. 661, 669.

Individuals with Disabilities Education Act (IDEA), P.L. No. 94-142, 89 stat. 773 (1975), amended by Pub. L. No. 101-476, 104 stat. 1141 (1992) and codified 20 U.S.C. §§1400–1487.

Kull, A. (1992). *The color-blind constitution* (Harvard University Press ed.)

Lawrence, C. R., III. (1983). *"Justice" or "Just us": Racism and the role of ideology*, 35 Stan. L. Rev. 831, 845.

Lawrence, C. R., III. (1987). *The id, the ego and equal protection: Reckoning with unconscious racism*, 39 Stan. L. Rev. 317, 355.

Losen, D. J., & Welner, K. G. (2001). *Disabling discrimination in our public schools: Comprehensive legal challenges to inappropriate and inadequate special education services for minority children*, 36 Harv C.R.-C.L.L. Rev. 407.

Pillai, K. G. J. (2003). *Incongruent disproportionality*, 29 Hastings Const. L. Q. 645.

S. Rep. No. 94-168, P.9 (1975), U.S. Code Cong. & Admin. News 1975, p. 1433.

Schriver, T. (2000). *Establishing an affirmative governmental duty to protect children's rights: The European Court of Human Rights as a model for the United States Supreme Court*, 34 U.S. F. L. Rev. 379, 383.

Sealing, K. E. (1998). *The myth of a color-blind constitution*, 54 Wash U. J. Urb. & Contemp. L. 157.

Wong, H., *Warrior for the disabled; Brenda Premo fought on the front line to help win Landmark Rights Bill*, L. A. Times, July 25, 1990, at E1.

Wong, M-l. E. (1993). *The implications of school choice for children with disabilities*, 103 Yale L. J. 827.

U.S. Const. amend. XIV, §5.

FURTHER READING

Adarand Constructors, Inc. v. Pena, 515 U.S. 200, 237 (1995).

Benton v. Maryland, 395 U.S. 784, 794 (1969).

Bivens v. Six Unknown Named Agents of Fed. Bureau of Narcotics, 403 U.S. 388 (1971).

Board of Education of Oklahoma City v. Dowell, 498 U.S. 237 (1991).

Board of Education v. Rowley, 458 U.S. 176, 192 (1982).

Board of Trustees of University of Alabama v. Garrett, 531 U.S. 356, 366 (2001).

Brotherhood of Carpenter v. Scott, 463 U.S. 825, 839 (1983), Justice Blackmun dissenting.

Brown v. Board of Education, 347 U.S. 483, 495 (1954).

Brown v. Board of Education (Brown II), 349 U.S. 294, 301 (1955)

Chaplinsky v. New Hampshire, 315 U.S. 568, 572 (1942).

City of Boerne v. Flores, 521 U.S. 507, 520 (1997).

City of Cleburne v. Cleburne Living Center, 473 U.S. 432 (1985).

City of Memphis v. Greene, 451 U.S. 100 (1981).

City of Richmond v. J. A. Croson Co., 488 U.S. 469, 492 (1989), plurality opinion of O'Connor, J., joined by Rehnquist, C. J., White, J.

Civil Rights Cases, 109 U.S. 3 (1883).

College Savings Bank v. Florida Prepaid Postsecondary Educ. Expense Board, 527 U.S. 666, 669–670 (1999).

Contractors Association of E. Pa. v. City of Philadelphia, 91 F.3d 586 (3d Cir. 1996).

Correctional Services Corporation v. Malesko, 534 U.S. 61 (2001), majority opinion of Rehnquist, C. J.

DeShaney v. Winnebago County Department of Social Services, 489 U.S. 189 (1989).

Edmondson v. Leesville Concrete Co., 500 U.S. 614, 632 (1991), O'Connor, J., dissenting.

Fitzpatrick v. Bitzer, 427 U.S. 445, 456 (1976).

Flagg Brothers v. Brooks, 436 U.S. 149 (1978).

Freeman v. Pitts, 503 U.S. 467, 492 (1992).

Fuentes v. Shevin, 407 U.S. 67 (1972).

Greene v. City of Memphis, 610 F.2d 395, 404 (6th Cir. 1979).

Green v. County School Board, 391 U.S. 430, 437 (1968).

Gregory v. Ashcroft, 501 U.S. 452, 470 (1991).

Hopwood v. Texas, 861 F. Supp. 551, 573 (W.D. Tex. 1994).

Hopwood v. University of Texas, 78 F.3d 932 (5th Cir. 1996), *cert. denied*, 518 U.S. 1033 (1996).

Jackson v. City of Joliet, 715 F.2d 1200, 1203 (7th Cir. 1983).

Keyes v. School District No. 1, 413 U.S. 189, 202 (1973).

Kimel v. Florida Board of Regents, 528 U.S. 62, 83 (2000).

Lugar v. Edmondson Oil Co., 457 U.S. 922, 937 (1982).

Malloy v. Hogan, 378 U.S. 1, 6 (1964).

Mass. Bd. of Retirement v. Murgia, 427 U.S. 307, 312–316 (1976).

McInnis v. Ogilvie, 394 U.S. 322 (1969).

Milliken v. Bradley, 418 U.S. 717, 744–745 (1974).

Mills v. Board of Education of the District of Columbia, 348 F. Supp. 866 (D.D.C. 1972).

Miss. Univ. for Women v. Hogan, 458 U.S. 718, 724 (1982).

Missouri v. Jenkins, 515 U.S. 70, 89 (1994).

Monroe v. Pope, 365 U.S. 167, 236 (1961), Frankfurter, J., dissenting.

North Georgia Fishing, Inc. v. Di-Chew, Inc., 419 U.S. 601 (1975).

Palmer v. Thompson, 403 U.S. 217 (1971).

Pennsylvania Association for Retarded Children v. Pennsylvania (PARC), 343 F. Supp. 279 (E.E. Pa. 1972).

Pers. Adm'r of Mass. v. Feeney, 442 U.S. 256, 279 (1979), citing *Arlington Heights v. Metropolitan Housing Dev. Corp.*, 429 U.S. 252, 266 (1977).

Podberesky v. Kirwan, 956 F.2d 52, 54 (4th Cir. 1992) (*Podberesky I*).

Podberesky v. Kirwan, 38 F.3d 147 (4th Cir. 1994) (*Podberesky II*), *cert. denied*, 514 U.S. 1128 (1995).

R.A.V. v. City of St. Paul, 505 U.S. 377 (1992).

Regents of the Univ. of Cal. v. Bakke, 438 U.S. 265 (1978).

Roth v. United States, 354 U.S. 476, 483 (1957).

Sable Communications of Cal., Inc. v. FCC, 492 U.S. 115, 124 (1989).

San Antonio Independent School District v. Rodrigues, 411 U.S. 1 (1973).

Seminole Tribe of Florida v. Florida, 517 U.S. 44, 54 (1996).

Sniadach v. Family Fin. Corp., 395 U.S. 337 (1969).

Swann v. Charlotte-Mecklenberg Board of Education, 402 U.S. 1 (1971).

Sweatt v. Painter, 339 U.S. 629 (1950).

United States v. Cruikshank, 92 U.S. 542 (1876).

United States v. Guest, 383 U.S. 745 (1966).

United States v. Harris, 106 U.S. 629 (1883).

United States v. Morrison, 529 U.S. 598, 624 (2000), Rehnquist, C. J., joined by O'Connor, Scalia, Kennedy, and Thomas, J. J.

United States v. O'Brien, 391 U.S. 367 (1968).

United States v. Virginia, 518 U.S. 515, 523 (1996).

Vance v. Bradley, 440 U.S. 93, 111 (1979).

Virginia v. Black, 123 S.Ct. 1536, 1541 (2003).

Washington v. Davis, 426 U.S. 229, 248 n. 14 (1976).

Webster v. Reproductive Health Services, 492 U.S. 490, 507 (1989).

Wygant v. Jackson Board. of Education, 476 U.S. 267, 276 (1986), Powell, J., plurality opinion.

3. DISPROPORTIONALITY OF AFRICAN AMERICANS IN SPECIAL EDUCATION PROGRAMS: A FORM OF RESEGREGATION

Warren J. Blumenfeld[*]

INTRODUCTION

No person in the United States shall, on the grounds or race, color, or national origin, be excluded from participating in, be denied the benefits of, or be subjected to discrimination under any program or activity receiving Federal financial assistance, or be so treated on the basis of sex under most education programs or activities receiving Federal assistance.

No otherwise qualified individual with disabilities in the United States shall, solely by reason of his disability, be excluded from the participation in, be denied the benefits of, or be subjected to discrimination under any program or activity receiving Federal financial assistance (U.S. Department of Education, 2001).

Integration

There are milestones in the history of education where conditions have come together to advance progressive social policy reforms. One such milestone was the

[*]Warren J. Blumenfeld is Assistant Professor in the Department of Curriculum and Instruction, Iowa State University, Ames, Iowa.

Administering Special Education: In Pursuit of Dignity and Autonomy
Advances in Educational Administration, Volume 7, 41–73
ISSN: 1479-3660/doi:10.1016/S1479-3660(04)07003-9

momentous United States Supreme Court decision, *Brown v. Board of Education* (Topeka, Kansas), rendered on May 17, 1954. In a unanimous decision, the court ruled that the "separate but equal" clause (set down in the case of *Plessy v. Ferguson*, 1896) was unconstitutional because it violated children's rights as covered in the Fourteenth Amendment of the U.S. Constitution when separating was solely on the classification of skin color. Delivering the court opinion, Chief Justice Earl Warren wrote that the "segregated schools are not equal and cannot be made equal, and hence they are deprived of the equal protection of the laws."

The *Brown* decision rested on accumulated social science research that emphasized the detrimental effects of school segregation on students of color (Balkin, 2001). Following the decision, intransigence on the part of a number of Southern political leaders prevented the law from fully taking effect. In fact, President Eisenhower was compelled to call out federal troops to ensure compliance in Little Rock, Arkansas in 1957. Some Southern governors chose to close some public schools in their states rather than comply with desegregation orders.

The Civil Rights Act of 1964 strengthened the *Brown* decision. Prior to this act, the Fourteenth Amendment of the United States Constitution applied primarily to the actions and laws of *states*. Following the Civil Rights Act of 1964, however, this was extended to include *individuals* who discriminate. The United States Congress passed the law to protect the constitutional rights of all people in the areas of public facilities and *public education*, and to prohibit discrimination in federally assisted programs. Title VI, Section 2000d of the Act stipulated: "Prohibition against exclusion from participation in, denial of benefits of, and discrimination under federally assisted programs on ground of race, color, or national origin." Title VI expressly mandated the withholding of federal funds from institutions, including public schools, which engaged in racial discrimination.

Another milestone in the history of education was an historic piece of legislation, Public Law 94–142, the 1975 Education of All Handicapped Children Act, passed by the United States Congress. This law mandated that to receive federal funds, school systems must provide "free appropriate public education" (FAPE) for every child between the ages of 3 and 18 (extended later to 3 and 21) regardless of how serious the disability. School districts were required to place students in the "least restrictive environment" (LRE) consistent with their educational needs, and, as much as possible, place them with students who do not have disabilities. The law also called for students to be evaluated for services in all areas of suspected disability in a process that is not biased by their language, cultural characteristics, or disability. Evaluation must be conducted by a multidisciplinary team, and no single evaluation procedure may be employed as the only criterion for planning or placement.

The act was reauthorized and amended by Congress in 1990. The amendments renamed this act the "Individuals with Disabilities Act" (IDEA) in keeping with the foundational understanding of emphasizing the person rather than merely the disability. Also, the term "handicapped student" and "handicap" was changed to "child/individual with disability."

On June 4, 1997, President Bill Clinton signed another amendment and reauthorization of IDEA into law. The act called for improvements in the performance of students in special *and* general education. Changes were also directed to focus on the provision of the law known as the "Individual Education Program," or IEP, which is the requirement that guarantees an individualized or tailored program to serve the specific needs of students with disabilities. Changes included the mandate that a statement be included in the IEP of measurable annual goals – which include a benchmark or short-term objectives – which would allow parents and educators to accurately determine a student's progress. The IEP team was also required to design and implement a behavioral management plan to be based on functional behavioral assessments. The amendment also directed educators to precisely measure and report students' progress, and also authorized options for parents and schools officials to mediate any conflicts or disputes they may have in the overall educational plans for students.

The thirteen current categories of special education outlined in IDEA are: Specific Learning Disability, Speech/Language Impairments, Mental Retardation, Emotional Disturbance, Multiple Disabilities, Hearing Impairments, Orthopedic Impairments, Other Health Impairments (of which Attention Deficit Hyperactivity Disorder is included), Visual Impairments, Autism, Deaf-Blind, Traumatic Brain Injury, and Developmental Delay. This latter category, Development Delay, differs from the other twelve categories since it is often considered as a precursor to the other categories of disability. This relatively new disability category, Developmental Delay, showed an incredible 62.1% increase in 1999–2000 over the preceding year (U.S. Department of Education, 2001). Valdivia (1999) defines developmental delay as a lag in development (either global or specific) where a child exhibits a functional level beneath her or his age. Eligibility into this category is open to children between the ages of birth and nine, which allows the child to receive early intervention assistance.

Resegregation

Since the 1970s, the pace of school segregation has slowed substantially. By the end of the 1990s, many U.S. public schools are largely segregated by race. For example, according to the Educational Testing Service in 1969, 77% of African American students attended predominantly minority schools. This figure declined somewhat by 1980 with 62% attending predominantly minority schools. By 1997, however, the figure had risen to 69%, with 35% of African American students attending schools with 90–100% minority students. For Latino/a students, in 1969, 55% were attending predominantly minority schools. By 1997, that number had risen to 75% (Educational Testing Service, in Balkin, 2001, p. B11).

Balkin charges that "resegregation" is due, at least in part, to Supreme Court decisions, which have accelerated the federal courts' attempts to terminate existing school desegregation orders. For example, in the 1974 case of *Milliken v. Bradley*, the Supreme Court virtually released white suburban school districts of Detroit, Michigan from participation in desegregation efforts. In addition, in *Board of Education of Oklahoma City v. Dowell* (1991), the Supreme Court held that lower courts could terminate previous desegregation orders in those school districts that had attempted "in good faith" to comply, even if this would result in abrupt resegregation. Other Supreme Court decisions that have increased the drive to resegregate include *Freeman v. Pitts* (1992) ending aspects of desegregation orders even when other aspects had never been fully implemented, and *Missouri v. Jenkins* (1995) overturning a plan for magnet schools in Kansas City, Missouri designed to attract white students back to inner-city schools. According to Balkin (2001), these legal decisions, along with social, political, and economic factors have been devastating to many children of color:

> Minority children in central cities are educated in virtually all-minority schools with decidedly inferior facilities and educational opportunities. More than half of black and Latino students around the country still attend predominantly minority schools (p. B12).

In addition, the Civil Rights Project at Harvard University (Frankenberg & Lee, 2002) found that although the 2000 national census reflected more racial and ethnic diversity in the United States than ever before, school children are relatively isolated from this diversity as reflected in data collected by the U.S. Department of Education from the year 2000 to 2001. According to the study:

> The racial trend in the school districts studied is substantial and clear: *virtually all* school districts analyzed are showing lower levels of inter-racial exposure since 1986, suggesting a trend toward resegregation, and in some districts, these declines are sharp. As courts across the country end long-running desegregation plans and, in some states, have forbidden the use of any racially-conscious student assignment plans, the last 10–15 years have seen a steady unraveling of almost 25 years worth of increased integration (p. 4, emphasis in original).

Among the study's additional finding were that white students in one-third of the school districts analyzed became more isolated from black and/or Latino/a students in the school years 1986–2000, and that blacks are the "most isolated" from white students in districts that do not have desegregation plans in place or where the courts have rejected city-suburban desegregation plans.

Balkin (2001) correlated the increasing trend toward resegregation with socioeconomic factors and with race, stating that only 5% of segregated white schools are in areas of concentrated poverty, whereas 80% of segregated black and Latino/a schools are in such areas. Schools in low-income areas have limited educational resources. As a consequence, students' educational outcomes in these schools are routinely lower than in wealthier districts.

Jonathan Kozol, in his groundbreaking book, *Savage Inequalities: Children in America's Schools* (1991), exposed in detail the segregated and unequal schooling in this country. He cited an example of a tale of two cities of sorts existing side-by-side: East St. Louis, Illinois that lies on the floodplain (the American Bottoms) on the east side of the Mississippi River, which is predominately black, and the towns on the Bluffs, which are predominately white. Kozol quotes James Nowlan, a professor of public policy at Knox College:

> The two tiers – Bluffs and Bottoms – have long represented...different worlds, [and their physical separation] helps rationalize the psychological and cultural distance that those on the Bluffs have clearly tried to maintain. [People on the Bluffs] overwhelmingly *want this separation to continue* (Nowlan, in Kozol, 1991, p. 9, emphasis added).

Blauner (1992) writes of a United States in which there exists "two languages of race" (p. 50), one spoken by blacks (and by implication, other people of color), the other by whites. By "language," he meant a system of meaning attached to social reality, in this instance a "racial language" reflecting a view of the world. This mirrors the conclusions of the Kerner Commission report released in 1968 in its study of urban unrest. It stated, in part, that the United States was moving toward two separate societies: one white and one black (though the report left it uncertain where other communities of color fit into this equation). Many blacks, and other peoples of color, see "race" and racism as salient and central to their reality. Many whites – excluding members of the more race-conscious extremists groups – consider "race" as a peripheral issue, and may even consider racism as a thing of the past, or, as in the Rodney King incident of March 1991 and in the rise of organized hate groups, as aberrations in contemporary U.S. society. Since the 1960s, blacks have embraced an expanded definition of "racism" to reflect contemporary realities, while many whites have not.

Although most whites are aware of what Batts (1989) terms "old fashioned racism" (taking such forms as slavery, lynchings, cross burnings, definition of people of color as inferior to whites, legal segregation between the "races," and others), many whites, asserts Batts, are either unaware of or unwilling to acknowledge the many manifestations of "modern forms of racism" by whites.

Batts lists these forms as dysfunctional rescuing, blaming the victim, avoidance of contact, denial of cultural differences, and denial of the political significance of differences.

These are among the many reasons Blauner (1992) gives for concluding that "blacks and whites talk past one another":

> Whites and blacks see racial issues through different lenses and use different scales to weigh and assess injustice (p. 50).

It must be added that by the 1960s, a number of national black leaders, including Stokely Carmichael of the Student Non-Violent Coordinating Committee, Malcolm X of the Nation of Islam, Huey P. Newton and H. Rap Brown of the Black Panthers, among others, questioned integrationist strategies generally and particularly in the schools – deprioritizing and even opposing desegregation – on the grounds that the notion that black children would learn best alongside whites was an inherently racist theory. They charged that an educational emphasis relying on integration was one that deemphasized systemic racist social structures, and one that pushed blacks to assimilate into dominant Eurocentric norms and cultural expressions at the expense of black culture and identity. Echoes of these sentiments reverberate to this day.

DISPROPORTIONALITY

In the U.S. during the years 1999–2000, 205,769 children and their families received early intervention services under Part C of IDEA, representing 1.8% of the country's infants and toddlers. Preschoolers served by provisions of IDEA accounted for 588,300 children with disabilities, or approximately 5% of all preschoolers residing in the United States. Students with disabilities ages 6 through 21 served under Part B of IDEA equaled 5,683,707, which was an increase over the 1998–1999 school year of 2.6% (U.S. Department of Education, 2001) (Table 1).

According to Losen and Orfield (2002), despite a number of substantial improvements in the system of special education,

> ... the benefits of special education have not been equitably distributed. Minority children with disabilities all too often experience inadequate services, low-quality curriculum and instruction, and unnecessary isolation from their nondisabled peers. Moreover, inappropriate practices in both general and special education classrooms have resulted in overrepresentation, misclassification, and hardship for minority students, particularly black children (p. xv).

In this regard, special education classes are used as a dumping ground for "difficult children."

Table 1.   Percentage and Number of Children Served Under IDEA by Disability and Age Group During the 1999–2000 School Year: *High-Incidence Disabilities.*

	Ages 6–11		Ages 12–17		Ages 18–21	
	Number	Percentage	Number	Percentage	Number	Percentage
Specific learning disabilities	1,118,152	39.9	1,608,645	61.9	145,169	51.1
Speech or language impairments	958,182	34.2	126,724	4.9	5,058	1.8
Mental retardation	238,714	8.5	308,802	11.9	66,917	23.5
Emotional disturbance	159,879	5.7	283,934	10.9	26,298	9.3
Multiple disabilities	51,312	1.8	47,010	1.8	14,671	5.2
All disabilities	2,802,385	100.0	2,597,134	100.0	284,188	100.0

Source: U.S. Department of Education, Office of Special Education Programs. (2001). Data Analysis System (DANS), p. II-26.

During the 1970s, the Office for Civil Right (OCR) of the United States Department of Education found that while black children represented 16% of the overall school-age population, they accounted for 38% of what was then referred to as "educationally mentally retarded" (what today is referred to as "mild" or "mild to moderately mentally retarded").

Meier et al. (1989) published results from their large-scale research project assessing 174 school districts throughout the United States to determine factors that limit educational equity for black students. The authors discovered that, in addition to other forces, "the sorting practices of schools are associated with racial disproportions" (p. 5). In addition, they found that African Americans were placed in classes for students with mild mental retardation three times more often than white students. The reverse was found in the assignment of students in classes for "gifted and talented," with white students 3.2 times more likely to be placed than African American students. The authors termed this uniform pattern as "second-generation educational discrimination," which is, basically a practice of resegregation.

According to a U.S. Department of Education study in 1992, while African Americans comprised 16% of the overall school population, they accounted for 32% of students designated in special education programs for students with mild retardation, 29% of students in programs for moderate mental retardation, and 24% of students in programs for students with serious emotional disturbance or behavioral disorders (in Zhang & Katsiyannis, 2002).

By 1998, the U.S. Department of Education's Office of Civil Rights (OCR) found only moderate improvements in this equation. While black children represented 17% of the total number of school-aged students, they represented 33% of those classified as "mentally retarded" (U.S. Department of Education, 2000). The National Research Council (in Donovan & Cross, 2002) found that over this same time period, black student disproportionality in the classification of emotional disturbance (ED), as well as the relatively rare diagnosis of ED combined with learning disabilities (SLD) rose significantly.

The most recent report of the U.S. Department of Education (2001) to Congress on the Implementation of IDEA found that "[b]lack students with disabilities exceeded their representation among the resident population." (p. xxii). According to this report, African Americans exceeded representation in all of the 13 special education disability classifications. The most glaring disparities were in the categories of mental retardation (34%), developmental delay (30.5%), and emotional disturbance (27.3%) (U.S. Department of Education, 2001). Included in this problem is the overrepresentation of blacks and other students of color in special education programs as well as the underrepresentation of these students in classes for students classified as "gifted and talented" (Table 2).

The issue of overrepresentation of students of color in special education has been documented for a number of years. Artiles and Trent (2000) define "disproportionate representation" as the "unequal proportions of culturally diverse students in special education programs" (p. 514).

In 1968, Lloyd Dunn brought to the attention of educators the disproportionality of students of color (primarily blacks and Latino/as) diagnosed with "educable mental retardation" in settings segregated from general education classrooms. From the time of Dunn's initial investigations, reports of overrepresentation have expanded to include additional special education categories. Though the figures for individual groups sometimes differ depending on the study or the agency reporting or interpreting the data, since Dunn's research, primarily black students have been consistently overrepresented in special education programs and underrepresented in programs for gifted and talented students.

The overrepresentation of African American children and youth in special education programs for students with learning disabilities, severe emotional or behavioral disorders, and mental disabilities remains a persistent reality even after more than 20 years of recognition (Patton, 1998, p. 2).

In their study, Oswald et al. (2002) found that biological sex and ethnicity/race were key determinants associated with identification for special education classification. In comparison to white females (who were statistically lowest in proportion to overall numbers within the school-aged population), white males, for example were

Table 2. Percentage of Students Ages 6 Through 21 Served by Disability and Race/Ethnicity, 1999–2000 School Year.[a, b, c]

Disability	American Indian/ Alaska Native	Asian/ Pacific Islander	Black (Non-Hispanic)	Hispanic	White (Non-Hispanic)
Specific learning disabilities	1.4	1.6	18.4	16.6	62.1
Speech or language impairments	1.2	2.4	16.1	12.7	67.6
Mental retardation	1.1	1.8	*34.2*	9.1	53.8
Emotional disturbance	1.1	1.2	*27.3*	8.9	61.5
Multiple disabilities	1.5	2.3	20.0	11.5	64.8
Hearing impairments	1.3	4.6	16.4	17.9	59.8
Orthopedic impairments	0.8	3.0	14.7	14.8	66.8
Other health impairments	1.1	1.4	14.9	8.0	74.7
Visual impairments	1.1	3.5	18.6	14.0	62.9
Autism	0.7	4.8	20.5	9.2	64.9
Deaf-Blindness	2.0	7.5	24.7	11.2	54.6
Traumatic brain injury	1.6	2.4	16.9	10.5	68.5
Developmental delay	0.9	0.8	*30.5*	4.1	63.7
All disabilities	1.3	1.8	20.3	13.7	62.9
Resident population	1.0	3.8	14.5	16.2	64.5

Source: U.S. Department of Education, Office of Special Education Programs (2001). Data Analysis System (DANS), p. II-27.

[a] Due to rounding, rows may not sum to 100%.

[b] Race/ethnicity distributions exclude Outlying Areas because current population estimates by race/ethnicity were not available for those areas.

[c] Population counts are July 1999 estimates from the U.S. Census Bureau.

3.8 times more likely to be identified with SED, black males were 5.5 times more likely, and American Indian males were 5.024 times as likely. However, compared to white females, black females were 1.376 times as likely to be identified with SED, and American Indian females, 1.376 as likely. In the classification of Mental Retardation, compared to white females, white males were 1.21 times as likely to be classified, while black males were 3.26 times as likely, and American Indian males 1.66 times as likely. Black females showed a 2.2 odds ratio, and American Indian females a 1.21 odds ratio.

Students identified in the categories of emotional disturbance, mental retardation, and multiple disabilities were more likely compared to students in other disability categories to receive services outside the regular classroom for more than 60% of the school day. MacMillan and Reschly (1998) assert that overrepresentation of primarily black students in the categories of mild

Table 3. Number and percentage of Students Age 14 and Older with
Disabilities Graduating with a Standard Diploma by Race/Ethnicity, 1998–1999.

Race/Ethnicity	Graduated with a Standard Diploma		Dropped Out	
	Number	Percentage	Number	Percentage
American Indian/Alaska Native	1,544	47.9	1,420	44.0
Asian/Pacific Islander	2,033	56.6	675	18.8
Black	19,653	43.5	15,251	33.7
Hispanic	13,150	52.9	8,029	32.3
White	100,900	63.4	42,820	26.9

Notes: The percentages in this table were calculated by dividing the number of students ages 14 through
21 in each racial/ethnic group who graduated with a standard diploma or dropped out by the
number of students ages 14 through 21 in that racial/ethnic group who are known to have left
school (i.e. graduated with a standard diploma, received a certificate of completion, reached
the maximum age for services, died, or dropped out).

New York, North Carolina, Washington, and the District of Columbia have not yet reported
1998–1999 exiting data by race/ethnicity and are thus not included in this table.

Source: U.S. Department of Education, Office of Special Education Programs (2001), Data Analysis
System (DANS), p. I-5.

mental retardation and emotional disturbance is, indeed, a problem because it
is restricted to what they term "judgmental" disability categories, as opposed to
some of the biologically-grounded conditions where there is a disproportional
representation of whites with, for example, PKU, Jews with Tay Sachs disease,
and African Americans with sickle cell anemia – conditions that are not contested
in overrepresentation discussions. Discussions around disproportionality in special
education, rather, center on the issue of *misplacement*.

In addition, overall graduation rates of students in special education varied by
race and ethnicity ranging from the highest (63.4%) among whites to the lowest
(43.5%) among black students. The lowest graduation rate among all the categories
of disability was in the area of emotional disturbance. Most students in special
education who drop out of high school "lack the social skills necessary to be
successfully employed; they consequently suffer from low employment levels and
poor work histories" (U.S. Department of Education, 2001, p. xxi) (Table 3).

A recurring question arising from the extant literature focusing on
disproportionality of black students in special education programs is, "Is
overrepresentation, indeed, a problem?" Most researchers in this field answer in
the affirmative. For example, Articles and Trent (1994) assert:

We argue that it is [a problem], and we maintain that the fact that disproportionate numbers
of minority students are placed in special education classrooms questions the efficacy of our

professional practices and challenges the basic notion of honoring the diversity that we as a field presumably embrace (pp. 410–411).

In addition, Artiles et al. (in press) see overrepresentation as a problem not only because it stigmatizes students, "but it can also deny individuals the high quality and life enhancing education to which they are entitled" (p. 4). Overrepresentation has been a problem for many African American students across the United States for a number of reasons, including the issue that many children of color have been denied access to the general education curriculum, some do not receive the services they need, and some are at risk of misclassification (The Council for Exceptional Children, 2002).

Heller et al. (1982) use the following criteria to determine whether disproportionality in special education is, indeed, a problem:

(1) if children are invalidly placed in programs for mentally retarded students; (2) if they are unduly exposed to the likelihood of such placement by virtue of having received poor-quality regular instruction; and (3) if the quality and academic relevance of the special instruction programs block students' educational progress, including decreasing the likelihood of their return to the regular classroom (p. 18).

Losen and Orfield (2002) claim that overrepresentation in special education programs often reflects similar overrepresentation in a number of undesirable school- and youth-related areas – including dropping out of school, placement in low academic tracks, school suspensions, and involvement with the juvenile justice system – and *under*representation in the desirable category of gifted and talented. The Office for Civil Rights (2000) of the U.S. Department of Education supports this claim. For example, while black students represent 17% of the total school population, they account for 33% of those suspended, 33% of those classified as "mentally retarded," and only 8% labeled "gifted and talented."

Losen and Orfield (2002) remind us that legally in the mandates set down by IDEA, students must be placed in the *least* restricted environment possible, and they claim that students receive the most benefit when educated with their general education peers to the maximum extent appropriate to their needs and their disability:

... students with disabilities are entitled to receive supports and services in a setting best suited to their individual needs, and not to be automatically assigned to a separate place, subjected to low expectations, or excluded from educational opportunities (Losen & Orfield, 2002, p. xxi).

They argue, however, that two groups in particular, Latinos and blacks, are "far less likely than whites to be educated in a fully inclusive general education classroom and far more likely to be educated in a substantially separate setting" (p. xxi).

Special education identification can and often has proven to benefit a great number of children who otherwise would have been denied services and programs to fully address their special educational needs. Overrepresentation of black and Latino/a students would not be considered a problem by educational researchers and government officials if the evidence supported the conclusion that overidentification and segregation from the general education classroom significantly benefited these students. However, Judy Heumann, Assistant Secretary of Education and Director of the Office for Special Education and Rehabilitative Services during the Clinton administration asserted that the system is discriminatory against racial minorities because

> Minority children are more likely not to receive the kinds of services they need in the regular ed. system and the special ed. system. . . . And special education is used as a place to move kids from a regular classroom out into a separate setting (Public Broadcasting Service, 1996).

Patton (1998) asserts that the majority of these black students are being denied the "quality and life enhancing-education" that has been proposed by the special education system because they are generally placed in segregated environments where they are stigmatized while being denied access to general education curricula.

Minority students are not only disproprotionally represented in special education programs, but are also likely to be overrepresented in resource rooms, separate classrooms, and separate school facilities as compared to their white counterparts (Grossman, 1991; Harry, 1992). Lipsky and Gertner (1997) continue that, "the negative consequences of the separate special education system are greater for students from racial minorities" (p. 33). Education of minority students in these restrictive placements has, in turn, lowered their levels of achievement in elementary and secondary schools, and has decreased their chances for post-secondary education, which has limited their options for employment (Patton, 1998). Patton asks a number of serious and important questions:

> What common good is served by having disproportionately large numbers of African Americans, specifically males, in special education programs? Whose common good is served and for what purpose? What kind of disservice does this arrangement, and the subsequent lack of contact with African American students, provide for non-African American people individually and collectively? How does society benefit when the potentialities of large numbers of African Americans lie in a program for those with emotional disturbance or mental disability? (p. 5).

In terms of post-secondary school employment prospects, approximately 75% of African American students categorized as having a disability, as compared to 47% of white students, have not found employment two years out of school. In addition, more than half (52%) of young African Americans adults as compared to 39% of their white counterparts remain unemployed three to five years out of school (Osher, 2001).

In the past three years, OSEP [the Office of Special Education Programs] has found that noncompliance regarding transition requirements persists in many States. Although more IEPs for students age 16 or older now include transition content, the statements of needed transition services do not meet Part B requirements (U.S. Department of Education, 2001, p. xxv).

CAUSES OF THE PROBLEM

Social Reproduction Theory

Definition

While the United States prides itself on being a country with enormous opportunity for those who have the motivation and drive to succeed, and it rests on the guiding principle of meritocracy, the reality often does not live up to the promise. The United States is a beautiful and noble concept, a vibrant idea, a vital and enduring vision, a process and progression toward, but not yet attaining, not yet reaching that concept, that idea, that vision. It is, rather, a work in process. This is true in the larger society as well as within the schools.

In my investigation of the literature focusing on disproportionality in special education, I discovered a number of causes to the problem. To situate my findings, I use the following conceptual organizer. Termed "Social Reproduction Theory," this philosophy asserts that schools basically reproduce the social inequities, especially in terms of socioeconomic class and also race, found within the larger society. Major exponents of this theory are economists Samuel Bowles and Herbert Gintis (1976) who contend that the schools often reflect, in microcosmic perspective, and maintain the divisions and unequal opportunities evident in the larger society.

Losen and Orfield (2002) list a number of factors in the overrepresentation problem including:

> . . . unconscious racial bias on the part of school authorities, large resource inequalities that run along lines of race and class, unjustifiable reliance on IQ and other evaluation tools, educator's inappropriate responses to the pressures of high-stakes testing, and power differentials between minority parents and school officials (p. xviii).

School practices that promote the reproduction of social inequalities include tracking, ability grouping, teacher expectations (and biases), counseling methods, and unequal funding expenditures.

Tracking

Tracking, a practice primarily found in high schools, divides students into separate and often distinct curricula "tracts" such as advanced placement (or "AP"), college preparatory, general level, basic level, career or occupational training, and others. While this sorting process can have some benefits, it can also pose a number of hardships upon students. According to a student of mine, Jamie Timmons, in my course, The American School at Colgate University in central New York State:

> Schools . . . have a habit of focusing on a select group of students to be groomed for college. Separating students into vocational or college prep classes may be an obvious way to narrow the focus of education, but it also takes away from a student's self-determination. Not only is it detrimental to the student who is told he is not "college material," it can also hurt the student who is told that being a mechanic or working with wood is beneath him (Timmons, 2003).

Stanford University professor of psychology, Claude Steele (2003), has coined the term "stereotype vulnerability," where minority students fear conforming to the myth of intellectual inferiority. They, therefore, decrease their academic efforts in an attempt to protect themselves psychologically from the potentially devastating prospects of trying hard with poor results.

In terms of special education, many educators believe that labeling students and placing them in classes with others of similar behavioral, learning, or physical characteristics enhance their changes for academic and/or social success. Some believe, however, that the negative effects of labeling far exceeds the benefits in that the labels themselves often stigmatize students.

Ability Grouping

Ability Grouping, though much like tracking, places students into different classes or groups within a given class based on their abilities. The students' abilities are determined by a combination of teacher assessment and standardized testing. Joel Spring (2002) asserted that the level of a student's placement is often dependent on that student's socioeconomic class and/or ethnoracial background:

> Often, the family income of students parallels the levels of ability grouping and tracking. That is, the higher the family income of the students, the more likely it is that they will be in the higher ability groups or a college-preparatory curriculum. Conversely, the lower the family income of the students, the more likely it is that they will be in the lower ability groups or the vocational curriculum (p. 77).

Teacher Expectations

Teachers' expectations, assumptions, and biases also play a large part in the placement equation. Teachers and other school officials often expect students to act and respond in certain stereotypical ways, often dependent on the students' socioeconomic and ethnoracial backgrounds. For example, teachers may expect working-class and poor students and black students to do poorly and middle-class and upper-class white students to do well in school. Students often respond accordingly to these expectations. This is termed the "self-fulfilling prophesy." In terms of special education labels, often teachers respond to the label attached to the students rather than emphasizing students' individuality and individual needs. The teacher might, therefore, expect less from a student labeled within a special education category. This is often exacerbated when the student is a student of color.

Meyen and Skrtic (1995) claim that the teacher's temperament and level of tolerance greatly impact whether students are referred to special education. Also, students with behavioral issues are more often referred (Craig et al., 1978).

In terms of perceptions, for example, Charles and Massey (2003) questioned 3,924 college students on their perceptions of themselves and of other racial groups and found that:

> [B]lack people are rated most negatively on traits that are consistent with American racial ideology. White, Latino, and Asian students are all likely to perceive blacks as violence-prone and poor. They also rate black people more negatively than themselves in traits like lazy, unintelligent, and preferring welfare dependence (B-11).

These results represent larger social notions associated with racial groupings. Teachers are increasingly less familiar with the cultural diversity associated with students' ethnicity and race. This, in turn, can lead to teachers' mistaken assumptions or diagnosis whereby the teacher mistakes cultural diversity with behavior disorders. McDermott (1987), for example, maintains that school failure of students of color can be, at least partially, explained by looking at clashes between the students' cultural background and the dominant culture reflected in the classroom.

> If the teacher frequently devalues or ignores these children's cultural backgrounds, they will often reject the teacher's messages as worthless . . . . Reciprocally, if the behaviors of the child are not consistent with the expectations and standards espoused by the teacher and the dominant culture as a whole, the child may be seen as behaviorally and/or academically deficient (quoted in Artiles & Trent, 1994, p. 423).

Harry (1992) has reported that teachers' expectations, prejudices, and biases have influenced their special education referral decisions of students of color. In addition, Ysseldyde et al. (1982) report that the factors of gender, physical appearance, as well as socioeconomic background effect special education eligibility decisions especially in the category of "learning disabilities." Following an extensive review of the literature, Artiles and Trent (1994) postulate that biased stereotypes regarding the academic abilities of children of color are advanced, "and to some extent perpetuate the placement of disproportionate numbers of minority students in special education classes" (p. 422).

Especially in the category of "emotional disturbance," one primary problem is that many teachers do not have the training to identify this disorder. Meyen and Skrtic (1995) define "seriously emotionally disturbed" (SED) as:

... a condition exhibiting one or more of the following characteristics over a long period of time and to a marked degree, which adversely affects educational performance: (a) an inability to learn which cannot be explained by intellectual, sensory, or health factors; (b) an inability to build or maintain satisfactory interpersonal relationships with peers and teachers; (c) inappropriate types of behavior or feelings under normal circumstances; (d) a general pervasive mood of unhappiness or depression; or (e) a tendency to develop physical symptoms or fears associated with personal or school problems (p. 48).

Polite and Davis (1999), assert that within general education classrooms, students who do not conform to educators' expectations of appropriate speech and action are often judged as disabled and are determined to be unsuited to general classroom instruction. In this regard, teachers influence whether a student is classified as emotionally disturbed, since the label of SED often is dependent on the interpretation of observable behaviors.

The SED classification itself depends significantly upon the moods of those who perceive the behavior as disordered, rather than upon professional concerns related to cognitive deficits, academic failure, superior ability, or sensory or physical differences (Polite & Davis, p. 40).

The criteria are bias laden, especially if the teacher has lowered expectations of the student based on that student's ethnoracial and/or class background, which is often the case for African American students, whom teachers often expect to be more disruptive and defiant than white students. Grossman (1991) asserts that teachers' negative and biased views of African American working-class students, in particular, can and does lead to overrepresentation in special education programs.

This may help to explain why both regular educators and special educators are more likely to choose a special education placement program for minority and working class students and a regular education placement for Euro-American middle-class students with the exact same behavioral and academic problems (p. 3).

Moreover, Grossman has found that teachers praise their African American student less often and criticize them more – verbally and nonverbally – than their white counterparts. When African Americans are given positive feedback by teachers, it is more often related to the student's behavior rather than their academic performance. Grossman continues that this preferential treatment also results in teachers interacting more with white students than with blacks. Teachers, for example, are more likely to respond to questions from and direct more questions to the white students, and are least likely to respond to African Americans, in particular, African American females.

Although Euro-American teachers typically demonstrate considerable concern and interest in Euro-American females' academic work, they pay less attention to African American female students' academic work than to their social behavior (Grossman, 1991, p. 3).

Grossman found that, in general, teachers in classes with higher percentages of African Americans respond in more authoritarian ways to African American students, and they are less inclined to employ an open classroom pedagogical approach. In addition, to address students' misbehavior, educators more often criticize the African American males' behavioral expression and are more inclined to use methods of punishment, including corporal punishment and school suspension.

> The evidence of prejudicial treatment . . . has led many educators to conclude that prejudice in school and in society in general drives many minority and working-class students to actively resist both their teachers and the system by purposefully misbehaving, tuning out teachers, disrupting their lessons, refusing to do their homework, coming late to school, and dropping out before graduating (Grossman, 1991, p. 5).

Because teacher perceptions are used in the evaluation process for placing students into special education programs, it is imperative that these teachers have the experience and expertise to make accurate evaluations. According to the U.S. Department of Education (2001), teacher vacancies in special education present a glaring problem. "As of October 1, 1999, there were 12,241 funded positions [in special education] left vacant or filled by substitutes because suitable candidates could not be found" (p. xxiv). With the enormous shortage overall of qualified teachers – special education as well as general education – this has led to the use of substitute teachers, unqualified personnel, and paraprofessionals in both the general education classroom as well as in special education. No matter whether teachers are fully qualified or not, they are legally required to be involved in the process of the referral, assessment, classification, and treatment components. Ysseldyke and Agozzine (1981) warn that many of the untrained teachers are "more susceptible to problems related to behavior than those associated with other child characteristics" (p. 434). Harry and Anderson (1994) continue that this shortage of qualified teachers often results in an increase in the identification of students labeled as "disabled," and increases the overrepresentation of African Americans in special education.

In addition, the overwhelming majority of public school teachers are of European descent. In 1988, for example, whites comprised nearly 90% of the teaching population in U.S. public schools, while white students made up approximately 70% of the overall school population. Since 1988, the racial makeup of teachers has changed very little, despite the increase of students of color in the overall demographic distribution. Cook and Boe (1995) discovered that 86% of special education teachers and 87% of general education teachers were white. There is evidence to suggest that teachers are more likely to recommend students from racial background dissimilar to their own to the special education system. McIntyre and Pernelle (1985) found, for example, that white teachers generally recommend more students to special education than their faculty of color counterparts. "White teachers referred students five times more often than did minority teachers from other racial groups" (pp. 112–113). The Council for Exceptional Children (2002) warns that errors in assessment, eligibility, and placement in special education occurs frequently, when, in actuality, these students are the "victims of ineffective teaching" (p. 15) rather than appropriate candidates for special education services.

Counseling Methods

Counseling Methods, by teachers as well as guidance counselors, often vary depending on the socioeconomic and/or ethnoracial background of the students and their parents. Spring (2001) states that parents of children in the middle and upper classes are more likely requested to attend school meetings to discuss the *work* of their children, whereas parents of working-class children are more likely asked to come to school to discuss the *behavior* of their children. Spring asserts:

> Objectively, one would assume that if the school were acting free of social-class [and ethnoracial] bias, parents of lower-class children would receive more counseling about schoolwork than about behavior . . . [P]roblems related to children of the lower social class tend to be considered behavior problems in school, whereas those related to the upper classes tend to be considered learning problems (p. 78).

Collaboration between parents and school personnel is an important aspect in the referral process, as it is also an important component of IDEA, which provides parents the right to share in the decision-making process of their child's education. Sometimes parents do not fully understand the educational implications of their child's disability. Power struggles can often develop between school personnel and parents.

> Frequency of communication, lack of communication, lack of follow up, misunderstood communications, and timing of clarifying attempts were given as factors that escalate conflicts between parents and schools (Grossman, 1991, p. 10).

In addition, the U.S. Department of Education (2001) concluded: "Families that expressed reservations about their level of involvement in the individualized education program process were disproportionately from black, Hispanic, and Asian/Pacific Islander families and from low-income households" (p. xxiii).

Unequal School Expenditures

Unequal school expenditures occurs when school districts with higher rates of taxable wealth have greater educational resources and spend more on children than districts with lower rates of taxable wealth resulting in glaring inequities in spending between school districts. According to a study conducted by the National Center for Education Statistics (NCES) (1997–1998),

> Districts with high percentages of disabled, limited-English-proficient and poor children may have to raise more revenue to provide education comparable to those in districts with lower percentages of these children (quoted in Spring, 2001, p. 84).

The NCES reports that wealthier school districts spend as much as 36% more per student than do poorer districts. Even when differentials in the cost of living between districts is accounted for, wide gaps remain in terms of financial *and* educational disparities.

Poverty and Not Poverty

Poverty has both direct and indirect influence on school academic outcomes generally, and on special education placement specifically (Artiles et al., in press). While greater numbers of white people live in poverty, the percentages of people of color living in poverty as compared to their numbers in the overall population far exceeds that of white people. For example, in 1999, the poverty rate was 11.9% of the overall population. For whites, the rate was 8%, 11% for Asian/Pacific Americans, 23% for Latino/as, 24% for African Americans, and 26% for American Indians (statistics from Artiles et al., in press, manuscript p. 8).

As is evident from the statistics, communities of color are disproportionately poor. This might explain, at least in part, the racial discrepancies in disability identifications. Objectively, one might expect that poverty would cause a higher frequency of what are known as the "hard" disabilities (e.g. blindness and deafness) among groups living in poverty due to the negative influences of substandard nutrition and inadequate pre- and post-natal care. Losen and Orfield (2002), after conducting an exhaustive literature review, are unequivocal, however, in their conclusion that African Americans throughout the nation are significantly *less likely* to be overrepresented in these "hard" categories. *"The effects of poverty cannot satisfactorily explain racial disparities in identification for mental retardation or emotional disturbance"* (Losen & Orfield, 2002, p. xxiii, emphasis in original). Poverty alone, then, cannot explain the overrepresentation problem. Race and racism is a, possibly *the*, significant factor.

Oswald et al. (2002) asked the question: Taking into account the effects of social, demographic, and school-related variable, are gender and ethnicity significantly associated with the risk of being identified for special education. They found that though the incidence of disabilities often increases with poverty, when wealth-related and poverty factors are controlled for, the significant predictors of cognitive disability identification in school are ethnicity and gender. What was most revealing in their survey was that even in the *wealthier* districts, black children, especially males, were, again, more likely to be labeled "mentally retarded." In addition, poverty alone cannot explain the vast gap between racial groups in the identification of males over females (see, e.g. National Research Council, 2002).

According to Losen and Orfield (2002), race and systemic societal racism rather than poverty alone are the most significant factors in overrepresentation. They report persistent trends or themes in their research. First, they found "pronounced and persistent racial disparities" in the identification and labeling between black and white children in the special education categories of mental retardation and emotional disturbance, and far less disparity in the category of special learning disability. They also found only a minimal level of racial disparity in the "hard" medically diagnosed disabilities when compared to the great level of disparity in the "subjective" or "soft" categories of cognitive disabilities. They also witnessed enormous differences in the incidence of disability from state to state and region to region. For example, in states "with a history of racial apartheid under *de jure* segregation" – Mississippi, South Carolina, North Carolina, Florida, and Alabama – these accounted for five of the seven states with the greatest disproportionality of African Americans labeled "mentally retarded." Losen and Orfield (2002) term this the "soft bigotry of low expectations," which they suggest may be the latest incarnation of "the undeniable intentional racial discrimination in education against blacks that once pervaded the South" (p. xxiii). Also, in the categories of mental retardation and emotional disturbance, they found "gross disparities" between African Americans and Latino/as and between African American males and females.

Additional Causes

Culturally Insensitive Evaluation Instruments
The Office of Special Education of the U.S. Department of Education (2001) reported that "culturally and linguistically diverse students may be disadvantaged in the assessment and evaluation process" (p. xxiii). Valdivia (1999) warned that we must determine whether the norms within the process of assessment and evaluation are inclusive of diverse families, whether diverse children represent variations that typify the communities in which the tool is being applied, whether the tool or process include provisions to conduct the evaluation in the student's dominant language, and whether the trained personnel have familiarity with the

family's culture, practices, and beliefs. All these criteria have an effect on proper identification. For example, Coll (1990) conducted a study in which she looked at tactile stimulation, verbal interaction, non-verbal interaction, and feeding routines in families in a variety of cultural traditions, including African Americans. She found that

> ... minority infants are not only exposed to different patterns of affective and social interactions, but that their learning experiences might result in the acquisition of different modes of communication from those characterizing Anglo infants, different means of exploration of their environment, and the development of alternative cognitive skills (p. 274).

Grossman (1991) concluded that many working-class and ethnoracial minority students are referred to special education programs largely because "the Euro-American middle class and upper class design the structure, organization, instructional strategies, and curriculum contents of schools to conform to their values, interests, learning styles, and needs" (p. 5). He contends that a teacher's "cultural competence" and "cultural sensitivity" are of paramount importance to ethnoracial minority students because of the "discontinuities" and bicultural realities that exist between the student's home environment and the norms and values found in most public schools.

Grossman defines "cultural sensitivity" as:

> ... an awareness of the general problems culturally diverse students experience in school because of their cultural differences, how cultural differences influence students' preferred learning styles, how they may cause students to behave in ways that are acceptable in their cultures, but not in school, and how these differences may lead students to react in unanticipated ways to behavior management techniques (p. 6).

For Grossman, cultural sensitivity is not merely being "sensitive" to students' cultural background, as the term might imply, but going further by having an understanding, a knowledge base of the numerous cultures represented in the classroom with the ability to gear lessons to cultural differences.

European American and African American Cross-Cultural Styles in Conflict

A number of researchers have looked into the differing worldviews and perspectives between females and males centering on linguistic/communication and cultural styles and values (e.g. Eakins & Eakins, 1978; Gilligan, 1982; Tannen, 1984, 1990, 1994). Other researchers (e.g. Kochman, 1981, 1994; Visions, 1994) have centered their comparisons between African American and European Americans.

Table 4.   Cross-Cultural Comparisons Between Anglo-Americans and African
Americans.

Components of World View	Anglo-American	African American
Psychological-Behavioral	Individuality, difference, uniqueness	Group centered, sameness
Values & Customs	Competition, individual	Cooperation, collective
Ethos	Independence, survival of fittest	Interdependence, survival of group
Epistemology	Cognitive, evaluating, measuring, counting	Affect, symbolic imagery, rhythm, feeling
Logic	Dichotomous, either/or	Deunital, both/and
Concept of Self	Individual	Extended self-concept, individual *and* group identities
Time	Clock-time, "on time"	Event focused in time, "starts when I get there
Ontology (what is "real")	Material	Spiritual

While the chart above depicts *general* trends and styles, and not all individuals within a given culture fit at all times and contexts, so too, many variations exist within a group. Moreover, styles differ *within* a given "ethnic," "racial," or "religious" culture stemming from a number of variables: adherence to traditions, degree of assimilation into the dominant culture, level of contact with the dominant culture, class background, biological sex, as well as generational and geographic differences.

Table 4 outlines some of the themes comparing African Americans and (assimilated) European Americans (Visions, 1994).

In his extensive research into the differing linguistic and cultural patterns of blacks and whites in the United States, Kochman (1981, 1994) grouped his finding in a number of areas. In summarizing the different cultural styles between blacks and whites, he highlighted the fact that these divergent styles, and the often-divergent *meanings* attached to these styles, repeatedly clashed in educational settings, the workplace, and on the playing field. Kochman (1981) emphasized:

> Both white and black males and females interpret each others' behavior in accordance with the meaning and value that behavior has within their own culture (p. 83).

In addition, Patton (1998) claimed that a number of researchers and educators generally view and interpret the behavior of African Americans based upon their own "outsider" beliefs, values, and assumptions regarding the genesis and significance of the behavior. Patton refers to this as "epistemological racism."

Over-Determination of Placement on IQ Tests

Dunn (1968) was one of the first researchers to assert that some of the causes of the problem of overrepresentation rested in the assessment tools, in particular standard IQ testing:

> The purpose has been to find out what is wrong with the child in order to label him and thus make him eligible for special education services. In large measure this has resulted in digging the educational graves of many racially and/or economically disadvantaged children by using a WISC or Binet IQ score to justify the label "mentally retarded" (p. 9).

Deno (1970) proposed rather that educators develop a paradigm shift away from the current medical model, which emphasizes locating a "defect" that is believed to reside within the child. Instead, educators need to focus attention to a greater degree to the external factors that may be having a tremendous impact on the apparent problems the child is having.

Patton (1998) has found that a number of intelligence tests are, indeed, biased and harmful in that they are culturally insensitive to African American learners, and that these tests do not reliably quantify ability or intelligence. Rather, these tests are more tools to assess the child's current stage of *acculturation* into a dominant "white" culture (Artiles & Trent, 1994). Some researchers argue that IQ tests are *subjective* assessment tools at best, and are flawed by ambiguity. The very fact that the cutoff level signifying "mental retardation" has changed a number of times demonstrates the arbitrary nature and, indeed, the social construction of "normalcy." This construction, asserts Davis (1997), is highly problematic and has posed enormous hardships for people who fall outside of a currently-defined norm. As he states,

> ... the problem is the way that normalcy is constructed to create the "problem" of the disabled person ... [T]he idea of a norm is less a condition of human nature than it is a feature of a certain kind of society (p. 9).

Meyen and Skrtic (1995) ask a number of critical questions regarding intelligence test reliability. First, in terms of content validity: Will students from non-dominant cultures answer questions correctly? Second is predictive validity: Do these tests predict equally the performance of differing groups of students. Third is the inadequacy of norm groups: Do the standardization groups, on which the norms are based, adequately represent ethnoracial minority groups? The authors charge that the tests are biased against ethnoracial minorities, especially African Americans.

In the book *The Black-White Test Score Gap*, Jencks (1998) found that in general, "African Americans score lower than European Americans on vocabulary, reading, and mathematics tests, as well as on tests that claim to measure scholastic aptitude and intelligence" (p. 1). Jencks asserts that African Americans are not academically or intellectually inferior to European Americans, for "despite endless speculation, no one has found genetic evidence indicating that blacks have less innate intellectual ability than whites" (p. 1). Patton (1998) charges, however, that there is sufficient theoretical as well as statistical evidence to conclude that many current intelligence tests are biased and harmful to many African American learners. Unfortunately, however, these tests still remain as one of the primary means of evaluation leading to classification. According to the Board of Assessment and Testing (BOAT), "the usefulness of IQ tests in making special education decisions needs reevaluation" (in Patton, 1998, p. 3). Patton concurs that standardized tests often do not offer accurate measurements in determining whether students need special education services since there is a "lack of connection between assessment practices and effective treatments" (p. 3). IQ tests, therefore, have been linked as a possible factor in the misplacement of students in the categories of mental retardation, and also emotional disturbance, since these tests are used in the assessment process.

REFORM AGENDA

Some of the problems and the solutions are beyond and outside the purview of the school. Researchers, however, have proposed a number of reform strategies. Dunn (1968), for example, recommended two general areas of change in special education: the first is improving systemic procedures including diagnosis, placement, instruction, and curriculum; the second involves improvement in the quality of personnel preparation programs and in-service teacher training. He called for the integration of all "slower learners" – especially those who come from ethnic and racial minorities, or the economically disadvantaged – into mainstream classrooms to the fullest extent possible.

Artiles and Trent (1994) suggest a reform agenda that includes a variety of levels. The first is in the area of concept refinement. They assert that the field of special education needs

> ... to continue refining and operationalizing the different definitions of mild handicapping conditions to assist special educators in the implementation of differential diagnoses ... More attention to concept refinement and its dissemination are desperately needed in this area to start developing conceptual frameworks that would enable us to elucidate the complex interactions among culture, learning, disability, and instructional outcomes (p. 427).

The second area is in the development of a sound, culturally sensitive research agenda, one that emphasized the interaction between the child's culture and how this impacts development and learning, and looking at "certain mediating variables" (p. 428) on how these influence student outcomes.

Artiles and Trent's third area is systemic reform. In terms of prevention, they claim that although scientific researchers and practitioners possess the knowledge and experience to prevent some forms of mental retardation, learning disabilities, and emotional or behavioral disorders, this has not been a particularly high priority in the realm of intervention. In addition, they claim that functional assessment should be a part of any prevention model.

> In this model, the role of context is considered critical to explaining a student's academic success or failure . . .. The most important components of the functional assessment model are prereferral interventions, direct observation, and curriculum-based measurement" (p. 429).

Educators must also come to a self-knowledge and understanding of any biases they maintain. Artiles et al. (in press) assert that

> . . . bias is more than the personal decisions and acts of individuals. Rather, bias against minorities should also be thought of in terms of historical residua that are layered in social structures and that may lead to various forms of institutional discrimination. It is necessary that educators learn to recognize biases in educational settings and institutional practices and learn to deal with them appropriately (manuscript p. 15).

Grossman (1991) is likewise clear on this point, and he calls for educators to "recognize and eliminate" any and all prejudicial attitudes and perceptions of, and discriminatory behaviors toward students of color as well as working-class students.

Artiles and Trent (1994) state that culturally sensitive instruction based on critical reflection should be employed in the classroom. They contend that teachers must be trained to use a wide variety of pedagogical practices in order to reach learners and their wide range of learning styles, especially at-risk students. Moreover, Artiles and Trent call for a redefinition of home-school-community relations, and for the implementation of what they term a "community-multidisciplinary approach" (p. 429). Here, service providers in the schools, mental health agencies, and social service organizations would all coordinate efforts and services with individual families and with sub-communities to provide services in a fair, equitable, and culturally sensitive manner. They call on governmental agencies – federal, state, and local – to give incentives to these service-providing agencies that function within this comprehensive model.

In this regard, parent input in students' educational program is important. The National Association of Black School Educators (NABSE) provides ways to facilitate the communication process and, in turn, increase the involvement of African American parents:

> When school personnel adjust their approaches to the families' beliefs about disability, health and healing; respect the family's sense of propriety, and eliminate or reduce language barriers (Lake, 2000, p. 1).

The fourth general area in Artiles and Trent's recommendations for change involves reform in professional teacher preparation programs in which they call for all educators (current and preservice) to be or to become culturally sensitive while employing a culturally responsive, multicultural pedagogy. On this point, Agada and Obiakor (1994) concur. They suggest that with a predominately white teacher workforce, it is critical that all teachers become sensitive to the cultural backgrounds, the learning styles, etc. of their diverse student populations. Teachers need to be aware of any biases they may have regarding students from cultures different from their own. Also, teachers must be able to distinguish between what is a behavioral difference and a behavioral disorder.

Nieto (1996) enumerates basic characteristics of multicultural education, which she argues is, first of all, much more than simple inclusion of cultural festivals, ethnic foods, and famous people (the so-called "heroes and holidays" approach). Rather, it is in the fullest sense anti-oppression education (e.g. racism, sexism, anti-Semitism, classism, heterosexism, ableism, ageism, etc.). Multicultural education is also basic education. Teaching "multicultural literacy" is as basic as teaching reading, writing, and arithmetic. In this regard, Valles (1998) calls for specific multicultural curricular changes in terms of, for example, more native language instruction, language transition strategies, and culturally relevant curriculum and materials.

In addition, for Nieto, multicultural education is important for *all* students of every ethnic, racial, religious, linguistic, gender, age, ability, or sexual orientation. Moreover, multicultural education, for it to be truly effective, must be pervasive, for it must permeate everything within the school: the physical environment, the curriculum, and relationships among teachers, students, and the larger community. Ultimately, multicultural education is education for social justice and learning to think in more inclusive and expansive ways, while putting what is learned into action.

Blumenfeld (2001) views social justice education as a component of multiculturalism.

> Social justice education looks at the ways in which social structures promote and maintain issues of domination and subordination.... One cannot fully understand intergroup conflict between two or more groups *within* a given society without examining larger contextual societal (or systemic) structures related to relative power differentials and inequities. These systemic inequities are pervasive throughout the society. They are encoded into the individual's consciousness and woven into the very fabric of our social institutions, resulting in a stratified social order privileging dominant (agent) groups while restricting and disempowering subordinate (target) groups based on ascribed social identities (p. 13).

Nieto (1996) continues that multicultural education is education in process in that it is ongoing and dynamic. Multicultural education is also education that emphasizes critical pedagogy encouraging critical thinking, reflection, and action (praxis) helping students develop decision-making and social action skills.

In addition to multicultural awareness and competencies on the part of educators, Artiles and Trent (1994) suggest that schools recruit a greater number of faculty and staff of color. This would, they assert, benefit the entire educational setting in at least three important ways. First, it will provide *all* students and professionals alike with a greater number and representation of role modes. Second, it will enlarge and expand the curriculum to provide more diverse perspectives and worldviews. And third, it will give voice to educators of color allowing them to share their unique perspectives to students, other educators, and policy makers.

According to Russo and Talbert-Johnson (1997):

> African American teachers are better able to bridge the gap often found between students from low socio-economic status families and middle-class teachers who tend to have higher expectations than white teachers for students of color (p. 5).

Patton (1998) also calls for more African Americans at all levels of the educational hierarchy, from teachers and school counselors to administrators and other policy makers. He asserts that African Americans have not been traditionally the "script writers" in their own life drama, and that the problems of disproportionality of African Americans in special education can be, in part, attributed to the dearth of African American educators.

The area of advocacy and policy is Artiles and Trent's (1994) fifth recommendation in their reform agenda. Realizing that full access to and dissemination of information are critically important components in developing appropriate policy that benefits all students, especially students at risk,

> We contend that it is time to propose and test different hypotheses to understand the construction of failure among minority individuals and to challenge traditional notions in this arena (p. 431).

They propose that regional and national data base systems be developed to continually record and monitor overrepresentation of students of color. In addition, they call for the development of "a systematic model" to fully and equitably assess and interpret the data on overrepresentation.

Going back to our discussion of Social Reproduction Theory in which one of the practices that perpetuates social inequities is the unequal distribution of school funding, communities and school districts must push for legislation to equalize the overall distribution of school resources. In terms of special education, with the passage of the initial act in 1975, the federal government had agreed to pay 40% of the additional costs for providing special education services to local school districts. But, according to Senator James M. Jeffords of Vermont,

... we have fallen woefully short on our funding commitment. Today, the federal government pays only 17% of special education costs. The chronic underfunding of special education is inexcusable (Jeffords, p. x).

Jeffords claims that this was a major reason for his decision to leave the Republican Party in 2001 and to declare himself an Independent.

[Solutions] will require an infusion of funding for higher quality teaching in both general and special education, early intervention, increased training for school administrators and teachers, and greater access to effective special education supports and services in the least restrictive environment (Jeffords, 2002, p. ix).

Jeffords has proposed legislation to raise the funding of special education programs by an average of 2.5 billion dollars annually through 2007.

We must also push for more unbiased and culturally sensitive assessment instruments and procedures. Moreover, an effective prereferral process is needed, one that can assist in the appropriate placement of students in special education. "The prereferral process is such a strategy because it prevents referrals by assisting teachers and students with the presenting problems in the context of the general education classroom" (The Council for Exceptional Children, 2002, p. 15). According to the Council for Exceptional Children (2002), the purpose of the prereferral process is to document and record any difficulties with instruction that students may be experiencing. The prereferral team also helps determine any possible causes for the problem, and suggests possible instructional accommodations or modifications and other strategies. In addition, it assesses interventions that have been used to ensure whether they are appropriate and efficacious, and monitors a student's progress to identify those students whose learning and/or behavioral problems persist while suggesting possible interventions. These procedures have already been used in a number of school districts, including some urban districts, in special education placements, and, in particular, they have been used to guard against disproportionality of African Americans in special education programs. These procedures include:

- Identifying team members who have a background in the use and design of instructional methods that identify individual needs of students.
- Identifying team members with particular expertise in attending to the educational needs of African American students.
- Assuring that team members fully understand that their purpose is to recommend and support appropriate and effective interventions in general education rather than to act as a special education eligibility or placement group.
- Assuring adequate time for teams to develop and to become fully institutionalized as a school-based resource.

- Ensuring that bureaucratic paperwork requirements do not become counterproductive and burdensome.
- Providing adequate monetary and human resource to ensure success (Committee for Exceptional Children, 2002).

Post-Secondary Education

The authors of the 23rd Annual Report to Congress (U.S. Department of Education, 2001) proposed three primary strategies to provide better opportunities for students with disabilities in gaining employment after their secondary education. The first was to promote high expectations in the area of student learning and achievement. The authors suggested the adoption of a number of strategies to address this area, including the promotion of differential teaching, universal design, and integrated academic and applied learning practices. An additional suggestion covered the systematic and appropriate use of assessment and instructional accommodations.

> Regular education and special education teachers need information and skills on how to appropriately use accommodations in assessment and instructional situation (U.S. Department of Education, 2001, p. I-23).

The third suggestion was for students with disabilities to have access to the wide range of educational curricula and programs that includes not only academic subject areas, but also the options that "include community-based work experience, vocational education, drop-out prevention and re-entry programs, independent living skills programs, Tech Prep programs, and service learning opportunities" (U.S. Department of Education, 2001, p. I-23). The report went on to suggest that agencies work together before the student graduates from high school.

> Strategies such as formalizing agency responsibilities through interagency agreements or memorandums of understanding and formalizing follow-up procedures and actions when agencies are unable to attend should be considered (p. I-26).

CONCLUSION

The Education of All Handicapped Children Act (and its two subsequent reauthorizations under IDEA) has ushered in a new era, one that offers great promise and potential for all students – those with disabilities as well as students in general education programs. It seems clear, however, that enormous inequities exist in the system as it currently operates. Despite benchmark Supreme Court decisions and Congressional legislation, schooling (general education and special education alike) within the United States remains largely segregated by "race" and socioeconomic class.

While I focused on primarily African Americans, disproportionality in special education programs affects Latino/as and Native American Indian students as well. It is clear that there are no simple or easy solutions to the problem of overrepresentation of African Americans and other students of color in special education programs, for as the old saying goes, "When it takes a long time to walk into the forest, it will, most likely, take a long time to walk out of the forest." We must address the inequities within the school in both the short and long term. For these strategies to prove successful, however, we must also address, as a country, the larger systemic societal inequities that are very often reproduced and maintained within the school districts throughout the United States. Though many students are able to survive *in spite* of the educational system, we much ensure that students thrive *because* of the system. Only then can we be assured that the promise of a truly equitable and effective special education system matches the reality.

ACKNOWLEDGMENTS

I would like to thank John Palmer, my colleague in the Department of Educational Studies at Colgate University, and two of my students, Sophia Ward and Nadine Joseph, for their generous assistance in suggesting literature to investigate for this article.

REFERENCES

Agada, J., & Obiakor, F. (1994). The politics of education: Imperatives for African American males in the 21st Century. *Proceedings of 1994: Annual conference of the National Association for Ethnic Studies*. Kansas City, MO.

Artiles, A. J., Harry, B., Reschly, D. J., & Chinn, P. C. (in press). Over-identification of students of color in special education: A critical overview. *Multicultural Perspectives*.

Artiles, A. J., & Trent, S. C. (1994). Overrepresentation of minority students in special education: A continuing debate. *The Journal of Special Education, 27*(4), 410–437.

Artiles, A. J., & Trent, S. C. (2000). Representation of culturally/linguistically diverse students. In: C. R. Reynolds & E. Fletcher-Jantzen (Eds), *Encyclopedia of Special Education* (Vol. 1, 2nd ed., pp. 513–517). New York: Wiley.

Balkin, J. M. (2001, November 9). Is the "Brown" decision fading to irrelevance? *Chronicle of Higher Education*.

Batts, V. A. (1989). *Modern racism: New melody for the same old tunes*. Rocky Mount, NC: Visions Publication.

Blauner, B. (1992). Talking past each other: Black and white languages of race. *The American Prospect,* *10*(Summer), 55–64.

Blumenfeld, W. J. (2001). *Black and off-white: An investigation of African American and Jewish conflict from Ashkenazic Jewish American perspectives.* Unpublished doctoral dissertation. School of Education, University of Massachusetts, Amherst, MS.

Bowles, S., & Gintis, H. (1976). *Schooling in capitalist America.* New York: Basic Books.

Charles, C. Z., & Massey, D. S. (2003). How stereotypes sabotage minority students. *The chronicle review of the chronicle of higher education.* January 10, B-10–B-11.

Coll, C. T. (1990). Developmental outcomes of minority infants: A process-oriented look into the beginnings. *Child Development, 61*(2).

Cook, L. H., & Boe, E. E. (1995). Who is teaching students with disabilities? *Teaching Exceptional Children, 28,* 70–72.

The Council for Exceptional Children (2002). Addressing over-representation of African American Students in special education: The prereferral intervention process.

Craig, P. A., Kasowitz, D. H., & Malgoire, M. A. (1978). Teacher identification of handicapped pupils (ages 6–11) compared with the identification using other indicators (Research Rep. EPC 4537). Menlo Park, CA: Stanford Research Institute.

Davis, L. J. (1997). Constructing normalcy: The bell curve, the novel, and the invention of the disabled body in the nineteenth century. In: L. J. Davis (Ed.), *The Disability Studies Reader.* New York: Routledge.

Deno, E. (1970). Special education as developmental capital. *Exceptional Children, 37,* 229–237.

Donovan, M. S., & Cross, C. T. (Eds) (2002). *Minority students in special and gifted education.* National Research Council Publication, Committed on Minority Representation in Special Education.

Dunn, L. M. (1968). Special education for the mildly retarded: Is much of it justifiable? *Exceptional Children, 23,* 5–21.

Eakins, B. W., & Eakins, R. G. (1978). *Sex differences in human communication.* Englewood Cliffs, NJ: Prentice-Hall.

Frankenberg, E., & Lee, C. (2002). *Race in American schools: Rapidly resegregating school districts.* Cambridge, MA: The Civil Rights Project, Harvard University.

Gilligan, C. (1982). *In a different voice: Psychological theory and women's development.* Cambridge, MA: Harvard University Press.

Grossman, H. (1991). *Special education in a diverse society.* Needham Heights, MA: Allyn & Bacon.

Harry, B. (1992). *Cultural diversity, families, and the special education system: Communication for empowerment.* New York: Teachers College Press.

Harry, B., & Anderson, M. G. (1994). The disproportionate placement of African American males in special education programs: A critique of the process. *Journal of Negro Education, 63*(4), 602–619.

Heller, K. A., Holtzman, W. H., & Messick, S. (Eds) (1982). *Placing children in special education: A strategy for equity.* Washington, DC: National Academy Press.

Jeffords, J. M. (2002). Forward. In: D. J. Losen & G. Orfield (Eds), *Racial Inequity in Special Education.* Cambridge, MA: The Civil Rights Project, Harvard University Press.

Jencks, P. (1998). *The black-white test score gap.* Washington, DC: Brookings Institution Press.

Kochman, T. (1981). *Black and white styles in conflict.* Chicago: University of Chicago Press.

Kochman, T. (1994). Black and white cultural styles in pluralistic perspective. In: G. R. Weaver (Ed.), *Culture, Communication, and Conflict: Readings in Intercultural Relations.* New York: Simon & Schuster.

Lake, J. (2000). An analysis of factors that contribute to parent-school conflict in special education. *Remedial and Special Education, 21,* 1–14.

Lipsky, D. K., & Gartner, A. (1997). *Inclusion and school reform: Transforming America's classrooms.* Baltimore: Brookes.

Losen, D. J., & Orfield, G. (2002). Introduction. In: *Racial Inequity in Special Education.* Cambridge, MA: The Civil Rights Project, Harvard University Press.

MacMillan, D. L., & Reschly, D. J. (1998). Overrepresentation of minority students: The case of greater specificity or reconsideration of the variables examined. *The Journal of Special Education, 34,* 15–24.

McDermott, R. P. (1987). Achieving school failure: An anthropological approach to illiteracy and social stratification. In: G. D. Spindler (Ed.), *Education and Cultural Process: Anthropological Approaches* (2nd ed., pp. 173–209). Prospect Heights, IL: Waveland Press.

McIntyre, L. D., & Pernell, E. (1985). The impact of race on teacher recommendations for special education placement. *Journal of Multicultural Counseling and Development, 6,* 112–120.

Meier, K. J., Stewart, J., & England, R. E. (1989). *Race, class, and education: The politics of second-generation discrimination.* Madison: University of Wisconsin Press.

Meyen, L., & Skrtic, T. (1995). *Special education and student disability.* Denver: Love Publishing.

National Center for Educational Statistics. *Revenues and expenditures for public elementary and secondary education: School year 1997–1998.*

Nieto, S. (1996). *Affirming diversity: The sociopolitical context of multicultural education* (2nd ed.). White Plains, NY: Longman.

Osher, D. (2001). *Exploring relationships between inappropriate and ineffective special education services for African American children and youth and their overrepresentation in the juvenile system.* Cambridge, MA: Harvard University, The Civil Rights Project.

Oswald, D. P., Coutinho, M. J., & Best, A. M. (2002). Community and school predictors of overrepresentation of minority children in special education. In: D. J. Losen & G. Orfield (Eds), *Racial Inequity in Special Education.* Cambridge, MA: Harvard University Press, The Civil Rights Project.

Patton, J. (1998). The disproportionate representation of African Americans in special education: Looking behind the curtain for understanding and solutions. *Journal of Special Education, 32*(1), 25–31.

Polite, C. V., & Davis, E. J. (1999). *African American males in school and society.* New York: Teachers College Press.

Public Broadcasting Service (PBS) (1996, May 10). *The Merrow report: What's so special about special education?*

Russo, C. J., & Talbert-Johnson, C. (1997). The overrepresentation of African American children in special education: The resegregation of educational programming? *Education and Urban Education, 29*(2), 136–148.

Spring, J. (2002). *American education* (10th ed.). Boston: McGraw-Hill.

Tannen, D. (1984). *Conversational style: Analyzing talk among friends.* Norwood, NJ: Ablex.

Tannen, D. (1990). *You just don't understand: Women and men in conversation.* New York: Ballantine Books.

Tannen, D. (1994). *Talking from 9 to 5.* New York: William Morrow.

Timmons, J. (2003). *Learning to love learning.* Unpublished paper, The American School, Colgate University. Professor Warren J. Blumenfeld, February 24 (extract included with permission of the author).

U.S. Department of Education, Office for Civil Rights (2000). *Elementary and secondary school civil rights compliance reports.* Washington, DC: U.S. Government Printing Office.

U.S. Department of Education, Office of Special Education Programs (2001). *To assure the free appropriate public education of all children with disabilities: Twenty-third annual report to Congress on the implementation of the Individuals with Disabilities Education Act.* Washington, DC: U.S. Government Printing Office.

Valdivia, R. (1999). The implications of culture on developmental delay. ERIC Digest E589. Reston, VA: ERIC Clearinghouse on Disabilities and Gifted Education.

Valles, C. (1998). The disproportionate representation of minority students in special education: Responding to the problem. *Journal of Special Education, 32*(1), 52–54.

Visions, Inc. (1994). From lecture on Afrocentrism. Workshop: Changing racism: A personal approach to multiculturalism. Cambridge, MS.

Ysseldyke, J. E., & Agozzine, B. (1981). Diagnostic classification decisions as a function of referral information. *Journal of Special Education, 15.*

Ysseldyke, J. E., Agozzine, B., Ridley, L., & Graden, J. (1982). Declaring students eligible for learning disability services: Why bother with the data? *Learning Disability Quarterly, 5,* 37–44.

Zhang, D., & Katsiyannis, A. (2002). Minority representation in special education. *Remedial and Special Education, 23*(3).

4. YOUTH WITH DISABILITIES IN TRANSITION: STRATEGIES FOR POSITIVE CHANGE

Karen Rabren[*]

INTRODUCTION

Numerous social conditions directly impact young people with disabilities as they enter adulthood. One such condition is the difficulty these individuals face in obtaining competitive work in an integrated setting. The consequence of this social reality is further magnified when they have received inadequate preparation for employment. Additional quality of life inhibitors often include isolation, dependence, and lack of control over their own lives. These and other social challenges have prompted the United States to initiate a national movement known as transition, which refers to the process of helping young people with disabilities prepare to successfully assume adult roles and responsibilities in a more integrative, collaborative, and supportive community.

Federal initiatives have been enacted to address barriers to a successful transition. In addition to legislation, one large-scale reform effort has been systems change projects funded to individual states. This paper presents one such statewide program to improve the social conditions of youth and young adults through three major transition systems change strategies: (a) demonstration sites; (b) multidisciplinary training; and (c) follow-along student tracking.

*Karen Rabren is an Associate Professor in the Auburn Transition Leadership Institute, Rehabilitation & Special Education Department, College of Education, Auburn University, Alabama.

Administering Special Education: In Pursuit of Dignity and Autonomy
Advances in Educational Administration, Volume 7, 75–100
Copyright © 2004 by Elsevier Ltd.
All rights of reproduction in any form reserved
ISSN: 1479-3660/doi:10.1016/S1479-3660(04)07004-0

Highlighted are the preliminary results of these strategies for educational and social reform to enhance the quality of life for youth and young adults with disabilities.

The social conditions of persons with disabilities have been less than optimal throughout history. Much too often, these lives have been characterized by seclusion, discrimination, and dependence on others. Unfortunately, these adults rarely have been considered to be employable or capable of living on their own and caring for themselves. These assumptions foster prejudices that have plagued individuals with disabilities for centuries and, to some degree, have continued into modern times.

The social dilemmas facing persons with disabilities helped to initiate a large-scale disability rights movement in the United States in the 1970s. This movement gained momentum after the passage of three key pieces of legislation: (a) the Rehabilitation Act of 1973; (b) the Developmental Disabilities Assistance and Bill of Rights Act of 1975; and (c) the Education for All Handicapped Children's Act of 1975. The Rehabilitation Act of 1973 (P.L. 93-112) was civil rights legislation that protected the rights of persons with disabilities from discrimination by any recipient of federal funds in the provision of services or employment. Soon thereafter, the Developmental Disabilities Assistance and Bill of Rights Act (P.L. 94-103) provided federal monies to establish planning, administration, delivery of services, and advocacy for persons with developmental disabilities. That same year, the Education for All Handicapped Children's Act (EAHCA) of 1975 (P.L. 94-142) provided all qualified children with disabilities, ages 3–18 years, the right to a free and appropriate public education. By September 1980, the EAHCA service eligibility age was extended to 21 for students with disabilities (Yell, 1998). This legislative base of the 1970s set the foundation for the development and implementation of programs and services for the purpose of improving economic, social, and educational conditions.

In the early 1990s, several federal initiatives were enacted to address social barriers faced by individuals with disabilities, including programs that specifically targeted young people as they made the transition into adulthood. One large-scale initiative was the federally funded transition systems change projects provided to individual states. This paper provides an overview of the results of one statewide program to effect positive change in the social conditions of youth with disabilities. This program, made possible through the federal transition systems change initiative, used three major program reform strategies: (a) demonstration sites; (b) multidisciplinary training; and (c) follow-along student tracking. Select results are highlighted to reflect the impact of these strategies. To introduce the reader to the foundation underlying this national initiative a discussion of transition definition, student outcomes, and best practices follows.

TRANSITION DEFINITIONS

Youth and young adults with disabilities became the focus of federal initiatives in the United States during the early 1980s. During this time, Madeleine Will, the then Commissioner for the Office of Special Education and Rehabilitative Services (OSERS), United States Department of Education, introduced concepts and policies that guided efforts for improving the transition from school-to-work for all individuals with disabilities. To spearhead this initiative, a transition definition and a service delivery model were established (Will, 1984). Transition, as defined by Will, was described as:

> ... an outcome oriented process encompassing a broad array of services and experiences that lead to employment. Transition is a period that includes high school, the point of graduation, additional post secondary education or adult services, and the initial years of employment. Transition is a bridge between the security and structure offered by the school and the risks of life (Will, 1984, p. 1).

Will's transition service delivery model included three different levels or means of crossing *bridges* from school to adulthood: (a) no special services; (b) time-limited services; and (c) ongoing services. Each of these *bridges* focused on what the individual with disabilities might need in order to obtain his or her desired employment outcome.

While Will's definition focused on one of the more important adult outcomes for independence and self-sufficiency, some considered its singular focus on employment as being too narrow. Halpern (1985), a leader and early pioneer in the field of transition, broadened Will's definition to include community adjustment as a desired adult outcome. According to his definition, a person with a disability should achieve community adjustment through the successful attainment of a residential environment, social and interpersonal relationships, as well as employment. In this sense, community adjustment as an adult outcome encompasses a more inclusive approach to transition.

This concept of transition helped extend the focus of transition program administrators and practitioners to a broader array of desired student outcomes. Subsequently, this more comprehensive approach was adopted by the professional organization of the Council for Exceptional Children, Division of Career Development and Transition (DCDT) in 1994 (see below).

> Transition refers to a change in status from behaving primarily as a student to assuming emergent adult roles in the community. These roles include employment, participating in post-secondary education, maintaining a home, becoming appropriately involved in the community, and experiencing satisfactory personal and social relationships. The process of enhancing transition involves the participation and coordination of school programs, adult agency services, and natural supports within the community. The foundations for transition should be laid during

the elementary and middle school years, guided by the broad concept of career development. Transition planning should begin no later than age 14, and students should be encouraged, to the full extent of their capabilities, to assume a maximum amount of responsibility for such planning (Halpern, 1994, p. 117).

In 1990, the Education of All Handicapped Children Act of 1975 (P.L. 94-142) was amended and renamed the Individuals with Disabilities Education Act (IDEA, P.L. 101-476). For the first time, transition became a part of this legislation and was defined as:

> a coordinated set of activities for a student, designed within an outcome-oriented process, which promotes movement from school to post-school activities, including post-secondary education, vocational training, integrated employment (including supported employment), continuing and adult education, adult services, independent living and community participation. The coordinated set of activities shall take into account the student's preferences and interests, and shall include instruction, community experiences, the development of employment and other post-school adult living objectives, and when appropriate, acquisition of daily living skills and functional vocational evaluation [IDEA, P.L. 101-476, 20 U.S.C. Chapter 33, Section 140 (a)(19)].

This definition provided specific requirements as to the types of services that should be considered in developing a transition program for youth with disabilities (e.g. community experiences and functional vocational evaluation).

An understanding of the definition of transition is important because it sets the parameters for policy development, program implementation, and evaluation standards. The elements of the transition definition set specific requirements that must be implemented in transition programs (e.g. post-secondary education, vocational training, integrated employment). In addition, the outcomes of students who participate in these programs will be measured by the standards set forth in the definition.

STUDENT TRANSITION OUTCOMES

Early after the release of Will's definition in the mid-1980s, the transition initiative incorporated the objective to conduct post-secondary outcome studies of former students with disabilities. This timing was especially appropriate given that it would measure the outcomes of the first generation of students receiving special education services as provided by the 1975 Education for All Handicapped Children's Act.

Transition outcome studies have been conducted to examine post-school adjustment in areas such as employment, living arrangements, and social interaction with others. Unfortunately, the predominant finding of this area of programmatic research has been that the social and economic outcomes of former students with disabilities are sorely inadequate.

In the mid-1980s, OSERS, an administrative arm of the U.S. Department of Education, contracted with Stanford Research Institute to begin the *National Longitudinal Transition Study of Special Education Students* (NLTS). One of the more comprehensive studies investigating the outcomes of former special education students, the NLTS included a national representative sample of 8,000 youth, ages 13–21, enrolled in special education in secondary school during the 1985–1986 school year (Wagner, 1989).

Follow-up information collected from a few months to two years after exit from the 1985 to 1986 school year indicated that 46% of these former students who received special education services were competitively working. Three years later, 57% of this same group was employed. Blackorby and Wagner (1996) contrasted these same employment rates with that of a comparison group from the general population, and found that 46% of those with disabilities and 59% of those without disabilities were employed in 1987. They found that these comparative figures were 57 and 69% in 1990. This finding suggests that while the employment rates improved almost equally for both groups during these years, the employment rate for those with disabilities continued to lag 12–13 percentage points behind those without disabilities.

These diminished employment trends continued into the late 1990s and early 2000s. According to the Second Report of the Presidential Task Force on Employment of Adults with Disabilities (1999), 75% of the 30 million working age adults with significant disabilities are unemployed, or underemployed. The National Council on Disability (2001) reported that the unemployment rate of people with disabilities has remained stagnant at the 70% level for more than 12 years, in contrast to the single digit unemployment rates of those without disabilities. Likewise, a recent national poll found the employment rate to be 32% for persons with disabilities, versus 81% for those without disabilities (National Organization on Disabilities, 2001).

In his review of 41 outcome studies, Halpern (1993) found that employment was the predominant post-school variable. Other less frequently examined outcome indices included: (a) personal fulfillment; (b) physical and material well being; and (c) performance of adult roles. The category of *performance of adult roles* was the largest of the three and included the outcome of employment. It also included other variables associated with individual quality of life such as *mobility* and *community access*, *educational attainment*, *relationships*, and *social networks*.

Unfortunately, there has been relatively little attention given to outcomes other than employment. While attaining and maintaining a job certainly can impact one's life in numerous ways, there are other factors, such as developing social relationships and increasing autonomy in self-care, that also contribute to one's satisfaction with quality of life. All of these factors are related of course, but some are studied more than others. Status of employment is easier to measure and report than is quality of life; it is much less ambiguous to determine and report whether or not a person has a job than whether or not that same person is happy. The opportunity for inaccurate interpretation increases markedly when one moves from objective to subjective considerations, and this kind of difference in measurable outcome indicators may explain why most quality of life variables have been relatively understudied.

In summary, much has been learned about the social conditions of youth and young adults through outcome studies. Collective findings can be obtained from comprehensive reviews and analyses of this line of research (e.g. Browning et al., 1995; Chadsey-Rusch et al., 1991; Darrow & Clark, 1992; Halpern, 1990; Johnson & Rusch, 1993; Levine & Nourse, 1998; Peraino, 1992; Phelps & Hanley-Maxwell, 1997). One sobering summary offered by Halloran (1993) notes that student outcome research has found that large numbers of students with disabilities are exiting public education and entering "*segregated, dependent,* and *nonproductive lives*' " (p. 210). Because of outcome findings such as these, it is imperative for the field of education, rehabilitation, and other related transition service organizations to invest in best practices with the anticipation of improving the post-school outcomes of young people with disabilities.

BEST PRACTICES FOR SUCCESSFUL TRANSITION

The reported findings from post-school outcome studies substantiated the need for transition programming, planning, and the implementation of best practices. Numerous best practices have been reported in the literature (e.g. Browning, 1997; Flexer et al., 2001; Greene, 2002; Sitlington et al., 2000). Typically, these practices are referred to as: (a) vocational preparation; (b) student-directed practices; (c) family involvement; (d) collaboration; (e) functional assessment; (f) functional curriculum; and (g) outcome accountability. The assumption is that a successful transition is, in part, a function of the incorporation of these practices into programming and planning. Presented below is a brief description of each practice.

Vocational preparation. The low employment figures of former students with disabilities prompt our attention to the continued need for vocational preparation as a transition service area. Vocational assessment and vocational training have been identified as two of the most important factors in preparing students for employment (Asselin et al., 1998). Benz et al. (1997), for example, found that students with disabilities were two to three times more likely to be competitively employed if they scored high on work-based variables such as social skills, job search skills, and work experience during high school. There must be specific training and experiences provided in vocational skill development in order to improve students' vocational outcomes; therefore, this practice should be considered a critical element of all transition programs.

Student-directed practices. Student-directed activities occur when students are actively involved in the transition process. This means that students are not merely recipients of transition services, but rather the central persons who direct their own transition planning and programming (Wehmeyer & Ward, 1995). Students need self-determination skills in order to be actively involved in their transition programs and direct their own Individualized Education Programs (IEPs). Therefore, students should develop, to the greatest extent of their capability, their own post-school goals and work with the IEP team to develop plans to reach those goals.

Family involvement. Other than the student, family members are the most central persons in the transition process. It is the parents, siblings, and other family members who have had direct contact with the person with a disability throughout his or her young life. They are the people closest to the student and know what will and will not work with their loved one. Unfortunately, parents typically have held passive roles in making educational decisions regarding their child(ren)'s educational programs (Turnbull & Morningstar, 1993).

Collaboration. Transition, as defined by IDEA (1997), requires a "coordinated set of activities" (P.L. 105-17). As such, coordinated transition services and activities have become a critical *best practice* (Benz et al., 1995; Browning, 1997; Szymanski et al., 1992; Wehman, 1996). This shared responsibility involves educators, families, and adult service providers who must ensure that all necessary connections between and among these individuals and entities are established and maintained for the benefit of students with disabilities (Steere et al., 1990).

Functional assessment. Functional approaches to assessment are considered a best practice in order to adequately and appropriately address the needs of students in transition programs. Although the need for more traditional standardized assessment procedures will continue to serve its purpose for placement and comparison decisions, functional assessment provides the necessary information for transition personnel to determine the functioning ability and progress of the students in their programs. Functional assessment is an appropriate method for transition given that the transition process is: (a) longitudinal in nature; (b) individually plan-directed; (c) collaboratively implemented; and (d) outcome oriented (Browning & Brechin, 1993).

Functional curriculum. A functional curriculum "is practical, relevant, useful, and useable for an individual student, or a group of students" (Dunn & Rabren,

1997, p. 183). The content of this curriculum provides the student with the skills needed for what they need to know at the time they are in high school, as well as what they need to know in the future (Clark, 1992). As a result, a functional curriculum is broad in focus and includes the development of skills needed for many adult roles. This requires that the curriculum include not only academics, but also necessary skills for adult living (e.g. social interpersonal skills, daily living skills, recreation skills, etc.).

Outcome accountability. The most appropriate measures of the effectiveness of transition programs and services are the post-school outcomes of former students served. These young adult outcomes can serve as a transition accountability index. In order to obtain this index, however, transition programs must establish and systematically implement a student tracking program to gather post-school information from their former students. This information is most valuable in program development and refinement because it provides "warning signs when something can be improved, when something is not working right, when education is not producing expected outcomes" (Ysseldyke et al., 1991, p. 5).

Seven general *best practices* have been presented as a foundation for services for students with disabilities. These practices are identified in the literature and applied in the field as strategies to address the many unfavorable social conditions facing students with disabilities. The importance of these practices is reflected in a statewide study conducted in Alabama (Browning et al., 2001). Included in the seven target groups participating in this study were two groups of special education professionals. Using a 5 point Likert scale, special education coordinators ($n = 92$) and special education teachers ($n = 369$) were asked to rate seven best practices

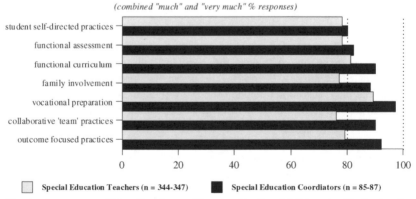

Importance of Best Practices in Transition
(combined "much" and "very much" % responses)

Fig. 1.   Importance of Best Practices as Perceived by Special Education Professionals.

in terms of their importance (i.e. *none, slight, moderate, much* and *very much*). Seventy-eight of the respondents considered each of these best practices as being *much* or *very much* important (Fig. 1).

TRANSITION SYSTEMS CHANGE

Coupled with federal disability legislation in 1990 was the emergence of a special grants program for systems change in transition. The purpose of this comprehensive initiative was to offer states one-time funds for a five-year period to improve and enhance their transition programs (Johnson & Halloran, 1997). These state grant programs, awarded on a competitive basis, provided funds for the foundational establishment of programs throughout the United States. The ultimate purpose of this federal initiative was to: *"increase the availability, access, and quality of transition assistance through the development and improvement of policies, procedures, systems . . . and create incentives for the implementation of lasting state-wide system changes in the transition of students with disabilities to postsecondary training, education, and employment"* (Federal Register, 1991, p. 66290).

In 1996, Alabama was awarded a transition systems change grant known as the *Alabama Transition Initiative* (ATI). This statewide reform program employed a decentralized approach to meet the goal of student-centered transition planning and implementation at the local school and community level. This goal was addressed through the establishment of demonstration sites that employed best practices in transition. The development of these sites provided the infrastructure so that all of Alabama's school systems could benefit from a network of leadership, resources, and opportunities to enhance the quality of life for Alabama's youth and young adults with disabilities. In addition to this systems change strategy, a multidisciplinary training program and a follow-along student tracking system were established for capacity building at the local level.

The remainder of this paper will describe how each of these reform strategies were implemented and measured. Selected results will be presented, followed by a discussion of program sustainability efforts and future directions for addressing the transition needs of youth and young adults with disabilities.

Reform Strategy 1: Transition Demonstration Site Program

The development of transition demonstration sites provided an opportunity to empower local education agencies and communities to implement proven effective programs, services, and best practices that result in positive post-school adult outcomes. These sites, which were selected through an annual RFP (request for funding proposal) competition for transition mini-grants, received funds and assistance to enhance their transition programs through the implementation of a set of best practices.

The selection process for choosing demonstration sites began with the distribution of an RFP application to all 128 school systems in the state. This application required those systems interested in becoming a transition demonstration site to complete a written proposal describing the current status of their transition program. Specifically, this proposal was to describe their school system's progress toward the establishment and implementation of best practices in transition.

Those systems choosing to participate in the demonstration site selection process returned their proposals to the state's education department. All completed RFP applications were distributed for blind review to an interdisciplinary selection committee. The committee members reviewed the submitted applications and scored each school system's degree of best practices implementation. Those systems with more complete implementation received the highest ratings and were ultimately the systems chosen. Since 1996, 49 transition demonstration sites have been established in local public school systems. The selected demonstration sites included city and county school systems in both urban and rural areas of Alabama's four major geographic regions (see Fig. 2).

The state's transition demonstration sites were expected to adhere to a set of guidelines designed to assist them in establishing model transition programs. First, each newly established site was required to send a five member representative

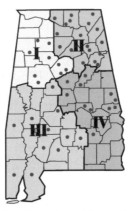

Fig. 2.   Alabama's Regional Locations of Transition Demonstration Sites.

multidisciplinary team to a one-week training on best practices in transition. This training provided participants an opportunity to spend an extended time focusing on the development and improvement of their local transition programs. Second, these demonstration sites were to contact ATI staff and consultants for technical assistance and specific training programs as needed throughout their two-year funding period. Third, after the first year of concentrated effort toward the improvement of their transition programs, these school systems were to serve as mentors to surrounding regional school systems and communities. Finally, these sites were to conduct on-site visits and regional training programs, and participate in the annual transition statewide conference.

Reform Strategy 2: Multidisciplinary Training Program

In order to continue the improvement of transition best practices in selected demonstration sites and other school systems and communities, a statewide multidisciplinary training program was established. This program focused on improving the understanding and ability of professionals, parents, and advocates to work effectively with youth with disabilities in transition from school to work and community. This type of training program has been recognized as one of the most important and effective strategies used by individual states to improve transition services (Cobb & Johnson, 1997; DeStefano et al., 1997; Guy & Schriner, 1997; Johnson & Guy, 1997). The establishment, implementation, and evaluation of this program was an instrumental change agent in the Alabama systems change project.

Training needs assessment is an essential activity for developing an effective training system (Goldstein & Gilliam, 1990). This fundamental principle was used to assist in the development of the statewide training program. During its early stages, a 37 item training needs questionnaire was mailed to all the city and county superintendents, special education coordinators, and principals of the Alabama public school systems. An analysis of 1,096 returned copies resulted in the identification of 10 content domains as training priorities and the feasibility of multiple training delivery strategies. These 10 domains were collapsed into eight best practices and two major training delivery modalities were identified. These findings provided the framework for developing the training delivery model and training content model.

The training program delivery model also provided the structure for various modalities and methods, as well as the many strategies used (see Fig. 3). The two major modes of training dissemination used in the training program were technology-based methods (compact discs, video tapes, Internet conferences) and

Alabama Transition Initiative
Training Model

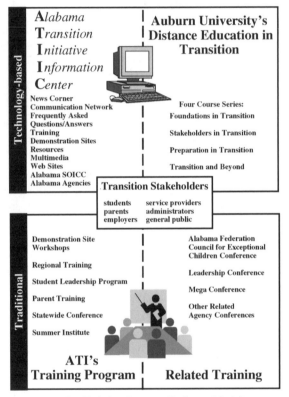

Fig. 3.   Training Program Delivery Model.

the more traditional face-to-face training provided once, at a single place and time (in-service programs, workshops, conferences).

The seven specific training implementation strategies employed were: (a) an interactive website; (b) distance education; (c) best practice seminars; (d) consumer training programs; (e) field-based training; and (f) an annual conference. These diverse strategies were used in order to maximize the options available to all persons involved in transition for students with disabilities.

The program content model identified training content, targeted persons for training, and measured training impact. This model included a set of best practices

"Best Practices" in Transition
Training Content Model

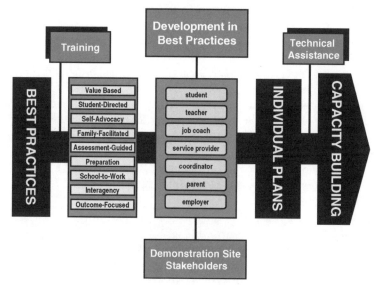

Fig. 4.   Training Program Content Model.

identified in the literature, as well as through the training needs assessment conducted in the state. For this model, these practices are classified under the generic headings of: (a) value-based; (b) student-directed; (c) self-advocacy; (d) family-facilitated; (e) assessment guided; (f) preparation; (g) school-to-work; (h) interagency; and (i) outcome-focused (see Fig. 4).

The content model assumes the need to match best practices to stakeholders in terms of their transition roles. Vocational practices, for example, are more suitable to job coaches and functional curricula are more applicable to teachers. This matching feature is in keeping with the notion that effective transition requires a *coordinated set of activities*, or in this case, activities based on a set of best practices aligned with stakeholder roles. Individualizing professional training in best practices to meet participant needs is especially relevant to team building at the local level.

Technology-based Strategies
An interactive website, the Alabama Transition Initiative Information Center (ATIIC), was developed to link all transition stakeholders and provide them with

a continuous resource and opportunity for communication, training, and technical assistance in transition. This educational resource went beyond static web pages and page linking, and created what Starr (1997) describes as truly interactive pages. ATIIC also connected users with different methods of communication ranging from traditional modes such as phone, fax numbers and e-mail addresses, to state-of-the art on-line exchanges available through chat rooms and desktop videoconferences.

Distance education provides many adults a learning opportunity that might not otherwise be available to them, especially those who are working full-time and/or reside in a rural setting. An Auburn University distance education program in transition provided students with an opportunity for intensive, yet convenient and flexible study. The learning strategies employed included: (a) reading materials; (b) workbook assignments; (c) video tapes; (d) compact discs (CDs); (e) field projects; and (f) Saturday sessions (Rabren & Browning, 2001). A total of 88 Alabama transition stakeholders successfully completed this 10-week training program.

Traditional Strategies

Weeklong training programs in best practices were provided to cross-disciplinary local teams from the transition systems change demonstration sites. Upon their award notification, each school system was required to identify up to five key stakeholders to participate in this extended training. These team members were instructed on 10 individual half-day training units (e.g. student-directed practices, family involvement practices). Since 1996, five, one-week best practices seminars have been conducted, serving 156 participants from transition demonstration sites.

A student leadership and self-advocacy training program was developed for high school students who were nominated by their high school to represent their demonstration site school systems. This program consisted of a one-day workshop aligned with the annual Alabama Transition Conference, followed by a one-week leadership summer camp on the Auburn University campus (*Counterpoint*, 1998). The program objectives included development of self-awareness, problem solving, decision-making, teamwork, goal setting, self-advocacy, and group development. Since 1998, a total of 116 high school students participated in either the one-day workshop and/or its companion one-week leadership program.

Parents of youth who attended the student leadership program participated in a separate, yet related training event during the same week. Other training programs available to parents of youth with disabilities included regional parent training workshops that ranged from two-hour sessions to two-day training events, and one-day statewide parent workshops. Since 1996, 28 training programs have been conducted in which 615 parents participated in one or more of these programs.

Field-based training sessions were short-term and usually conducted in half-day, one-day, or two consecutive day sessions held in the participants' respective city, county, or region. The purpose of these training sessions was to provide either an overview of a particular topic, or a general introduction to the foundations of best practices in transition. Since 1996, a total of 67 of these training programs have been conducted in over 30 local areas around the state, serving over 2,708 stakeholders.

The Alabama Transition Conference is a statewide training event that annually brings together transition professionals, family members, and students with disabilities for a concentrated time of sharing and learning. From 1991–2003 this conference has attracted over 7,000 participants and provided a total of 421 concurrent sessions and 64 full-day pre-conference workshops. Conference proceedings are typically published and distributed statewide (e.g. Browning & Rabren, 1999).

In summary, Alabama's systems change training program was established to provide a formalized method for ensuring that information on transition best practices was accurately and systematically disseminated to selected demonstration sites and other school systems and communities statewide. The value of training is further underscored by the fact that it was not an isolated change agent, but rather one that was integrated with other strategies in order to be effective. The Alabama systems change project, for example, established 49 transition demonstration sites that are considered to represent an effective strategy for systems change. In order to ensure that the sites incorporated contemporary best practices, it was stipulated that each site had to engage in training (e.g. best practices seminar). Few would argue that regardless of the initiative's nature, real systems change is unlikely in the absence of professional training.

Reform Strategy 3: Student Tracking Program

The very definition of transition requires an *outcome-oriented* focus; therefore, Alabama established a student tracking program to monitor student outcomes. This follow-along system provides the infrastructure for systematically obtaining and evaluating post-school outcomes of students who have participated in transition programs, and allows for comparison of these outcomes to the students' perceptions of their program while in school.

The rationale for building a student tracking program is best exemplified by the fundamental purpose of the national transition systems change initiative, which is the continued program improvement and policy development of transition programs. A student tracking program allows for systematic monitoring of a transition program and, in so doing, provides educators with information about how to continually develop and refine the program to best meet the educational needs of the students (Frey, 1993).

In addition to program evaluation and improvement, a student tracking program provides information needed for policy development. By examining the specific outcomes of students in relationship to program elements, considerations for effective transition programs and services can be determined. Program policy can then be developed to emphasize elements of transition programs (e.g. functional curriculum) that have a positive impact on the successful transition of the students they serve (DeStefano & Wagner, 1992).

Methods

The methods for establishing student tracking programs have varied. However, the literature describing post-school outcome studies indicates that two main types of research designs have been used: follow-up and follow-along. The follow-up design examines an individual's post-school status at one point in time, whereas, the follow-along design requires measurement of an individual's post-school status along multiple points in time (Halpern, 1990). The follow-along design is longitudinal in nature and is preferred in that it provides the structure necessary to collect and measure predictive information (during high school) and compare it to outcome information obtained at a later point in time (after high school). The Alabama Student Tracking Program includes both an in-school and post-school transition survey instrument (Browning et al., 2001).

From 1996–2003, this follow-along system had gathered information on 10,315 students with disabilities in the state. The post-school survey form is an adaptation of Vermont's Post-School Indicators Follow-Up Questionnaire (Hasazi et al., 1992). Minor modifications of Vermont's questionnaire were made based on recommendations from an Alabama feasibility task force that included one of the authors of the Vermont instrument. From this questionnaire, an accompanying in-school survey was developed. The in-school and post-school instruments include demographic sections, as well as questions about the students' high school programs and post-school goals and outcomes. Many of the items appear in both surveys; however, there is an additional section on the post-school survey to be completed if the respondents are working at the time of the interview. Prior to participating in the administration of the student tracking instruments, Local Education Agency (LEA) personnel received special training with respect to the nature and importance of the student tracking system and the use of standardized interview procedures as written in the *Alabama Student Tracking*

Program Administration Manual. The purpose of this training is to address the issue of fidelity of treatment across settings and interviewers.

Procedures

In-school. The in-school instrument is administered to youth with disabilities in their 11th grade year. This survey is administered in a group setting by the students' special education teacher. Students complete the survey by listening to the teacher read each item, then responding to the choices read aloud by filling in the circle next to the answer of their choice. The teacher follows a script that provides specific wording for the administration of the survey. Special administration procedures allow alternative response formats for those students, who, by the nature of their disability, cannot respond in the paper and pencil format.

Upon the students' completion of the surveys, the special education teacher returns the students' in-school instruments to the immediate LEA special education supervisor (e.g. special education coordinator). This individual reviews the collected surveys from the participating high schools, and then forwards them to the Alabama Student Tracking Program administrators. Once received, these forms are reviewed for completeness and processed for analysis.

Post-school. The post-school instrument is administered through phone interviews with former special education students, or with an immediate family member, approximately one year after the students' exit from high school. The interviews are conducted by local education agency (LEA) personnel from the schools that these former students attended. Each LEA determines who will conduct the interviews. In the majority of the school systems, secondary special education teachers are assigned three to five students each to interview. As indicated in the administration manual, interviewers make at least three attempts to contact each student. Once completed, the survey results are returned to a central site and state and university personnel review the surveys for completeness. If necessary, the interviewee, or a representative from the student's former school, is contacted for further verification of information. Finally, the data are coded and entered into a data storage file.

In summary, one method employed by the Alabama systems change project to ensure that transition programs in the state are *outcome-focused* was to implement a student tracking program. The predictive information (in-school) and evaluative information (post-school) allows for comparison of programs along parallel data points. For example, if a student responds that he or she plans to live independently upon exit from high school, whether or not this has occurred can be determined based on his or her response to a similar item one year after exit. This and other information obtained from Alabama's follow-along system provides invaluable information for program evaluation and improvement.

IMPACT OF SYSTEMS CHANGE

The impact of Alabama's transition systems change program can be measured through the results of the three main strategies implemented through this program: (a) demonstration sites; (b) training; and (c) student tracking. A sample of results from each of these strategies to improve the social condition of youth with disabilities is presented as an indicator of the impact of systems change in this statewide program.

Demonstration Sites' Impact

Alabama transition stakeholders were surveyed during the time period of the implementation of the systems change project and asked if their local school had shown *positive change* over the past several years in preparing its high school students for a successful transition (Browning et al., 2001). A total of 985 survey forms were completed for an average return rate of 64% across the six target groups (i.e. special education coordinators, special education teachers, career technical teachers, job coaches, rehabilitation counselors, and parents). A representative sample of 792 respondents indicated the degree of change was either *none* (4%), *slight* (16%), *moderate* (37%), *much* (30%), or *very much* (13%).

It is presumptuous to conclude that the systems change project was the only reason for this high level of response indicating that a positive change had occurred in these transition programs. The fact is, however, that respondents who were relatively new to the demonstration site program, or who were not associated with a demonstration site, had overall lower levels of positive change response, as compared to the higher levels reported from established demonstration sites. This finding suggests that the systems change program had a positive influence on the development and implementation of local transition programs.

Another impact indicator evolving from this same study pertained to the provision of networking and technical assistance. Specifically, all special education coordinators and special education teachers whose local school system had an ATI transition demonstration site were asked if they *had assisted* other schools in their geographic proximity regarding their transition programs and services. In response, 37 and 38% of these special education personnel answered *yes*. They described providing assistance to others such as: "... on site training for Job Coaches from other school systems"; "several [school] systems have visited our site"; "training to other schools"; "We helped others develop transition brochures for their schools."

Demonstration sites were considered a central pillar for implementing systems change in Alabama. Although the federal funding has subsided, these sites have continued to serve the state as a foundational network for quality programs and services in transition. Furthermore, personnel from these sites continue to provide leadership to the state. Each year, for example, site representatives present at the state's annual transition conference and serve on numerous task force committees for the state department of education.

Training Program Results

The effectiveness of Alabama's systems change training program was evaluated using the Training Evaluation Kit (TEK) (Browning & Foss, 1983). TEK is a formal evaluation tool designed to systematically obtain short-term training information. This evaluation method provides trainers with a demographic profile of all training participants, a measure of the trainees' perception of the accomplishment of training objectives, and the degree to which the training program was successful in impacting change within each training participant.

Demographic information is an essential part of the training data collection system in training evaluation. As such, the Participant Input Questionnaire (PIQ), which is part of the TEK instrument, was used to collect demographic information. The PIQ is comprised of six items, including: (a) gender; (b) educational level; (c) stakeholder role; (d) geographic region; (e) school system (city vs. county); and (f) population (rural vs. urban). Since 1996, trainees have responded to one or more of these input variables, thus providing staff with a data-based trainee profile for planning and reporting.

TEK includes the evaluation of both participant and trainer objectives, since they may not be the same. Preferably, there would be high correspondence between these two sets of objectives, which could be interpreted that the participants are attending training that meets their expected needs and interests. Figure 5 presents a four-year cumulative profile of trainee and trainer objectives across five, one-week best practices training programs, representing a total of 134 participants. These participants had a combined total of 276 training objectives, which they generated at the beginning of their respective programs. At the end of training, they indicated that 89% of these objectives had been either *somewhat met* (27%) or *highly met* (62%). By contrast, each of the five programs had the same trainer objectives. The first of six objectives across all programs, for example, was "To provide trainees with a common frame of reference regarding transition in terms of its history, definition, problems, issues, and post-school performance outcomes." Of the 579 ratings for the six trainer objectives, 98% were either *somewhat met* (20%) or *highly met* (78%) according to the participants. These results suggest that the seminars met the objectives identified by both the trainees and trainers.

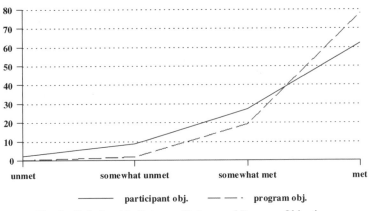

Fig. 5. Relationship Between Trainee and Program Objectives.

At the conclusion of selected training programs, participants were asked the type and degree of change they experienced due to training. The degree of choices the trainees responded to ranged from *no change, slight change, moderate change,* to *much change.* The definitions of the four change areas were printed in their TEK booklet and read to them by a trainer before they answered this outcome item. Table 1 presents the results from trainees who attended these selected programs in which this information was obtained. Training outcome results, as measured by the TEK system, indicate that trainees had *moderate* and *much* informational 82%, behavioral 78%, attitudinal 76%, and motivational 84% change as a result of participating in a systems change training program between 1997 and 2000.

Table 1.   Change Due to Training ($N = 1,879–1,905$), 1997–2000.

Change Area	Degree of Change								Total
	None		Slight		Moderate		Much		
	N	$\%$	N	$\%$	N	$\%$	N	$\%$	N
Informational	84	4	247	13	673	35	901	47	1,905
Behavioral	116	6	287	15	813	43	663	35	1,879
Attitudinal	152	8	288	15	705	37	738	39	1,883
Motivational	94	5	201	11	611	32	986	52	1,892
Total	446	6	1,023	14	2,802	37	3,288	43	7,559

Student Tracking & Outcomes

Several outcome studies have been conducted using data obtained through the Alabama Student Tracking System (Austin, 1999; Dunn et al., in press; Dunn & Shumaker, 1997; Holder, 2001; Rabren et al., 2002; Whetstone, 2002). These studies were conducted using information from the post-school instrument; however, comparative analysis is currently being conducted using student responses from both the in-school and post-school survey instruments. As previously mentioned, the effectiveness of any high school preparation program can, in part, be measured by the successful post-school outcomes of its former students.

One outcome variable that has been examined through Alabama's student tracking system is the employment status of former students one year after exit from high school. Over a five-year period, of the 2,691 of the students with disabilities who responded to the question as to whether or not they were employed one year after exit, 71% were employed and 29% were unemployed. While these figures indicate that a high percentage of students are working a year after high school, the type of work in which they are engaged must be taken into consideration. For example, of those who indicated they were working, 52% were working full-time, and 48% were working part-time.

Rabren et al. (2002) examined the employment status of 1,393 former students who received special education services and who exited from 37 of Alabama's 128 school systems between 1996 and 2000. These 37 school systems served as demonstration sites through the state's transition systems change grant. Follow-up telephone interviews revealed that 73% ($n = 1,013$) of these former students were employed one year after exit. Using a hierarchical logistic regression analysis, there was an 87% probability that these students would be employed one year after high school if they held a job at the time they exited school. Other significant findings include the relationship between employment status and student gender, disability, and urban or rural setting.

The probability of the student having a job one year after high school, for example, was greater if the student was male, had a learning disability, was from an urban school, and had a job at the time of school exit. In contrast, the probability of employment was less likely for females with a disability other than a learning disability, from rural schools, and without a job at the end of high school. These findings suggest that students with disabilities can benefit from participating in paid work experiences during high school and that females in rural settings need more aggressive transition planning and programs.

The findings from Rabren et al. (2002) suggest that programming initiated through the systems change project may have had an impact on the social condition of youth with disabilities (e.g. employment). Specifically, participation in an occupational diploma program that required students to enter paid employment during high school may have significantly improved the chances for employment one year after high school.

Following this study, another investigation was conducted to examine factors that might prevent students with mental retardation or learning disabilities from dropping out of high school (Dunn et al., in press). Between 1996 and 2001, a total of 4,676 former students provided post-school information on their current status one year after high school. This number included 228 students who had dropped out of school and a randomly selected sample of 228 who had not dropped out. Two sets of predictor variables (student demographics and post-school interview responses) were analyzed using hierarchical logistic regression analysis in terms of their relationship to the outcome variable of high school dropout. Model 1 examined demographic variables; *learning disability* was the only variable that contributed significantly to this model. In Model 2, interview questions were examined and *helpful person* and *general preparation* were found to be significant. In the final model, *learning disability*, *helpful person*, *helpful class*, and *general preparation* were the variables retained.

Specifically, it was found that the probability of dropping out for a student with a learning disability who did not feel he or she was being prepared for life after high school and did not identify a helpful class and a helpful person was 0.86. By contrast the probability of dropping out was 0.16 for a student with mental retardation who found a particular class and person helpful and felt that school was preparing him or her for what he or she wanted to do after high school.

The limited results obtained from these few studies using the Alabama Student Tracking System data provides enlightening information for program improvement and direction. These and other outcome results can provide local school systems with information regarding the status of their former students with disabilities and their successes or difficulties as compared to former students across the state. Using this information, school systems can identify strengths and weaknesses in their programs and positively influence those factors shown to affect the social conditions of their former students.

SUSTAINABILITY AND FUTURE DIRECTIONS

Alabama joined other states in the United States in implementing transition systems change projects to improve services and programs for young persons with disabilities. The three main strategies employed through its statewide program included the development and implementation of: (a) 49 demonstration sites;

(b) a multidisciplinary training program; and (c) a follow-along student tracking system. Sample results from each of these strategies have been presented as indicators to the change brought about by the Alabama Transition Initiative.

A major concern for Alabama and other participating states in the systems change initiative is how to sustain commitment and enhancement of transition programs and services once federal funding has ceased (Johnson & Guy, 1997). Fortunately, Alabama has addressed this problem, in part, by obtaining continued support for its systems change reform strategies through the establishment of the Auburn Transition Leadership Institute at Auburn University. Carefully planned and implemented sustainability efforts may now be continued through this newly established transition resource to the state. This sustained commitment can support the proactive and systematic strategies necessary for breaking through the social barriers commonly experienced by persons with disabilities. We must continue to embrace and expand the mission of successfully preparing youth and young adults with disabilities to assume responsible and productive roles in more integrative, collaborative, and supportive communities.

REFERENCES

Asselin, S. B., Todd-Allen, M., & DeFur, S. (1998). Transition coordinators: Define yourself. *Teaching Exceptional Children, 30*(3), 11–15.

Austin, P. E. (1999). *Post-school student outcomes of Alabama students with disabilities: The impact of existing transition services.* Unpublished doctoral dissertation, University of Alabama, Tuscaloosa.

Benz, M. R., Johnson, D. K., Mikkelsen, K. S., & Lindstrom, L. E. (1995). Improving collaboration between schools and vocational rehabilitation: Stakeholders identified barriers and strategies. *Career Development for Exceptional Individuals, 18*(2), 33–144.

Benz, M. R., Yovonoff, P., & Doren, B. (1997). School-to-work components that predict post-school success for students with and without disabilities. *Exceptional Children, 63*(2), 151–165.

Blackorby, J., & Wagner, M. (1996). Longitudinal post-school outcomes of youth with disabilities: Findings from the National Longitudinal Transition Study. *Exceptional Children, 62*(5), 399–413.

Browning, P. L. (1997). *Transition in action for youth and young adults with disabilities.* Montgomery, AL: Wells Printing.

Browning, P. L., & Brechin, C. (1993, Winter). Assessment in transition: A functional definition and collaborative program for practice. *Vocational Evaluation and Work Adjustment Bulletin, 26,* 123–127.

Browning, P. L., Dunn, C., Rabren, K., & Whetstone, M. (1995). Post-school outcomes for students with disabilities: A U.S. synopsis. *Issues in Special Education and Rehabilitation, 10*(1), 31–37.

Browning, P., & Foss, G. (1983). Evaluation of rehabilitation continuing education. In: E. Pan, E. Backer & C. Vash (Eds), *Annual Review of Rehabilitation* (Vol. 3, pp. 64–92). New York: Springer.

Browning, P., & Rabren, K. (1999). *Transition VII & VIII Alabama: A profile of commitment.* Auburn, AL: Transition Leadership Institute, Department of Rehabilitation and Special Education, Auburn University. (Proceedings of the 1997 and 1998 annual conference on transition in Alabama).

Browning, P., Rabren, K., & Hall, G. (2001). *A statewide study to examine Alabama's high school programs' for students with disabilities.* Auburn, AL: Transition Leadership Institute, Department of Rehabilitation and Special Education, Auburn University.

Browning, P. L., Whetstone, M., Rabren, K., & Dunn, C. (2001). An Alabama tracking system for youth and young adults with disabilities. In: P. Browning, C. Cox, K. Rabren & S. Tew-Washburn (Eds), *Transition in Alabama: Service, Training and Research* (pp. 221–229). Transition Leadership Institute Rehabilitation, Auburn University.

Chadsey-Rusch, J., Rusch, F. R., & O'Reilly, M. (1991). Transition from school to integrated communities. *Remedial and Special Education, 12*(6), 23–33.

Clark, G. M. (1992, April). Providing transition services through a functional curriculum and functional instruction. Paper presented at the Council for Exceptional Children annual conference. Baltimore.

Cobb, B., & Johnson, D. (1997). The statewide systems change initiative as a federal policy mechanism for promoting educational reform. *Career Development for Exceptional Individuals, 20*(2), 179–190.

Counterpoint (1998, Fall). National Association of State Directors of Special Education Newsletter, *19*(1).

Darrow, M., & Clark, G. M. (1992). Cross-state comparisons of former special education students: Evaluation of a follow-along model. *Career Development for Exceptional Individuals, 15*, 83–99.

DeStefano, L., Hasazi, S., & Trach, J. (1997). Issues in the evaluation of a multi-site federal systems change initiative. *Career Development for Exceptional Individuals, 20*(2), 123–139.

DeStefano, L., & Wagner, M. (1992). Outcome assessment in special education: What lessons have we learned? In: F. R. Rusch, L. DeStefano, J. Chadsey Rusch, L. A. Phelps & E. M. Szymanski (Eds), *Transition from School to Adult Life: Models, Linkages, and Policy* (pp. 173–208). Champaign, IL: Sycamore.

Dunn, C., Chambers, D., & Rabren, K. (in press). *Predictive factors in dropping out of school for students with disabilities. Remedial and Special Education.*

Dunn, C., & Rabren, K. (1997). Preparation practices. In: P. L. Browning (Ed.), *Transition in Action for Youth and Young Adults with Disabilities.* Montgomery, AL: Wells Printing.

Dunn, C., & Shumaker, L. (1997). A follow-up study of former special education students from a rural and urban county school system. *Career Development for Exceptional Individuals, 20*(1), 43–54.

Federal Register (1991). State systems for transition services for youth with disabilities: Final rule. *U.S. Department of Education, 56*(245), 66290–66295.

Flexer, R. W., McMahan, R. K., & Baer, R. (2001). Transition models and best practices. *The expected outcomes of education for students with disabilities.* East Lansing, MI: Center for Quality Special Education.

Frey, W. D. (1993). *Outcome indicators for special education. A model for studying the expected outcomes of education for students with disabilities.* East Lansing, MI: Center for Quality Special Education.

Goldstein, I. L., & Gilliam, P. (1990). Training system issues in the year 2000. *American Psychologist, 45*(2), 134–143.

Greene, G. (2002). Best practices in transition. In: G. Greene & C. A. Kochhar-Bryant (Eds), *Pathways to Successful Transition for Youth with Disabilities* (pp. 154–196). Columbus, OH: Merrill-Prentice Hall.

Guy, B., & Schriner, K. (1997). Systems in transition: Are we there yet? *Career Development for Exceptional Individuals, 20*(2), 141–164.

Halloran, W. D. (1993). Transition services requirement: Issues, implications, challenge. In: R. C. Eaves & P. J. McLaughlin (Eds), *Recent Advances in Special Education and Rehabilitation* (pp. 210–224). Boston, MA: Andover Medical.

Halpern, A. S. (1985). Transition: A look at the foundations. *Exceptional Children, 51*(6), 479–486.

Halpern, A. S. (1990). A methodological review of follow-up and follow-along studies tracking school leavers from special education. *Career Development for Exceptional Individuals, 13*(1), 13–28.

Halpern, A. S. (1993). Quality of life as a conceptual framework for evaluating transition outcomes. *Exceptional Children, 59,* 486–498.

Halpern, A. S. (1994). The transition of youth with disabilities to adult life: A position statement of the Division on Career Development in Transition, The Council for Exceptional Children. *Career Development for Exceptional Individuals, 17*(2), 115–124.

Hasazi, S. B., Hock, M., & Cravedi-Cheng, L. (1992). Vermont's post school indicators: Using satisfaction and post school outcomes data for program improvement. In: F. Rusch, L. DeStefano, J. Chadsey-Rusch, J. A. Phelps & E. M. Szymanski (Eds), *Transition from School to Adult Life: Models, Linkages, and Policy* (pp. 485–508). Champaign, IL: Sycamore.

Holder, C. (2001). *A critical analysis of student outcomes and "best practices" for Alabama's secondary special education transition-to-work initiative: Implications for policy and practice.* Unpublished doctoral dissertation, University of Alabama, Tuscaloosa.

Johnson, D., & Guy, B. (1997). Implications of the lessons learned from a state systems change initiative on transition for youth with disabilities. *Career Development for Exceptional Individuals, 20*(2), 191–199.

Johnson, D. R., & Halloran, W. H. (1997). The federal legislative context and goals of the state systems change initiative on transition for youth with disabilities. *Career Development for Exceptional Individuals, 20*(2), 1121–1909.

Johnson, D., & Rusch, F. R. (1993). Secondary special education and transition services: Identification and recommendations for future research and demonstration. *Career Development for Exceptional Individuals, 16,* 1–18.

Levine, P., & Nourse, S. W. (1998). What follow-up studies say about postschool life for young men and women with learning disabilities: A critical look at the literature. *Journal of Learning Disabilities, 31*(3), 212–233.

National Council on Disability (2001). *Investing in Independence: Transition Recommendations for President George W. Bush* (Retrieved November 20, 2001, from http//:www.ncd.gov).

National Organization on Disability (2001). *Employment rates of people with disabilities* (Retrieved November 2, 2002, from http:///nod.org).

Peraino, J. (1992). Post-21 follow-up studies: How do special education graduates fare? In: P. Wehman (Ed.), *Life Beyond the Classroom: Transition Strategies for Young People with Disabilities* (pp. 21–70). Baltimore: Paul H. Brookes.

Phelps, L. A., & Hanley-Maxwell, C. (1997). School-to-work transitions for youth with disability: A review of outcomes and practices. *Review of Educational Research, 67*(2), 197–226.

Public Law 94-142, Education for All Handicapped Children Act of 1975, 20 U.S.C. §1400 et seq.

Public Law 101-476, Individuals with Disabilities Act (IDEA) of 1990, 20 U.S.C. §1400 et seq.

Public Law 93-112, Rehabilitation Act of 1973, 19 U.S.C. §794 et seq.

Public Law 94-103, Developmental Disabilities Assistance and Bill of Rights Act of 1975, 42 U.S.C.
§6009 et seq.

Public Law 105-17, Individuals with Disabilities Education Act (IDEA) of 1997, 20 U.S.C. §1400 et
seq.

Rabren, K., & Browning, P. (2001). Distance education program in transition. In: P. Browning, C. Cox,
K. Rabren & S. Tew-Washburn (Eds), *Transition in Alabama: Service, Training and Research*
(pp. 166–172). Transition Leadership Institute Rehabilitation, Auburn University.

Rabren, K., Dunn, C., & Chambers, D. (2002). Predictors of post high school employment among
young adults with disabilities. *Career Development for Exceptional Individuals, 25*(1), 25–40.

Second Report of the Presidential Task Force on Employment of Adults with Disabilities (1999).
Recharting the course: If not now, when? (Available from the Presidential Task Force on
Employment of Adults with Disabilities, 200 Constitution Avenue, NW, Room S2220d,
Washington, DC. 20210).

Sitlington, P. L., Clark, G. M., & Kolstoe, O. P. (2000). *Transition education & services for adolescents
with disabilities* (3rd ed.). Needhem Heights, MA: Allyn & Bacon.

Starr, R. M. (1997). Delivering instruction on the world wide web: Overview and basic design principles.
Educational Technology, 37(3), 7–14.

Steere, D. E., Pancsofar, L., Wood, R., & Hecimovic, A. (1990). Principles of shared responsibility.
Career Development for Exceptional Individuals, 13, 57–65.

Szymanski, E. M., Hanley-Maxwell, C., & Asselin, S. B. (1992). Systems interface: Vocational
rehabilitation, special education, and vocational evaluation. In: F. R. Rusch, L. Destefano,
J. Chadsey-Rusch, L. A. Phelps & E. M. Szymanski (Eds), *Transition from School to Adult
Life: Models, Linkages, Issues* (pp. 153–171). Champaign, IL: Sycamore.

Turnbull, A. P., & Morningstar, M. E. (1993). Family and professional interaction. In: M. E. Snell (Ed.).
Instruction of Students with Severe Disabilities (4th ed., pp. 31–60). Upper Saddle River, NJ:
Merrill-Prentice Hall.

Wagner, M. (1989). *Youth with disabilities during transition: An overview of descriptive findings from
the national longitudinal transition study.* Menlo Park, CA: SRI International.

Wehman, P. (1996). *Life beyond the classroom: Transition for young people with disabilities* (2nd ed.).
Baltimore, MD: Paul Brookes.

Wehmeyer, & Ward (1995). The spirit of the IDEA mandate: Student involvement in transition planning.
Journal of the Association for Vocation Special Needs Education, 12, 108–111.

Will, M. (1984). *OSERS programming for the transition of youth with disabilities: Bridges from school
to working life.* Washington, DC: Office of Special Education and Rehabilitation Services, U.S.
Office of Education.

Yell, M. L. (1998). The history of the law and children with disabilities. *The law and special education*
(pp. 53–67). Upper Saddle River, NJ: Prentice-Hall.

Ysseldyke, J. E., Thurlow, M. L., Bruininks, R. H., Deno, S., McGrew, K., & Shriner, J. (1991). A
conceptual model of educational outcomes for children and youth with disabilities (Working
Paper 1). Minneapolis: University of Minnesota, College of Education, National Center on
Educational Outcomes.

5. RETHINKING THE ASSESSMENT OF MALADAPTIVE BEHAVIOR

Richard England[*]

ABSTRACT

Children with disabilities that exhibit maladaptive behaviors as a result of abuse and neglect require consideration of a more comprehensive, alternative method of assessment to determine the source and patterns of the behaviors. The need exists to go beyond an assessment of the current level of intellectual functioning, individual academic achievement, and functional behavior to a more ethological approach that considers the dynamics in the home and social settings that influence development. The careful analysis of the child's social and academic records; patterns and frequency of movement for those in out-of-home placements; interviews and records of primary care givers; along with the intellectual and academic assessments enables special educators, social workers, school staff, and health care professionals to more effectively address the individual needs of the child. This paper discusses assessment methods that utilize a more comprehensive approach to determine the factors that lead to high levels of maladaptive behavior in special needs children. Additionally, alternative intervention strategies are recommended that include establishing the child's perceived primary care giver with the most stable environment to facilitate the child's development of more appropriate behaviors.

[*]Richard England is Associate Professor of Special Education, Freed-Hardeman University, Tennessee.

Administering Special Education: In Pursuit of Dignity and Autonomy
Advances in Educational Administration, Volume 7, 101–118
ISSN: 1479-3660/doi:10.1016/S1479-3660(04)07005-2

INTRODUCTION

Behavior, particularly the term "maladaptive behavior" is difficult to precisely define. Behavior considered acceptable in one society, culture, social setting, or other environment may be highly inappropriate in another. Behavior is observable. Therefore, the observed actions, or behaviors, of an individual are judged based on the context of the respective behavior. For children, the context must also include the anticipated behaviors demonstrated at the varying developmental stages the child experiences during growth. The child's behavior at age two is expected to be markedly different from the behavior of the same child at age five, fifteen, and in adulthood. If children exhibit age inappropriate behaviors, whether acting beyond their years or well below what is expected, their behavior is considered atypical. Maladaptive behavior then refers to those observable actions of a child that are considered inappropriate either for the age, setting, or both.

Assessing maladaptive behavior in children is indeed the acknowledgement that the current behaviors of the child are inappropriate. The majority of definitions and assessment instruments focus on assessing "adaptive behavior" instead of "maladaptive behavior" with the general intent to determine, as much as possible, the parameters of the adaptive behavior within two contexts: "(a) the degree to which individuals are able to function and maintain themselves independently; and (b) the degree to which they meet satisfactorily the culturally imposed demands of personal and social responsibility" (Sattler, 1992, p. 376). The assessments are designed to examine the situational determinants with an emphasis on trying to understand the antecedents and consequences of the behavior and to attempt to determine ways to change the behavior (Groth-Marnat, 1997).

For school age children, the most common approach to assessing behavior includes the use of one or more standardized adaptive behavior scales. These standardized assessment instruments are used in conjunction with observations; interviews; background information on the child, including relationship with parents; cultural and socioeconomic analysis; and reasons for assessment (Salvia & Ysseldyke, 2001; Sattler, 1992). A focal point of many standardized instruments is the parental interview. "These instruments permit a study of how each parent views the child's problems, how parents' views compare with teachers' views, and how behavior may change as a result of therapeutic or remedial interventions" (Sattler, 1992, p. 376). When the behavioral assessment is combined with the information gathered from an assessment of intellectual functioning and academic achievement, the composite picture is to provide enough information to begin the appropriate level of intervention. The intervention may include a component designed to strengthen desirable behaviors while encouraging alternative behaviors for those considered unacceptable (Salvia & Ysseldyke, 2001).

There are difficulties with the assessment process, however, that still emerge with children who have significant problem behaviors. Early studies of children's behavior and the interventions that occurred, "were unable to distinguish improvement due to passage of time from the amount of improvement due to the treatment alone" (Bickman, 2000, p. 3). A common problem, that in many ways still exists today, was that "Researchers and clinicians alike assumed that treatments delivered in strict laboratory settings to carefully selected clients would also be effective when delivered by community practitioners to real world clients" (Bickman, 2000, p. 3). Consequently, the changes in a child's behavior could very well have been the result of maturation, change in environment, change in primary care giver, or other unknown factors instead of the intervention implemented.

Another factor providing a strong influence on both the traditional assessment and intervention process is the relationship the child maintains with the individual implementing the intervention. For many children in school settings this person is the teacher. The positive teacher-child relationship has been shown to serve as a buffer against risk (Stuhlman & Pianta, 2002). The positive aspect described is the "relationship" instead of a specific intervention. The nature of a relationship may have a direct impact on children's behavior more than the nature of the behavioral intervention. The possibility exists that the maladaptive behavior of the students also influences the behavior of others responsible for care, such as the teacher. Considering that teachers may frequently have negative emotions toward certain children, how those negative emotions are managed can have a direct impact on the development, or lack of development, of appropriate behavior patterns in the children. "For example, children who were more negative in the classroom had teachers who expressed more negative affect when talking about them, whereas children who were less compliant in the classroom had teachers who were less positive when discussing them... This is also suggestive of a dyadic systems perspective on relationships, particularly relational negativity in which child and teacher hold mutually negative beliefs and expectations of one another that are reinforced or confirmed in their behavioral interaction" (Stuhlman & Pianta, 2002, pp. 159–160).

The mutual negative interactions and expectations can lead to greater levels of social withdrawal by the children. Without opportunities to learn and develop appropriate behavior, children develop greater risks for serious behavior problems (Moroz & Jones, 2002). Positive response to interventions will in theory allow the child to develop a greater sense of socially appropriate behaviors. A major problem occurs, however, when the interventions fail to consider that the individual differences among children can have a tremendous impact on the effectiveness of the interventions. Children may exhibit temporary gains in appropriate behaviors, but these gains may also be attributed to the unique response of each individual child to the delivery and withdrawal of the intervention (Moroz & Jones, 2002). Further, children who have behavior problems in school generally have the initial roots of the problem well established prior to school age. As a result of the beginnings of maladaptive behavior occurring early in the life of many children who exhibit high levels of behavior problems, "Primary prevention strategies are not of sufficient intensity and strength to effectively remediate the problems of children and youth who require secondary prevention strategies" (Walker & Sprague, 2000, p. 8).

In the absence of effective interventions for the children who have high levels of maladaptive behavior there is the growing number of children who are experiencing emotional disturbances and serious mental health issues. The end result for many of these children is that they become victims of the "get tough" policies in schools and in the community. The Office of Juvenile Justice and Delinquency Prevention (2000) indicates that "it is safe to estimate that at least one out of every five youth in the juvenile justice system has serious mental health problems" (p. 6) In addition to the behavioral problems that resulted in their involvement with the juvenile justice system, the children may also have co-occurring problems such as substance abuse which further complicates the issues associated with appropriate interventions.

THE MALADAPTIVE ENVIRONMENT

The environment for children has changed, and is changing dramatically. In addition to social observations about access to information, technology, and the mobility of society, there also is a need to recognize a fundamental change in the type of care, and the importance placed on the care, of children. There is a substantial increase in the number of children who must seek an alternative setting to the traditional home and family structure in order to secure the environment that allows them to have some chance for an acceptable quality of life. For example, the American Public Welfare Association (March, 1997), and the Child Welfare League of America (1998) indicate a dramatic rise in the number of children in out-of-home care in the United States from 1990 to 1996. Though definitions vary from state to state, out-of home care may be described as foster care, kinship care, pre-finalized adoptive placements, group homes, institutional placements, and state's custody. Based on data provided by these organizations, in 1990 approximately 405,989 children were in out-of-home care. This figure grew to approximately 442,205 children in 1993, and then to 531,311 children in 1996. While these figures represent approximations, difference in reporting among the states, and levels of incompatibility in reporting the data, the overall trend provides a disturbing profile of the changing environment for a significant number of children.

In addition to the significant number of children who are now in out-of-home placements, there is a growing concern about the number of reported incidents of child abuse and neglect. Special needs children are especially vulnerable due to the fact that many are incapable of adequately articulating what is happening to them. Further, many may doubt the truthfulness of claims made by special needs children simply because they are "special needs" children and the assumption may be they simply do not understand what they are talking about.

Reports of abuse and neglect in the United States are staggering. The number of cases referred for investigation grew from 2,577,882 in 1990 to 2,893,409 in 1993, to 3,007,578 in 1996 (U.S. Department of Health and Human Services, 1997, 1998). These figures represent an increase in the numbers reported of approximately 16% with the child population growing only at approximately 7% (Child Welfare League, 1998). The total number of reported cases from 1990 to 1996 is an amazing figure of 19,598,331. Keeping in mind that these figures represent only reported incidents, the actual number of potentially neglectful and abusive circumstances for children probably far exceed the reported figures. It is uncertain how many childhood fatalities are the direct result of the neglect and abuse due to difficulties with both the investigation of the instances and reporting. Further, with fewer than 30 states able to provide reasonable information regarding children who died as a result of abuse and neglect with a primary caregiver as the alleged perpetrator, the number of children killed by those who were to take care of them cannot be accurately determined. While homicide is the eleventh leading cause of death for those living in the United States, it is the third leading cause of death for children between the ages of 5 and 14. The Children's Defense Fund further defines the seriousness of the problem by indicating that there was a 300% increase in the number of children seriously injured, primarily by violent parents, between 1986 and 1993.

Issues exist in the lives of many behavioral disordered children that serve as an insight into the reasons why certain behaviors developed. Such issues do not excuse inappropriate behavior, but do assist those with the responsibility of implementing interventions with understanding the behavior. In examining approximately 40 cases of children served in the State of Tennessee, the Tennessee Commission on Children and Youth (2000) identified several critical issues involving children in state's custody. Of the cases examined, 75% had little or no relationship with their fathers with 35% having little or no relationship with their mother; 69% of the parents had substance abuse issues; 60% lived in homes below the poverty level; 58% of the parents had been incarcerated; 46% of the parents were never married to each other; 81% of the children above the age of 13 were sexually active; 33% were physically abused; 21% sexually abused, with six of these allegedly involving incest; 17% came into state custody from squalid living conditions; 15% of the children had been abandoned; and 63% of the children came from families with three or more siblings (Tennessee Commission on Children and Youth, 2000). Children in these situations frequently are at a loss when trying to determine who can be relied on as the primary care giver. The sense of insecurity, and perhaps hopelessness, becomes the norm instead of the exception. These emotions, with the true unmet need to have a secure home, may result in a general sense of distrust, academic failure, and high levels of inappropriate and/or at-risk behavior (England, 1997, 1999, 2000, 2001). The long term outcome for children who come with these experiences can be positive, but the probability of more serious behavioral problems associated with delinquency, school failure, depression, substance abuse, dependence on the social service system, incarceration, and higher mortality rates is greatly increased (England, 2001; Robbins & Szapocznik, 2000; Walker & Sprague, 2000).

The inability to develop socially acceptable behavior can result in an alternative residential placement for the child. A significant increase was seen in the number of cases in which children were placed on probation or ordered to a residential treatment facility between 1987 and 1996. Adjudicated delinquency cases that resulted in residential placement increased by 51% from 1987 to 1996, with a total of 159,400 delinquency cases ordered to residential placement in 1996. From 1987 to 1996 the number of cases involving children that resulted in formal probation increased 58%, with 306,900 children placed on formal probation in 1996. Other sanctions, such as community service and/or restitution, were placed on an additional 75,800 adjudicated cases in 1996 (Stahl, 1999a–c).

Another by-product of the instability experienced by children in our society is the number referred to juvenile detention, correctional, or shelter facilities. The Office of Juvenile Justice and Delinquency Prevention indicates that on February 15, 1995, over 108,700 juveniles were in such placements. Of this number, approximately 74% were in public facilities. Further, when compared with previous information regarding children placed in public facilities due to crimes, the one-day count rose 47% from 1983 to 1995, with the number of juveniles held for violent crimes doubling during that same period (Sickmund, 1998a–f).

Children in alternative settings due to criminal acts are further subjected to the sense of displacement when the amount of time spent in these facilities is considered. In 1994, the Office of Juvenile Justice and Delinquency Prevention indicates that there were 723,547 released with the average length of stay at approximately 40 days. Those committed to public facilities during 1994 (133,239) had an average stay of approximately 147 days. In contrast to the children in detention verses those who were committed, the average stay for those in detention was about two weeks, and for those who were committed the stay approached five months. Juveniles who were committed to private facilities had an average length of stay of approximately three and one-half months.

From 1983 to 1995, juveniles held for violent crimes became an even greater number percentage of the public facility population increasing from 19% in 1983 to 25% in 1995. In 1996, juvenile courts, or courts that had juvenile jurisdiction, disposed in excess of 1.7 million delinquency cases. Of the 1,757,600 cases, a total of 381,500 were person offenses (i.e. criminal homicide, forcible rape, robbery, aggravated assault, simple assault, violent sex offense, other person offense). During the same year, a total of 874,000 property offenses were committed; 176,300 drug law violations; and 325,400 public order offenses. These offenses represented an increase of 49% in the juvenile court delinquency caseload from 1987 to 1996 (Stahl, 1998).

Based on information from the Office of Juvenile Justice and Delinquency Prevention, law enforcement agencies arrested approximately 2.8 million persons under the age of 18 in 1997. There were approximately 2,500 arrested for murder and manslaughter; 5,500 for forcible rape; 39,500 for robbery; and 75,900 for aggravated assault (Snyder, 1998a–h). Other figures indicate that approximately 52,200 were arrested for carrying a weapon; 18,500 for sex offenses excluding forcible rape and prostitution; 220,700 for drug abuse violations; 158,500 for liquor law violations; and 215,100 for disorderly conduct.

While many times the popular press will focus on violent crimes perpetuated by males, it is necessary to understand that these issues are not necessarily exclusive to the male population. Based on an analysis of unpublished arrest data from the Federal Bureau of Investigation from 1981 to 1994, Snyder (1998a–h) indicates that between 1988 and 1994 the Violent Crime Index arrest rate almost doubled for females while increasing 60% for males. Still the Violent Crime Index arrest rates (arrests per 100,000 persons age 10–17) remained far lower for females (145) than males (772) (Snyder, 1998a–h).

When considering juvenile crimes, certain actions on the part of the juveniles raise the level of concern about the increase in violence toward others. For example, the juvenile arrest rate for aggravated assault increased more than 120% from 1983 to 1994 (Snyder, 1998a–h). Between 1988 and 1994, the arrest rate for robbery increased 70%. The especially violent crime of murder has also seen a significant increase in the past years. Approximately 25,000 juveniles were murdered in the United States between 1985 and 1995, with approximately 2,600 murdered in 1995. Of these 2,600 approximately 72% were male – 49% black and 47% white. Especially interesting is that 22% of the juvenile murder victims were murdered by family members and 13% by strangers. Sixty-one percent of the juveniles murdered in 1995 were murdered using a firearm. The victims of family members were more likely to be younger children, with the other significant population of murder victims being black males. Approximately 83% of the older children who were murdered were killed with a firearm, while firearms accounted for only 17% of the younger victims. With a 66% increase in the murder of juveniles between 1985 and 1995, nearly all of the increase was among the older victims and related to the use of firearms (Federal Bureau of Investigation, 1997; Snyder, 1998a–h).

Homicides involving juvenile offenders have also increased substantially during the past years. In 1980, juveniles were the offenders in approximately 8% of all homicides, but by 1994 juveniles were determined to be the offenders in approximately 16% of homicides. In 1995, estimates indicate that approximately 2,300 juvenile offenders were involved in about 1,900 homicides. From the period between 1987 and 1993, the juvenile arrest rate for murder more than doubled (Federal Bureau of Investigation, 1997; Snyder, 1998a–h). While the increase in violent juvenile behavior does not necessarily imply a causality between delinquency and the increase in the number of children experiencing maladaptive environments, and periods of maladaptive behavior, the reality appears to be that with the instability many children face in their home life there is the increased probability that the children will begin to manifest their frustration in deviant behavior (England, 1996, 2001).

ATTACHMENT AND MALADAPTIVE BEHAVIOR

The basic premise that children need a secure, loving, caring environment that provides for their needs is certainly not a new idea. Children need the opportunity to grow in such an environment to develop as capable individuals who are able to function in society as well as learn those developmental skills necessary to provide a secure environment for their own family. Bowlby (1969, 1980, 1988), a primary proponent of attachment theory argued that, "giving time and attention to children means sacrificing other interests and other activities. Yet I believe the evidence for what I am saying is impeachable . . . that health, happy, and self-reliant adolescents and young adults are the products of stable homes in which both parents give a great deal of time and attention to the children. I want also to emphasize that, despite voices to the contrary, looking after babies and young children is no job for a single person" (p. 2) Further, additional research using the concept of attachment as a primary force in guiding research shows that emotion is also a key component in developing securely attached relationships (Waters et al., 2002). Considering that the family is one of the most important and influential systems in the lives of children it therefore stands to reason that the dysfunctional family can have an impact on the type of attachment the child will develop toward those considered to be primary care givers.

Recent arguments have been made that attachment not only may include ties to a specific individual as a primary care giver, but also includes the behavioral system that exists for the child. This behavioral system is viewed as flexibly operating in terms of set goals, mediated by feeling, and in interaction with other behavioral systems. In this view, behavior is predictably influenced by context rather than constant across situations (Sroufe & Waters, 1977). When attachment is viewed as an organizational construct rather than a trait (Sroufe & Waters, 1977) the variations that may occur in the reliability and sensitivity of the care provided to the child may lead to individual differences in the security the child develops as a result of the relationship. The result is that the different types of experiences in the care giving situation will be seen in the different types of behavior, based on the type of attachment, exhibited by the child (Ainsworth, 1972, 1973, 1974; Lewis & Goldberg, 1969; Sroufe & Waters, 1977).

Bowlby advocated that understanding the importance of the family was basic to having children grow to well adjusted adults. "Paradoxically it has taken the world's richest societies to ignore these basic facts. Man and woman power devoted to the production of material goods counts a plus in all our economic indices. Man and woman power devoted to the production of happy, healthy, and self-reliant children in their own homes does not count at all. We have created a topsy-turvy world ... There is in consequence a great danger that we shall adopt mistaken norms. For, just as a society in which there is a chronic insufficiency of food may take a deplorably inadequate level of nutrition as its norm, so may a society in which parent of young children are left on their own with a chronic insufficiency of help take this state of affairs as its norm" (Bowlby, 1988, pp. 2–3). The secure base for a child's development is to serve as the environment that allows the child to explore and learn, but always have a place of safety and security to which the child can retreat. Such a base provides reassurance and a place of refuge in times of distress (Bowlby, 1988; Waters et al., 2002). The secure base, however, is at times absent in the lives of children. If a parent, or primary care giver, refuses to accept the responsibility of providing the security necessary for the growth of the child the resulting behaviors will be strongly impacted. "No parent is going to provide a secure base for his growing child unless he has an intuitive understanding of and respect for his child's attachment behaviour and treats it as the intrinsic and valuable part of human nature I believe it to be" (Bowlby, 1988, p. 12).

THE ATTACHMENT TO CHAOS

When considering the basic postulates in the theories of anxiety and fear within the ethological approach to studying attachment Bowlby (1973) argued, "Perhaps the most basic and pervasive of these traditional assumptions is that the only situation that properly arouses fear is the presence of something likely to hurt or damage us; with the corollary that fear arising in any other situation must be in some way abnormal, or at least requires special explanation. While this assumption may appear plausible at first sight, there are two distinct ways in which it proves to be mistaken. One type of mistake concerns the nature of the stimuli and objects that frighten us and lead us to retreat. Not infrequently, it is found, they bear only an indirect relationship to what is in fact dangerous. The second type of mistake is just as basic. We are frightened not only by the presence, or expected presence, of situations of certain sorts, but by the absence, or expected absence, of situations of other sorts" (p. 78). It is the second mistake that perhaps brings the greatest challenge to understanding how better to assess the nature of maladaptive behavior in children. When attachment is viewed as an organizational construct (Sroufe & Waters, 1977) the "situations" described by Bowlby must be considered important elements in determining the causes of maladaptive behavior, especially for children.

A basic underlying premise necessary to assessing the level of maladaptive behavior is that a child can become attached to anything, and in fact will become attached to whomever or whatever becomes the realm of security. In the absence of a primary caregiver(s), consistently present to meet the needs of reassurance, compassion, love, security, and overall well-being, the child becomes ambivalent about who or what to trust. The element of trust is a key to attachment. A child becomes attached to those things or people that give a sense of trust and dependability. Given a stable environment early on, a child is then able to develop a sense of independence that develops within the context of a "secure base" allowing for the exploration of the child's self, always knowing that there is something secure to which the child can return. With multiple caregivers, or multiple care systems, the child may become confused and/or ambivalent about who is actually providing the care. If there are multiple primary care givers, i.e. mother, father, sister, brother, or extended family engaged in positive interactions with the child, and among themselves, that child has a greater chance to grow with a strong sense of security. This sense of security, belonging, and family allows the child to more fully reach her or his potential as a responsible adult. The development includes a sense of social adaptation exhibited by appropriate behaviors, according to the age and/or stage of development.

The absence of this sense of stability increases the probability, though not inevitability, of maladaptive behavior. The maladaptive behavior becomes a manifestation of fear with perhaps the greatest fear being the fear of isolation (Bowlby, 1973). The increase in the maladaptive behavior may very well be in direct proportion to the lack of security provided by the primary care giver(s). As a result, the child who has multiple caregivers within a system of caregivers who have little or no consistent contact with the child, or who have only a passing professional interest in the child, has an increased chance of higher levels of maladaptive behavior. Therefore, the child who is completely alienated from a consistent level of interaction with a caring, primary caregiver, in all probability will exhibit a high level of maladaptive behavior. Consequently, the roots of the behavior must be examined carefully before implementing any intervention strategy to bring the behavior more in line with social, societal, and cultural norms.

The early establishment of attachment provides the child with the frame of reference for acceptable behavior. Just as love, comfort, and reassurance that is common place in a stable home provide a model of development for the child, the absence of love, comfort, and reassurance also provide a model for the development of the child. The difficulty is the type of development that occurs. One setting leads to a child that is considered to be a productive member of society. The other produces a child void of any sense of societal responsibility beyond self-preservation, if indeed the child survives. Given these set of assumptions, it is reasonable that the child who exhibits high levels of maladaptive behavior is probably more concerned with self-preservation than cultural and/or societal expectations. For example, a child who grows in an environment that requires multiple placements either within the foster care system, or among various family members, runs the risk of developing the sense that she or he actually "belongs" nowhere and to no one. The frame of reference, the secure base then becomes the system of movement and the egocentric sense of self. Anything that occurs that threatens the sense of self, as defined by the child, is seen as a threat to self-preservation. "Not infrequently, of course, a person is trying simultaneously to escape from one situation and, without success, to gain proximity to another. In such a case he would be described in this terminology as feeling both alarmed and anxious" (Bowlby, 1973, p. 95). The child begins to believe, whether acknowledged to others or not, that he or she is truly isolated, alienated, and even unlovable. The sense of isolation now becomes the comfort level. Anything that begins to break the sense of isolation is doing more than simply attempting to bring the child into compliance with behavioral expectations; it is viewed as an attempt to change the child's sense of self. Such drastic challenges to self-image result in resistance brought about by the fear of something new. It may be that changes in behavior due to temporarily secure relationships have been contemplated by the child only to have the primary caregiver(s) who instilled this new self-image within the child either be removed, or remove themselves from consistent interaction with the child. "Experience in a close relationship can shape beliefs" (Waters et al., 2002, p. 7). The shaping that occurs can either be positive, or something less than desired. If these with whom the child has developed the attachment completely abandon the child, the child must again go through the process of reassessing who he or she is, and resort back to whatever comfort level can be found. Should this same scenario be played out more than once, the child now becomes wary of anyone or anything that begins to produce a sense of security foreign to the self-established framework within the child. The sense of protection of one's self then manifests itself in maladaptive behavior. As observed in comments about anxious attachment and the susceptibility to fear, "once the frequency and effects of such threats are firmly grasped, a great many cases of separation anxiety and anxious attachment that otherwise appear inexplicable become intelligible" (Bowlby, 1973, p. 229).

As previously stated, maladaptive behavior is not easily defined. What is considered "normal" or "acceptable" behavior in one setting, culture, socio-economic climate, family, etc. may not be considered appropriate behavior by others. Further, acceptable behavior under one set of circumstances may not be acceptable given another set of circumstances. Such emphasizes the need for the secure base from which the child can explore their own avenues, and even limits of behavior without a sense of ultimate rejection, but rather secure guidance into appropriate levels of behavior. Consistent behavioral expectations further influence the manner in which a child begins to develop a sense of attachment. Repeatedly imposing, or attempting to impose, changes in the child's organizational construct impede the development of attachment. The child whose background includes multiple changes in the home situation, schools, teachers, primary care givers, etc. is not allowed to develop a frame of reference for acceptable behavior. These multiple factors, when considered independently, may actually present situations that could be addressed by the child with assistance from the appropriate caregivers. The combination of factors, however, presents a different situation. The child faced with multiple situations that serve to be stressors can begin to react to the entirety of these factors as opposed to one specific factor. "A finding of central importance to the argument is that two stimulus situations that, when present singly, might arouse fear at only low intensity may, when present together, arouse it at high intensity. Another and related one is that the presence or absence of an attachment figure, or other companion, makes an immense difference to the intensity of fear aroused. Only if these two findings are borne constantly in mind can the conditions that elicit intense fear be understood" (Bowlby, 1973, p. 97). Acceptable behavior for the child becomes simply survival-emotionally, psychologically, and perhaps even physically.

Bowlby, Ainsworth, and others laid a very strong foundation for exploring further the nature of attachment. The basic theoretical premise for attachment, however, includes the primary caregiver(s) as people. A step further would seem to indicate the possibility that children may become attached to situations in the absence of the security found in a person or persons who serve as primary care givers. For example, a child in the foster care system in the United States will probably have several individuals who will be identified as considering the "best interests" of the child. In fact, the motivation on the part of the adult care-givers in these situations is largely professional, not personal, and therefore it becomes inherently impossible for the child to formulate a strong sense of attachment to any individual(s) given the responsibility of care. With multiple caregivers, many times appearing and then disappearing with an alarming frequency, the child begins to become attached more to the "chaos" of the situation in place of the people involved. Multiple moves, multiple caregivers becomes the norm for the child. A situation that begins to be more permanent for the child, with the intent of establishing a permanent placement, becomes a threat to the child's sense of self, or what is normal. "Normal" for the child is "chaos" regardless of how others perceive the situation. Abused children frequently will demonstrate high levels of ambivalent attachment to abusive caregivers, but it is attachment. When placed in a situation where care, emotionally stability, and love is the norm, such a place is foreign to the child and may be perceived more as a threat than relief. The end result is the child's need to survive by engaging in behaviors inconsistent with the new physical placement. These behaviors are perceived to be maladaptive by the new caregivers, when in fact they are acceptable behaviors for the child as a matter of self-preservation.

IMPLICATIONS FOR ASSESSMENT
AND INTERVENTION

The first implication for the assessment of the maladaptive behavior exhibited by a child is quite simply the acknowledgment that those involved probably have little, if any, understanding of the complex nature of events that led to the behavior. Crowded schools; a backlog of assessments to be conducted for special education services; teachers inadequately trained to work with special needs children-especially those with severe behavior problems; lack of counselors and other behavior therapists; districting changes in schools; and a host of other variables contribute to the frustration of conducting adequate behavioral assessments and applying the determined interventions. The school system conditions then serve only to contribute to the confusion of the home situations for many of the children to be served. In a dysfunctional family, where the children are placed in state's custody for a period of time, the social well-being of the child will suffer as a result of questions about placement. As stated by a high school child in an interview whose behavior had become a source of concern in the school system, "You have no idea what it's like for me. You know where you are going to sleep. I have not slept in the same bed for a week in over a year. When I go to bed at night, I don't know if I will get to sleep in the same bed. You don't know what it's like."

Regardless of the inherent confusion that exists in schools when working with severe maladaptive behaviors there must be the acceptance of responsibility to work with these children and to try to address the needs presented. The typical assessment of children with behavioral problems includes an assessment of current level of intellectual functioning; individual academic achievement test(s); administration of a standardized adaptability scale; personality assessment; review of records; and interviews with those who have some knowledge about the background of the child. If possible, and especially if deemed necessary, a review of medical records also adds much information to this fairly standard process. Based on current special education law in the United States, the assessment is to take place within a specific period of time, the individual education program determined, the interventions started, and a continuous monitoring of the progress, or lack thereof, for the benefit of the child. While such a process is necessary by law, and is considered good practice due to the need to begin working with the children as quickly as possible, there is an element that should be considered when assessing the level of maladaptive behavior.

To effectively facilitate a process that allows the child to develop a desire to change his or her behavior there is more than just a need for continuous monitoring of the interventions to determine progress. There is the need for the individual to actually begin the process of trying to form an attachment to the child. As previously shown children need a sense of attachment to increase the probability of developing appropriate behavior. In the absence of a secure base at home, for school age children, the school by default becomes the most secure environment. It is the place where the child has a sense of safety, warmth, security, and perhaps even the place where more care is shown directly toward the child. Again, regardless of the inadequacies of the school systems, the educational environment mandated for all children in the United States becomes the constant in the life of the child. The school setting may be the traditionally oriented public or private school, or may be an alternative that exists within the system either through an alternative school, home-bound instruction, or other option.

For children who consistently exhibit high levels of maladaptive behavior there is the danger of removal from the traditional school setting. This is especially true when the behavior escalates to the point of concern for the safety of the child or other students. Making the assumption that a consistent environment is necessary to develop appropriate behaviors, the removal of the child only adds to the problem. Therefore, the educational setting must allow the child with maladaptive behaviors to have enough security in the educational setting to engage in the maladaptive behaviors without the fear of expulsion. The safety of the child and others must be considered, but dismissing the child from the therapeutic environment, whether school, classroom, or other setting, simply reinforces the idea that the child's security is more within the detached relationships or organizational chaos instead of the sense of positive attachment necessary for the development of more appropriate behaviors.

The assessment of the maladaptive behavior now becomes an on-going evaluation of the child to develop and maintain a sense of positive attachment to the constant of those individuals with whom the child interacts on a daily basis in the education environment. With the use of this setting as the controlled environment, and the security on the part of the child that must be developed that when engaged in high levels of maladaptive behavior there is still this constant, secure base, the situation is now set to truly facilitate effective behavior change. Simply put, the educational setting becomes the secure home. The special education teachers, home-bound teachers, regular classroom teachers, counselors, therapists, or whoever is designated to work with the child become the surrogate parents. The interventions are modified much as modifications are made when raising children in the home with an emphasis on the attachment between the child and the new organizational construct. Again, the ideal situation would be for the home to be the secure base. The reality is that the "ideal situation" for many children who have high levels of inappropriate behavior does not exist within the context of the home.

The risks in this process, though inherent if the child is susceptible to multiple moves, far exceed the reality that if the child who has strong levels of inappropriate behavior is not placed in a situation to learn more appropriate behaviors there is a high probability that the child will continue to digress. The child then becomes the adult dependent on the system, and a perpetuator of the cycle of maladaptive behavior.

This type of intervention, allowing the educational setting to become the secure base, requires rethinking how students are assessed for placement in special education. Further, such a high level of involvement on the part of the personnel involved requires a higher level of interaction among those working with the child, regardless of the interpretation of the "need to know" policies designed to ensure a child's civil rights. Finally, such an intervention requires consistency in application, regardless of setting. If the child is indeed susceptible to multiple moves due to a dysfunctional home, placement in state's custody, foster care, or other alternative form of care, it is imperative that the same level of interaction be consistently followed regardless of the placement of the child. Ultimately, the interventions used to address maladaptive behaviors of children must always be considered within the context of the true best interests of children.

ACKNOWLEDGMENTS

The author wishes to gratefully acknowledge the assistance of Dr. Jake Morris, Dr. Deryl Hilliard, and Dr. Barbara England in the preparation of this paper. Their review and comments are deeply appreciated.

REFERENCES

Ainsworth, M. (1972). Attachment and dependency: A comparison. In: J. Gewirtz (Ed.), *Attachment and Dependency*. Washington, DC: Winston.

Ainsworth, M. (1973). The development of infant-mother attachment. In: B. Caldwell & H. Ricciuti (Eds), *Review of Child Development Research* (Vol. 3). Chicago: University of Chicago Press.

Ainsworth, M. (1974). Infant-mother attachment and social development: Socialization as a product of reciprocal responsiveness to signals. In: M. Richards (Ed.), *The Integration of the Child into the Social World*. Cambridge: Cambridge University Press.

American Public Welfare Association (1997). *Voluntary cooperative information system, 1990–1995*.

Bickman, K. (2000, Winter). Improving children's mental health: How no effects can affect policy. *Emotional and Behavioral Disorders in Youth, 1*(1), 2–3.

Bowlby, J. (1969). *Attachment and loss: Vol. 1: Attachment*. New York: Basic Books.

Bowlby, J. (1973). *Attachment and loss: Vol. 2: Separation*. New York: Basic Books.

Bowlby, J. (1980). *Attachment and loss: Vol. 3: Loss, sadness and depression*. New York: Basic Books.

Bowlby, J. (1988). *A secure base: Parent-child attachment and healthy human development* (pp. 1–19, 77–98). New York: Basic Books.

Child Welfare League (1998). *State agency survey*.

England, R. (1996). Adoption, foster care or other: An overview of critical aspects of psychological adjustment in children. In: Henry R. Zurhellen (Ed.), *Research Symposium*. University of Memphis.

England, R. (1997). Theoretical considerations in the psychological adjustment of fostered, adopted, or other placements of children with human immunodeficiency virus infection. Paper presented at the Tennessee Joint Conference on Children and Youth with Disabilities.

England, R. (1999). Evaluation of personality characteristics of adjudicated and institutionalized youth: Critical aspects of psychological adjustment in children, Report I: Demographic Profile of Institutionalized Children (Report Summary). Report prepared for the Tennessee State Department of Mental Health.

England, R. (2000). Theoretical considerations for special educators in the psychological adjustment of fostered, adopted, or other placements of children. ERIC ED435165.

England, R. (2001). *Displaced children in crisis: Our enabling system for high risk behavior*. New York: Edwin Mellen.

Federal Bureau of Investigation (1997). *Supplementary homicide reports 1980–1995*. In: H. Snyder (Ed.), *Number of Juvenile Murder Victims, 1980–1995*.

Groth-Marnat, G. (1997). *Handbook of psychological assessment*. New York: Wiley.

Lewis, M., & Goldberg, S. (1969). Perceptual-cognitive development in infancy: A generalized expectancy model as a function of the mother-infant interaction. *Merrill-Palmer Quarterly, 15*, 81–100.

Moroz, K., & Jones, K. (2002). The effects of positive peer reporting on children's social involvement. *School Psychology Review, 31*(2), 235–245.

Robbins, M., & Szapocznik, J. (2000, April). Office of Juvenile Justice Bulletin Brief Strategic Family Therapy.

Salvia, J., & Ysseldyke, J. (2001). *Assessment* (8th ed.). Boston: Houghton Mifflin.

Sattler, J. (1992). *Assessment of children* (3rd ed.). San Diego: Sattler.

Sickmund, M. (1998a). States with judicial waiver, 1997. In: P. Torbet & L. Szymanski (Eds), *State Legislative Responses to Violent Juvenile Crime: 1996–97 Update*. Washington, DC: Office of Juvenile Justice and Delinquency Prevention.

Sickmund, M. (1998b). Minimum transfer age specified in statute, 1997. Adapted from P. Griffin, P. Torbet & L. Szymanski (Eds), *Trying Juveniles as Adults in Criminal Court: An Analysis of State Transfer Provisions*. Washington, DC: Office of Juvenile Justice and Delinquency Prevention.

Sickmund, M. (1998c). One day count of juveniles in public or private custody facilities. In: M. Sickmund et al. (Eds), *Juvenile Offenders and Victims: 1997 Update on Violence*. Washington, DC: Office of Juvenile Justice and Delinquency Prevention, 1997.

Sickmund, M. (1998d). Change in the offense profile of juveniles in custody in public facilities, 1983–1995. In: M. Sickmund et al. (Eds), *Juvenile Offenders and Victims: 1997 Update on Violence*. Washington, DC: Office of Juvenile Justice and Delinquency Prevention, 1997.

Sickmund, M. (1998e). Average length of stay for juveniles released from custody in 1994. In: M. Sickmund et al. (Eds), *Juvenile Offenders and Victims: 1997 Update on Violence*. Washington, DC: Office of Juvenile Justice and Delinquency Prevention, 1997.

Sickmund, M. (1998f). Percent change in the public custody facility population, 1983–1995. In: M. Sickmund et al. (Eds), *Juvenile Offenders and Victims: 1997 Update on Violence*. Washington, DC: Office of Juvenile Justice and Delinquency Prevention, 1997.

Snyder, H. (1998a). Estimated number of juvenile arrests, 1997. In: H. Snyder (Ed.), *Juvenile Arrests 1997*. Washington, DC: Office of Juvenile Justice and Delinquency Prevention.

Snyder, H. (1998b). Juvenile arrest rates for aggravated assault, 1981–1997. In: H. Snyder (Eds), *Juvenile Arrests 1997*. Washington, DC: Office of Juvenile Justice and Delinquency Prevention.

Snyder, H. (1998c). Number of juvenile murder victims, 1980–1995. In: M. Sickmund et al. (Eds), *Juvenile Offenders and Victims, 1997 Update on Violence*. Washington, DC: Office of Juvenile Justice and Delinquency Prevention.

Snyder, H. (1998d). Juvenile arrest rates for murder, 1981–1997. *Juvenile arrests 1997*. Washington, DC: Office of Juvenile Justice and Delinquency Prevention.

Snyder, H. (1998e). Murders known to involve juvenile offenders, 1980–1995. *OJJDP Statistical Briefing Book*.

Snyder, H. (1998f). Juvenile arrest rates for forcible rape, 1981–1997. In: H. Snyder (Ed.), *Juvenile Arrests 1997*. Washington, DC: Office of Juvenile Justice and Delinquency Prevention.

Snyder, H. (1998g). Juvenile arrest rates for robbery, 1981–1997. In: H. Snyder (Ed.), *Juvenile Arrests 1997*. Washington, DC: Office of Juvenile Justice and Delinquency Prevention.

Snyder, H. (1998h). Male and female juvenile arrest rates for violent crime index offenses, 1981–1997. *OJJDP Statistical Briefing Book*.

Sroufe, L., & Waters, E. (1977). Attachment as an organizational construct. *Child Development, 48*, 1184–1199.

Stahl, A. (1999a). Delinquency cases judicially waived to criminal court, 1987–1996. In: A. Stahl (Ed.), *Delinquency Cases Waived to Criminal Court, 1987–1996*. Washington, DC: Office of Juvenile Justice and Delinquency Prevention.

Stahl, A. (1999b). Adjudicated delinquency cases by disposition, 1987–1996. In: A. Stahl, M. Sickmund, T. Finnegan, H. Snyder, R. Poole & N. Tierney (Eds), *Juvenile Court Statistics, 1996*. Washington, DC: Office of Juvenile Justice and Delinquency Prevention.

Stahl, A. (1999c). Delinquency cases, 1996. In: A. Stahl et al. (Eds), *Juvenile Court Statistics 1996*. Washington, DC: Office of Juvenile Justice and Delinquency Prevention.

Stuhlman, M., & Pianta, R. (2002). Teachers' narratives about their relationships with children: Associations with behavior in classrooms. *School Psychology Review, 31*(2), 148–163.

Tennessee Commission on Children and Youth (2000, April 14). Southwest Region Preliminary System Observations.

U.S. Department of Health and Human Services (1997).

U.S. Department of Health and Human Services (1998).

Walker, H., & Sprague, J. (2000, Winter). Intervention strategies for diverting at-risk children and youth from destructive outcomes. *Emotional and Behavioral Disorders in Youth, 1*(1), 5–8.

Waters, E., Crowell, J., Elliott, M., Corcoran, D., & Treboux, D., (2002). *Bowlby's secure base theory and the social/personality psychology of attachment styles: Work(s) in progress*. Unpublished manuscript to appear in Attachment and Human Development.

6. RISK SCREENING STRATEGIES FOR PROTECTING THE WELL-BEING OF THE CHILD

Verle Headings[*]

INTRODUCTION

The premise of this work is that in most societies significant proportions of children do not experience optimum well-being. The goals of this work are: (1) to delineate and illustrate the tangled web of multifactorial causation and heterogeneity of causation for impaired well-being; and (2) to develop the proposition that these very characteristics of causation necessitates particular risk screening strategies which allow for timely interventions. The essence of such screening is to assess target effects which may be consequence of multiple factors, by cost-effective and universally applicable means. This screening paradigm will be examined briefly in relation to selected long standing screening systems, such as "triple test" screening of the fetus, and universal newborn genetic screening. The accumulated experiences with these systems provide some insights on strategic designated planning for risk screening which could be applied in areas of universal newborn screening for prenatal teratogen exposure effects, screening for indicators of systemically imposed disadvantages in the child's experience, screening the child for inattention to quality of health, and screening for indicators of risk for violent behavior. Such applications of risk screening, if appropriately embedded

* Verle Headings is Professor, Department of Pediatrics & Child Health, Division of Medical Genetics, Howard University College of Medicine, Washington, DC.

Administering Special Education: In Pursuit of Dignity and Autonomy
Advances in Educational Administration, Volume 7, 119–133
ISSN: 1479-3660/doi:10.1016/S1479-3660(04)07006-4

in universal service structures, e.g. newborn nurseries and schools, can allow for timely interventions for the most vulnerable children.

OBJECTIVES OF THIS WORK

The outcomes of risk exposure are not evenly distributed among those exposed. However, among those identified as exposed and before signs of substantially impaired well-being there is opportunity to remove the risk or to offer countering intervention.

Based on the domains of risk to child well-being, particularly in the United States, as reviewed here we will:

(1) Formulate strategies for risk screening in four domains of risk to well-being in children.
(2) Design the strategies to be universally accessible for all children in a population.
(3) Tailor the screening strategies to life stages which allow for beneficial intervention.

Pursuit of these objectives is here offered as a report of a work in progress.

A MACRO LEVEL PERSPECTIVE

The developing knowledge on: (1) circumstances which allow for optimal child development; (2) variables in fetal and childhood environments which correlate with impaired physical, cognitive, psychological, and social functioning in later life stages; (3) differences over time and geography in social practices and technologies which impact adversely on child well-being; and (4) the sheer scale of adverse effects which overwhelm resources, present sobering occasion to reflect on how best to strategize interventions.

Risks to fetal development through teratogen exposures, systemic disadvantages of children, inattention to quality of health and variables which promote violent behavior by children, follow from behaviors of adults in the child's environment. This being the case one must conclude that the well-being of children cannot be entrusted without qualification to the self-interested judgments of adults in their environments. If it be true that it takes a village to raise a child, professionals allied with other local citizens might consider applying this precept also to universal screening of children's vulnerabilities to adverse effects of life style and economic decisions made by adults in their environments.

In this chapter, four domains of vulnerability for the child in North America early in the 21st century will be set forth. These four will represent both high frequency vulnerabilities as well as permit us to focus on strategies which permit universal screening for impairments with poorly defined endpoints. This is not an inclusive set of vulnerabilities.

We may easily claim that local programs are in place to address these domains of risk for children. However, the literature documents glaring failure to prevent adverse effects in these areas throughout the culture. We will both document this failure and examine approaches to universal screening for risks in the interest of discovering particularly vulnerable children in advance of major adverse outcomes.

CONCEPTUALIZING WELL-BEING OF THE CHILD

Well-being, a characteristic subject to multiple subjective definitions, has been formally presented as – "the state or condition of being well: a condition characterized by happiness, health or prosperity: moral or physical welfare" (Webster's Third New International Dictionary, 1996). These are elements of both material and immaterial qualities, existing in an essential unity, and are rooted in shared common sense experiences in most cultures (Machuga, 2002).

We may further note a distinctively *human* (as distinguished from other creatures) appreciation of well-being as one embedded in a capacity to differentiate between right and wrong, better and worse – "the ability of an individual to recognize the rights, freedoms, and obligations defined by society" (Loike & Tendler, 2002). To the extent that actions and social arrangements in the adult world impede the child's success in maturing into this competence of "moral intelligence," we might well expect impaired psychological and social functioning which in turn compromises well-being.

Finally, the creative work of research neurologist Antonio Damasio concerning feelings of joy and sorrow posits that body states accompanied by modes of thinking about perception of given body states yield the subjective experience of well-being (Damasio, 2003). Thus, we here return to the close affinity of objective physical indication of well-being and the subjective lived experience of well-being.

This set of understandings provides some guide to how we might identify markers of impaired well-being which could be screened for universally.

LESSONS FROM NEWBORN AND PRENATAL SCREENING

Newborn Screening service was introduced in the early 1960's with the pioneering work of Dr. Robert Guthrie (Fox et al., 2000). As applied to universal screening of newborn infants for genetic disorders a medical test is applied to all individuals in the absence of any presenting medical complaint. The objective is to identify individuals who bear silent (presymptomatic) indicators of future overt disease (Headings, 1988, 1998). In some instances this in effect represents a molecular definition of disease during a clinically benign stage of disease when intervention can achieve prevention of progression to clinical presentation.

Two diseases by which this principle can be illustrated are congenital hypothyroidism and phenylketonuria (PKU), each occurring in the United States with incidences of 1/4,000 and 1/10,000, respectively (Levy & Albers, 2000). For hypothyroidism the variable commonly screened for is thyroxin concentration in blood, the hormone product of the thyroid gland. Significant deficiency will impair development of cognitive function and physical growth, which is preventable by daily intake of thyroxin beginning within the first two weeks following birth. PKU screening focuses on an excess of an essential amino acid, phenylalanine, in blood which cannot be metabolized because of an inherited enzyme deficiency. Restricting dietary phenylalanine, beginning in the first two weeks is required in order to ensure near-normal cognitive development.

Universal application of screening and intervention strategies for these two disorders is mandated by state laws in all 50 states and the District of Columbia. Each state additionally screens for other inborn error disorders universally within the state but which are not screened for among all states. In addition to inherited metabolic errors newborn infants in some states are universally screened for impaired hearing and for infectious diseases (toxoplasmosis, HIV). It is estimated that the aggregate incidence of inborn errors which could be screened for the benefit of infants is on the order of 1/600, and that new technology recently introduced may eventually allow for cost effective expanded screening.

The criteria for disease screening in general were formulated in 1968 (Wilson & Jungner, 1968) and have contributed to developing the elements of newborn screening services.

With suitable adaptations these criteria can serve in the design of screening for risks of impairments by multifactorial and more heterogeneous causation than is the case for most disorders currently included in newborn screening programs.

Reservations about universal newborn screening programs have included the fact that as presently constituted they include a very modest number of all genetic disorders; that there are risks of ill advised use of the resulting information within families; there can be moral disagreements among members of society on the use of genetic information derived through screening (Rowley, 1984); less than ideal outcomes from interventions following screening (Treacy et al., 1995); and divergent opinions on how narrowly the criterion of intervention (benefit) should be construed (Ross, 2002). For example universal newborn screening for

Duchenne muscular dystrophy and cystic fibrosis currently are not widely accepted by professionals because efficacy of presymptomatic treatment of the disease is equivocal. However, limited offerings of voluntary newborn screening for such disorders suggests some parents may have a different perspective which is founded in a broader appreciation of benefit for the family unit.

Universal prenatal screening for neural tube closure defects and two chromosome abnormalities is accomplished by assaying amounts of three chemicals in mother's blood, the so-called "triple screen." Characteristics of such screening are that these chemicals serve as secondary markers, which when yielding a positive screen requires confirmatory diagnostic testing involving relatively invasive procedures. Such screening yields significant rates of false negative and false positive screen results. Finally, interventions, while of benefit, are substantially less than ideal.

The following lessons may be gleaned from newborn and prenatal screening, which contain insights for how to design screening for impairments with poorly defined endpoints.

- For most disorders screening has been directed to outcome markers which lend themselves to cost effective universal screening, rather than to identifying causes. In part this circumvents the problem of heterogeneity of causation.
- Screening can be justified even if false positive and false negative rates of detection fall short of the ideal. Justification for offering screening under such circumstances takes account of the interests of lay persons, the nature of benefits to be achieved, and provision of appropriate pre-screening education/counseling of persons offered screening.
- Less than *ideal* efficacy of intervention does not exclude justifiable screening, provided that *benefit* of a screening service in human and monetary terms unambiguously exceeds *cost* of not screening.
- Universal offering of screening which provides an opt-out opportunity reasonably protects the interests of parents who may disagree with the goals of screening.

THE PREMISE THAT PREVENTION
IS PREFERABLE TO TREATMENT

Newborn screening for inborn errors provides for a narrow window of opportunity following birth to effect prevention since injury done by inattention to risk typically is not reversible when brain-based functions are impaired. Analogously, infants born with genetic disorders for which there is no preventive treatment, e.g.

Down Syndrome, nonetheless may derive some benefit from neuromotor training programs beginning in early infancy.

Informal clinical experience with fetal alcohol spectrum disorder in humans suggests that in the absence of interventions beginning in early infancy one can anticipate about a 90% prevalence of mental health problems (Streissguth & O'Malley, 2000).

Exposure to alcohol prenatally also predisposes to a range of cognitive/learning impairments in humans and animal models. Neuromotor training during infancy of rats which were prenatally exposed to alcohol reportedly improves later proficiency with the skills taught in infancy. This offers significant promise for enhancing well-being by early intervention for humans with history of prenatal alcohol exposure.

It is commonly acknowledged that *early* identification and interventions for children with learning disabilities are of more benefit for the child and family. At the least early intervention avoids the difficult task of unlearning counterproductive patterns of learning and coping before productive skills can be learned.

POSITIONING SCREENING STRATEGIES AND INTERVENTIONS SO AS TO BE UNIVERSALLY ACCESSIBLE IN A POPULATION

Equitable access to screening for all children at a life stage when beneficial interventions can be applied is difficult to achieve if this activity is left to the initiatives of individual parents or clinicians. Neither is a local "special project" approach likely to achieve universal and enduring screening service. A much more reliable design is to apply screening at a "gateway" point through which essentially all children must pass under observation of a clinician. Two of these are the newborn nursery and the entry into school.

Which of these gateways are selected will be governed by life stage at which available interventions can be most efficacious and safely administered.

If the screening design and methodology can be fitted into the context of other service delivery, both cost containment and likelihood of universal implementation are enhanced.

DISTINCTIVE CHARACTERISTICS OF MULTIFACTORIAL CAUSATION AND HETEROGENEITY OF CAUSATION

Screening for health problems during latent or early symptomatic stages typically has required establishing commonly agreed risk thresholds for the variable being

Table 1. Domains of Risk to Well-being.

Teratogen exposure
Systemically imposed social and economic disadvantages
Inattention to quality of health
Inattention to variables which foster a mentality of problem solving by violent behavior

measured by the screening test. The four domains of risk to well-being (Table 1) we are now considering present additional challenge.

The model of multifactorial causation as it is commonly invoked for explaining complex inheritance of genetic disorders posits a set of liability factors for a phenotype in a population. These multiple factors, which may be either mutant genes or environmental variables, present in individuals in multiple combinatorial arrays with a resulting spectrum of phenotype severities.

The most simplistic version of this model assumes that each liability factor presents a small and equivalent effect to all other factors contributing to the measured phenotypic value. Furthermore, the effects of each factor are additive, not multiplicative. As displayed below (Fig. 1) these conditions will yield a symmetrical unimodal frequency distribution of measured phenotypic values (differing severities) in a population, with specified mean and standard deviations (the Gaussian or normal distribution).

Of course, changing the conditions whereby the liability factors contribute unequally to the phenotypic value, and interact with one another in non-additive relationships will change the shape of the distribution of phenotypic values in a population. The latter includes a concept of gene epistasis, whereby product of one gene modifies the effect of another gene's product. Individual liability factors may contribute to chains of risk factors for an adverse outcome. Furthermore, a given risk factor may function as such only in the presence of another risk factor.

A second model of phenotype inheritance is genetic heterogeneity, or more generally heterogeneity of causation, whereby *alternative* liability factors yield *similar* phenotypic values *among* families or among different environmental contexts. Thus, there is potential for both alternative combinations and interactions of risk (liability) factors yielding similar outcome.

A substantial literature on both cross-sectional and longitudinal studies concerning multiple risk factors in childhood which associate with antisocial and criminal behavior illustrates the complexity of liability and protective factor interactions which operate through child-specific factors, family factors, school context, life events, community and cultural factors (Pathways to Prevention, 2004). Teasing apart relevant liabilities for an adverse outcome in a particular child is diagnostically critical. However, at the level of risk screening, which is our

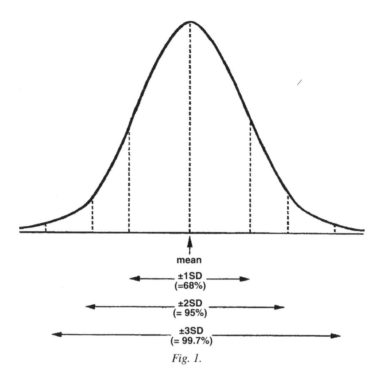

Fig. 1.

task here, we must seek methods which can in a timely manner identify each child in need of diagnostic evaluation. This comports with the current political climate of "leaving no child behind."

UNIVERSAL SCREENING FOR IMPAIRMENTS WITH POORLY DEFINED ENDPOINTS

*Primacy of a Child's Parents as Source of Information
to be Screened for Indicators of Risk*

For each of the four domains of risk screening (Table 1) a strategy of screening includes parents as a prime source of the requisite information. This is both because parents possess the inside longitudinal perspective on the information to be sought about their child, and their collaboration at this stage prepares them for subsequent diagnostic and intervention efforts should these be indicated.

Outcomes of Teratogen Exposure

Fetal Alcohol Syndrome (FAS) was so named in 1973 to denote children with specific minor anomalies of the face, deficiency of growth, and cognitive/behavioral disorders, and who are born to mothers who use alcohol during pregnancy. In time longitudinal studies revealed a range of alcohol related neurodevelopmental and neurocognitive impairments spanning childhood, adolescence and adult stages, even in the absence of physical signs, leading to designation of Fetal Alcohol Spectrum Disorder (FASD). Through careful study by Streissguth and colleagues the incidence of FASD is estimated at nearly 1/100 live births (Streissguth & O'Malley, 2000).

The *scale* of this spectrum of disability in children through choices made by adults itself invites measures for universal early identification and intervention. However, this does not fully reflect the additional other drugs with physical and behavioral teratogenic potential, which commonly are used in conjunction with alcohol. In a study now underway we have documented through a screening questionnaire administered to an unselected series of new mothers in the maternity ward that 39% of women delivering infants at Howard University Hospital acknowledge using one or multiple agents with reported teratogenic potential (Taylor et al., 1999). Based on other studies this is expected to be an under-estimate. These included alcohol, nicotine, cocaine, marijuana, heroin, methadone and PCP. Each of the exposed neonates pointed to an average of 2.8 older siblings who could also be considered at risk for teratogen exposure (Taylor, 2000).

Our continuing research focuses on devising and field testing tools for universal screening of newborn infants for outcome of teratogen exposure regardless of the specific teratogen (Scott et al., 1999). Employing craniofacial photographs on 516 unselected infants in our nursery, measurements were recorded on distances among 23 standard landmarks on the face, a method reported by Clarren (Clarren et al., 1987). Infants were assigned to an unexposed group or to one of seven exposure groups. Distance measurements will be analyzed as triangulated sets, with each triangle apex serving as a morphometric marker.

Analyses of these data is not yet completed. If the method yields statistically distinguishable differences between morphometric markers of exposed and unexposed infants this methodology lends itself to universal screening of all newborn infants for "subclinical" dislocations of face landmarks, implemented through electronic transmittal of digital photographs to a laboratory for analysis. Prior to application of such a screening test its power to predict subsequent impaired development during early childhood must be established through longitudinal studies.

Table 2.   Wilson-Jungner Criteria for Screening.

Condition should be an important health problem
There should be a latent or early symptomatic stage
The natural history of the disease should be understood
There should be a suitable screening test
The test should be acceptable to the public
Facilities for diagnosis and treatment should be available
There should be accepted treatment for the health problem
There should be an agreed upon policy on whom to treat
Cost should be economically balanced
Case finding should be a continuous process

The goal of defining an early predictor (in the nursery) of teratogen-induced cognitive and behavioral impairment is to justify studies on remedial behavioral training in early childhood. Finally, the methods and the goal must be evaluated in light of each of the screening criteria in Table 2. Clearly, a new screening service can entail extensive and detailed research.

Systemically Imposed Disadvantage

In the United States a cluster of social and economic characteristics have been catalogued, which by any judgement would be interpreted as disadvantage for children. Our primary task here is not to disentangle the webs of causation for these disadvantages nor their interactions, but to recognize their impact on children and to consider tools for early universal screening of risk for these disadvantages. However, one perspective offered by John Wall (2003) points to a possibility that multiple common disadvantages for children and youth, a small sample of which are listed below (Table 3), are unintended consequences of a set of cultural characteristics:

> Certainly we are a country that increasingly has come to value individual autonomy, freedom, and competition for resources, and this ethic is likely to sideline children, given their special vulnerability, neediness, and dependence on others. But children are also the objects of deliberate social attack, for example through – the targeting of children by the movie and television industries for violent entertainment, and diminishing government support for schools and families. Although there is much rhetoric about children as the promise of America's future and although parents themselves generally work hard to raise their own children well, we have not as a society developed the language or commitment to address child-rearing as a public moral concern (Wall, 2003).

One author estimates that on some 40 indicators of emotional and social well-being, children in North America present evidence of decline over time (Goleman, 1995).

Table 3.   Social and Economic Disadvantages of Youth.

About 17% live below the official poverty rate (U.S. Census Bureau, 2000).

Ten million are without health insurance (Hewlett & West, 1998).

Amount of contact between child and parent has decreased by about ten hours per week since 1970s (Fuchs, 1988).

More than half of all children live separately from one parent some or all of their childhood (McLanahan & Sandefur, 1994).

In the past 30 years numbers of children born outside marriage rose from 5.3 to 32.8% (Popeno et al., 2000).

By the time of eighteen years an estimated one in four girls is physically or sexually abused (McKenzie, 1995).

Following a far ranging cataloguing of disadvantages imposed on children by choices in the adult world, David Orr concludes as follows:

> We are unwittingly undermining our children's physical health, mental health, connection to adults, sense of continuity with the past, connections to nature, the health of ecosystems, a sense of commonwealth, and hope for a decent future. But we have difficulty in seeing whole systems in a culture shaped so thoroughly by finance capital and narrow specialization (Orr, 2002).

That such outcomes impair well-being of children needs no further documentation. What is additionally sobering, however, is a body of literature that points to relationships between low socioeconomic position and limited education in childhood, and poorer health and morbidity in adulthood, as well as more limited cognitive function in adulthood (Hertzman, 1998, 1999; Hertzman & Wiens, 1996; Kaplan et al., 2001; Lynch et al., 1997; Turrell et al., 2002).

Thus, considering markers of impaired well-being pointed to by the above observations, some embedded in endemic social circumstances and others in economic disadvantage, there is a case to be made for research on approaches to universally screening the social and economic liability factors which surround each newborn infant and each child at the point of entering school. This could be approached through a carefully designed and field tested risk rating scale.

Inattention to Quality of Health

Despite school health programs, public health programs, and government assistance programs for low income populations, the children and youth of North America seem beset by multiple risks to health through the inattention of their responsible adults.

One postulate about such a cluster of preventable adverse effects on the health of children is that economic and social pursuits in the adult world of much of North

Table 4.   Health Problems Among Children.

Poor nutrition
Obesity in one-fourth of children
Sedentary, entertainment driven life style
Sexually transmitted diseases
High prevalence of depression
Undetected high blood concentrations of cholesterol and sugar
Violent deaths

America foster an inattentiveness to or ignorance of the necessary conditions for avoiding such risks to health of children.

Screening each child and its family context for health liability factors of the types suggested in Table 4 at two or three points during the child's elementary and secondary education can provide a vehicle for focusing the attentiveness of the family unit on the special needs of a child identified by screening. If schools offer health education classes for children, then the appropriate accompanying laboratory learning exercise for the child and it's family is periodic universal health risk screening, with due diligence to designing the screening system in conformity with the Wilson-Jungner criteria for disease screening.

Improvement in this domain of a child's well-being is likely to exert salutary effects on other domains of well-being as well.

Inattention to Markers for Violent Behavior

During the past 30 years more than 1000 research studies have permitted public health professionals to conclude that violence in various media is associated with increased aggressive and violent behavior among children. The introduction of violent interactive media, such as video games, introduces the child to learning the same conditioned reflex skills as a soldier or police officer in training (Grossman, 1996; Grossman & Degaetano, 1999; Joint Statement, 2000). Most recently L. Rowell Huesmann et al. published a longitudinal study on several hundred adults whose degree of exposure to televised violence had been assessed in the 1970s. Now as adults they were rated by various indicators of aggressive behaviors by which they attempt to solve problems. For both males and females magnitude of exposure to entertainment violence in childhood correlated with severity of aggressive behavior when these children became adults.

Whatever the multiple sources of violent and aggressive behavior by children the prevalence has become of epidemic proportions. Concerned parents and professionals require a tool for screening behavioral development of the child as pertains to solving problems by behaviors of domination or overt violence. Behavioral rating scales on items such as persistent fascination with instruments of violence, rehearsing violent behavior via interactive video games, etc. merit research as to their predictive value for aggressive behavior.

Parents and teachers working together could apply such behavioral rating scales at selected intervals during childhood. Early identification of a child with special need in this domain allows for early intervention, with an expectation of enhanced well-being for both child and family. An analogous behavioral rating scale has been developed by the National Organization for Fetal Alcohol Syndrome (NOFAS) to be used by parents and professionals (Mitchell, 2002). NOFAS is a national advocacy group of parents and professionals.

THOUGHTS ON DESIGN OF SCREENING FOR POORLY DEFINED ENDPOINTS

We revisit here the core theme of screening for variables concerning which there is known association with risk of harm to a child's well-being. Thus, screening merely adjusts the risk for a given child; it is not diagnostic.

Poorly defined or variable endpoints of dysfunction can pose significant challenge to achieving ideal detection rates. However, experience with traditional newborn and prenatal screening services have demonstrated new benefit to many children and families even though the screening tools are imperfect. This outcome rests centrally on educating of individuals (parents) before participation in screening, and follow-up counseling, diagnostic work and recommendations on interventions when indicated for screen positive individuals. This paradigm is similarly relevant for dysfunctions presenting with poorly defined endpoints.

We conclude by highlighting the high standard to be satisfied by any screening service. Well founded estimates of early beneficial intervention as well as risks which may attend screening must meet the test of broad if not universal agreement by both professionals and laypersons.

REFERENCES

Clarren, S., Sampson, P., Larsen, J., Donnell, D., Barr, H., Bookstein, F., Martin, D., & Streissguth, A. (1987). Facial effects of fetal alcohol exposure: Assessment by photographs and morphometric analysis. *American Journal of Medical Genetics*, *26*, 651–666. http://www.ahrq.gov/news/press/pr2002/mepschpr.htm.

Damasio, A. (2003). *Looking for Spinoza: Joy, sorrow, and the feeling brain*. New York, NY: Harcourt Brace Jovanich.

Fox, C., Lloyd-Puryear, M., & Mann, M. (2000). Serving the family from birth to the medical home. *Pediatrics*, *106*(Suppl.), 383–427.

Fuchs, V. R. (1988). *Women's quest for economic equality*. Cambridge, MA: Harvard University Press, p. 111.

Goleman D. (1995). *Emotional intelligence*. New York: Bantam.

Grossman D. (1996). *On killing: The psychological cost of learning to kill in war and society*. Boston, MA: Little, Brown.

Grossman, D., & Degaetano, G. (1999). *Stop teaching our kids to kill*. New York: Crown Publishers.

Headings, V. (1988). Screening the newborn population for congenital and genetic disorders. *Pediatric Reviews & Communications*, *2*, 317–332.

Headings, V. (1998). The present state of genetic knowledge and implications for genetic screening. In: J. Kegley (Ed.), *Genetic Knowledge: Human Values and Responsibility* (pp. 113–129). St Paul, MN: Paragon House.

Hertzman, C. (1998). The case for child development as a determinant of health. *Canadian Journal of Public Health*, *89*(Suppl. 1), S9-14, S16-21.

Hertzman, C. (1999). The biological embedding of early experience and its effects on health in adulthood. *Annals of the New York Academy of Sciences*, *896*, 85–95.

Hertzman, C., & Wiens, M. (1996). Child development and long-term outcomes: A population health perspective and summary of successful intervention. *Social Science & Medicine*, *43*, 1083–1095.

Hewlett, S., & West, C. (1998). *The war against parents: What we can do for America's beleaguered moms and dads* (p. 250). New York, NY: Houghton Mifflin.

Joint Statement on the Impact of Entertainment Violence on Children, by the American Academy of Pediatrics, the American Academy of Child and Adolescent Psychology, the American Psychological Association, the American Academy of Family Physicians, and the American Medical Association. Congressional Public Health Summit, July 26, 2000.

Kaplan, G. A., Turrell, G., Lynch, J. W. et al. (2001). Childhood socioeconomic position and cognitive function in adulthood. *International Journal of Epidemiology*, *30*(2), 256–263.

Levy, H., & Albers, S. (2000). Genetic screening of newborns. *Annual Review of Genomics and Human Genetics*, *1*, 139–177.

Loike, J., & Tendler, M. (2002). Revisiting the definition of Homo Sapiens. *Kennedy Institute of Ethics Journal*, *12*, 343–350.

Lynch, J. W., Kaplan, G. A., & Shema, S. J. (1997). Cumulative impact of sustained economic hardship on physical, cognitive, psychological, and social functioning. *New England Journal of Medicine*, *337*(26), 1889–1895.

Machuga, R. (2002). *In defense of the soul: What it means to be human*. Grand Rapids, MI: Brazos Press.

McKenzie, M. (1995). *Domestic abuse in America*. Lawrenceville, VA: Brunswick.

McLanahan, S., & Sandefur, G. (1994). *Growing up with a single parent: What hurts, what helps* (pp. 2–3). Cambridge, MA: Harvard University Press.

Mitchell, K. (2002). Fetal alcohol syndrome: Practical suggestions and support for families and caregivers. National Organization on Fetal Alcohol Syndrome, Washington.

Orr, D. (2002). *The nature of design: Ecology, culture, and human intention*. New York: Oxford University Press.

Pathways to Prevention – Developmental and early intervention approaches to crime in Australia – Full Report. Selected developmental studies and concepts, pp. 1–43. http://law.gov.au/ncp/Publications/80917_pathways_report/selected_developmental.htm.

Popeno, D., & Dafoe Whitehead, B. (2000). *The state of our unions 2000: The social health of marriage in America*. Report of the National Marriage Project, Rutgers University, p. 33.

Ross, F. R. (2002). Predictive genetic testing of conditions that present in childhood. *Kennedy Institute of Ethics Journal, 12*, 225–244.

Rowley, P. (1984). Genetic screening: Marvel or menace? *Science, 225*, 138–144.

Scott, D., Bookman, E., Taylor, K., Ampy, F., & Headings, V. (1999). Craniofacial landmarks in human neonates exposed to alcohol and other teratogens. *Alcoholism: Clinical & Experimental Research, 23*, 109A.

Streissguth, A., & O'Malley, K. (2000). Neuropsychiatric implications and long-term consequences of fetal alcohol spectrum disorders. *Seminars in Clinical Neuropsychiatry, 5*, 177–190.

Taylor, K. (2000). *Identification of older siblings at-risk for developmental delay through ascertainment of a teratogen-exposed neonate*. Masters Thesis, Howard University Graduate School, Washington, DC.

Taylor, K., Bookman, E., Scott, D., Ampy, F., & Headings, V. (1999). Screening for teratogen exposures among unselected human neonates. *Alcoholism: Clinical & Experimental Research, 23*, 108A.

Treacy, E., Childs, B., & Scriver, C. (1995). Response to treatment in hereditary metabolic disease: 1993 survey and 10 year comparison. *American Journal of Human Genetics, 56*, 356–367.

Turrell, G., Lynch, J. W., Kaplan, G. A. et al. (2002). Socioeconomic position across the life course and cognitive function in late middle age. *Journal of Gerontology B Psychological Science and Social Science, 57*(1), S43–S51.

United States Census Bureau. Census 2000, pp. 60–210, vi.

Wall, J. (2003). Animals and innocents: Theological reflections on the meaning and purpose of child-rearing. *Theology Today, 59*, 559–582.

Webster's Third New International Dictionary (1996).

Wilson, J., & Jungner, G. (1968). *The principles and practice of screening for disease*. Geneva: World Health Organization.

7. INCLUSION OF CHILDREN WITH DISABILITIES IN GENERAL EDUCATION CLASSROOMS ☆

Wendy A. Harriott[*]

According to the U.S. Department of Education (2001), approximately 53% of all students with disabilities (ages 6–21) were receiving a major portion of their education within general education classrooms. Further, according to the National Center on Educational Restructuring and Inclusion (NCERI, 1995), students from IDEA's 13 disability categories, at all levels of severity, in all grade levels, are being included across the country. Additionally, the numbers of students who are being educated in inclusive settings has been increasing. However, it should be noted that inclusive programs serving students with disabilities vary among individual states in the United States. For example, some rural states (e.g. Idaho, North Dakota, Oregon, Vermont) serve more than 90% of their students with disabilities in general education for over 40% of the day (USDOE, 1998). Other states (e.g. District of Columbia, Louisiana, New York) serve fewer than 60% of students with disabilities in general education (USDOE, 1998).

Inclusive programs are advocated by some professionals for all students regardless of the severity of their disabilities (Sailor, 1991). Currently, there are

☆Portions of this paper are excerpted from: Harriott Godshall, W. A. (2001). Administrators' and teachers' perceptions of necessary resources for secondary general education inclusion classrooms in rural Pennsylvania school districts. (Doctoral dissertation, The Pennsylvania State University, 2001.) *Dissertation Abstracts International, 62*, 1792. Research for a majority of this paper was conducted during doctoral work at The Pennsylvania State University, University Park, PA.
*Wendy A. Harriott is Assistant Professor, Monmouth University, New Jersey.

Administering Special Education: In Pursuit of Dignity and Autonomy
Advances in Educational Administration, Volume 7, 135–166
Copyright © 2004 by Elsevier Ltd.
All rights of reproduction in any form reserved
ISSN: 1479-3660/doi:10.1016/S1479-3660(04)07007-6

many definitions of inclusion (i.e. the education of students with disabilities in general education) as well as disagreement among professionals if inclusion is recommended for students with disabilities.

In this chapter, terms used in the past and current definitions used for educating students with disabilities in general education classrooms in the United States are summarized. Next, outcomes of inclusion are presented for students with and without disabilities. Also, five resource areas (i.e. organizational climate, personnel, time, inservice training, and supplementary materials) necessary for inclusion will be reviewed based on a comprehensive literature review and data collected from general education teachers, special education teachers, and administrators. Finally, implications for practitioners and researchers are provided.

INCLUSION LEGISLATION AND DEFINITIONS

During the last decade, school districts throughout the United States have implemented inclusion programs utilizing a variety of models. A growing number of school districts are including all students with disabilities, even those with severe disabilities, into general education classrooms (Thousand & Villa, 1990). Although the term inclusion has no legal definition, and has been interpreted by educational professionals in a variety of ways, the concept has been in existence under the least restrictive environment (LRE) provision of PL 94-142, The Education for all Handicapped Children Act of 1975, PL 101-476, The Individuals with Disabilities Education Act (IDEA) of 1990 and most recently within PL 105-17, The Individuals with Disabilities Education Act Amendments (IDEA) of 1997. According to IDEA (1997), public education agencies are required to ensure that:

> to the maximum extent appropriate, children with disabilities, including children in public or private institutions or other care facilities, are educated with children who are nondisabled; and that special classes, separate schooling or other removal of children with disabilities from the regular educational environment occurs only if the nature or severity of the disability is such that education in regular classes with the use of supplementary aids and services cannot be achieved satisfactorily [Authority 20 U.S.C. 1412 (a) (5)].

The concept of inclusion has been defined in various ways within the literature. Catlett and Osher (1994) reviewed policy statements of professional organizations and found at least seven different definitions for inclusion. Currently, in education, inclusion is the term used when students with disabilities are placed in general education classrooms for a portion of the school day (Falvey et al., 1995b). The term inclusion is differentiated from mainstreaming. Mainstreaming refers to the placement of students with disabilities in general education classrooms with appropriate instructional support (Meyen, 1990). When students are mainstreamed, they are usually prepared prior to placement into general education and are expected to "keep up" with the general classroom expectations (Rogers, 1993). Students with disabilities who are mainstreamed receive the same or nearly the same curriculum as general education students and are expected to "fit" into the general curriculum and classroom. On the other hand, within inclusive programs, the general education teacher is expected to make adaptations to provide a suitable environment for students with disabilities. Within the literature on inclusion, there are a variety of interpretations of the definition of inclusion (e.g. Gartner & Lipsky, 1987; Rogers, 1993; Stainback & Stainback, 1984). For the purposes of this chapter, inclusion is defined as programs in which students with disabilities (with the exception of gifted) are eligible for special education, have an individualized education program (IEP), and receive their education in general education classrooms using different, modified, and/or additional curricula from students without disabilities. This definition of inclusion is similar to "selective inclusion" as described by Zionts (1997). Selective inclusion refers to partial general education class placement of students with disabilities (Zionts). The assumption that this definition is based on is that general education is not always appropriate for every student; some students may benefit by receiving individualized services in addition to general education.

RATIONALE FOR INCLUSION

Within this section are various issues relevant to the impetus of inclusion. Philosophical issues such as integration, the regular education initiative (REI), merging of special and general education, and the concept of full inclusion are summarized. Additionally, legal issues relevant to inclusion are reviewed such as least restrictive environment (LRE) and related court cases. Finally, the viewpoints of proponents of inclusion are summarized.

Integration

A landmark Supreme Court case, *Brown v. Board of Education* (1954), eliminated segregation in public schools. In this decision, racial segregation was declared unconstitutional. Specifically, the Brown decision "recognized that educating black children separately, even if done so in 'equal' facilities, was inherently unequal because of the stigma attached to being educated separately and because of the deprivation of interaction with children from other backgrounds" (Rothstein, 1990, p. 2). Additionally, in later years, more than 30 court cases cited the principles established by *Brown v. Board of Education* as support for equality issues for the education of students with disabilities (Calfapietra, 1996). Further, during the 1980s, professionals began to use the term "integration" relative to students with disabilities as the individuals who were being discriminated against (Gliedman & Roth, 1980).

Regular Education Initiative

The beginnings of the regular education initiative (REI) are usually referred to as a speech made in 1985 by Madeleine Will and a paper by Wang et al. (1986). In her speech (later published in *Exceptional Children*, 1986), Will argued that the "pull-out" approach had failed to meet the needs of students (i.e. those with mild and moderate disabilities) in those programs. She recommended that regular and special educators work together to benefit all students. Will also suggested that many children in regular education need extra help but do not receive it because they are not eligible for special education services. Similarly, Wang et al. (1986) were also critical of the "pull-out" approach. There are various REI advocates within the literature (e.g. Lilly, 1987; Reynolds, 1991). The major goals of REI advocates are to: (a) blend special and general education into one system; (b) increase the number of children with disabilities in general education classrooms; and (c) improve academic achievement of students with mild and moderate disabilities (Fuchs & Fuchs, 1994).

Merger

Some professionals challenge the philosophy of maintaining two separate systems (i.e. general education and special education). For example, Stainback and Stainback (1984) advocated for a "merger" of general and special education; Biklen (1985) supported "integrating" general and special education; Wang and Walberg (1988) used the term "shared responsibility." Similarly, today, there is a trend toward merging general and special educator preservice programs in higher education (Sapon-Shevin, 1988; Stainback & Stainback, 1987). Further, there is a trend in some public school districts across the United States to merge general and special education services (Reynolds et al., 1987; York & Reynolds, 1996).

Full Inclusion

Full inclusion advocates support the elimination of separate special education classrooms (Kauffman, 1994). Further, proponents of full inclusion, believe that the main focus should be on developing social skills and friendships, not academics (Fuchs & Fuchs, 1994). The term full inclusion is used by some authors to mean that all students, regardless of disability, attend their local schools with supports and services provided in general education classrooms (e.g. Rogers, 1993; Thousand & Villa, 1990).

Legal Issues: Least Restrictive Environment

The least restrictive environment (LRE) has been interpreted in various ways by different professionals. For example, Osborne and Dimattia (1994) defined LRE as the legal principle that students with disabilities should be educated in general education as much as possible. LRE was more broadly defined by Taylor (1988, p. 45), "The principle of LRE for residential, educational, vocational, and other services may be defined as follows: Services for people with developmental disabilities should be designed according to a range of program options varying in terms of restrictiveness, normalization, independence, and integration, with a presumption in favor of environments that are least restrictive and most normalized, independent and integrated."

Early cases tested the concept of placement in the least restrictive environment. In *Pennsylvania Association for Retarded Children (PARC) v. Commonwealth of Pennsylvania* (1971, 1972), children ages 6–21 with mental retardation were guaranteed a free public education program. Further, it was recognized that, "if appropriate," placement in the regular class is preferable to placement in a separate special class. Additionally, in *Mills v. Board of Education of the District of Columbia* (1972), the same rights were extended to children with all types of disabilities.

With the passage of The Education for all Handicapped Children Act of 1975 (PL 94-142), legislation provided for appropriate education for all children with disabilities in the least restrictive environment. Subsequent legislation [i.e. the Individuals with Disabilities Education Act (IDEA, 1990) (PL 101-476) and IDEA Amendments (1997) (PL 105-17)] continued to require placement in the LRE. In fact, IDEA (1997) has a specific focus on ensuring access to general education.

Legal Issues: Court Cases

Throughout the years, the courts have clarified the concept of LRE. For an in-depth analysis of the LRE principle, refer to Taylor (1988). In this section, three court decisions (since the late 1980s) are reviewed that have helped clarify legislation related to least restrictive environment.

The issue of mainstreaming children with mental retardation into general education with support services was examined in *Daniel R. R. v. Board of Education* (1989). This case helped to clarify when placement in general education is appropriate and when removal to special education settings is acceptable. The decision was that a separate class was appropriate for this child. The court stated that the school district must provide supplementary aids and modify general education to meet students' needs. The court also determined that the general education teacher is not required to devote all of his/her time to one child. The court also identified both social and academic benefits as considerations in determining the appropriateness of a placement. As a result of the Daniel case, a two part test was established: (a) can education in general education with supplemental aids and services be achieved; and (b) if the student is placed in a more restrictive setting, is the student integrated to the maximum extent appropriate? (Yell, 1998).

In *Oberti v. Board of Education* (1993), the emphasis was again on the use of supplementary aids and services to support a child with disabilities. The court acknowledged that many techniques used in separate classes could be used in general education classrooms and that general education teachers can be trained to use these techniques. Also, the court considered "reciprocal benefits" of inclusion for peers without disabilities in the classroom.

Finally, in *Sacramento City Unified School District v. Rachel H.* (1994), it was determined that the IEP could be delivered in general education with curriculum modifications and supplementary services. The court also acknowledged that Rachel gained nonacademic benefits from the general education placement. As a result of this case, the courts have been using a four factor test to determine if an inclusive placement is appropriate. The courts consider: (a) can the child receive academic benefits if the necessary supports are provided; (b) can the child receive nonacademic benefits; (c) the effect of the student with disabilities on the teacher and students without disabilities; and (d) costs (Yell, 1998). Overall, courts have supported the rights of students with disabilities to be educated in the LRE, sometimes interpreted as a more segregated special education classroom, sometimes a general education classroom.

Inclusion as a Right
Advocates of inclusion use a variety of rationales to support their beliefs. In this section, some of these views will be presented. It is important to note that many advocates of inclusion are quite passionate and some of their views are based on opinion, not necessarily empirical data.

One of the major views of inclusion advocates is that inclusion is a "right" and a comparison is often made between inclusion and civil rights. Advocates believe that all students have the right to attend school with their peers in their local neighborhood (i.e. general education classrooms) (Gartner & Lipsky, 1987; Stainback & Stainback, 1984). In fact, some proponents describe administrators as "blocking the classroom door" to keep students with disabilities outside (Villa & Thousand, 2000). One strong advocacy group for inclusion is The Association for Persons with Severe Handicaps (TASH). TASH (1993) describes inclusion as "a new way of thinking that embraces a sociology of acceptance of all children into the school community as active, fully participating members." Additional examples of this viewpoint of inclusion as a "right" according to the literature follow. "Inclusion is the opposite of segregation and isolation" (Falvey et al., 1995a, p. 8). Forest and Pearpoint (1991) differentiate between two roads, "the road to exclusion," and "the road to inclusion" (p. 2). These authors describe the road to inclusion as one of diversity and a celebration of differences. Furthermore, "the criterion for inclusion is breathing, not IQ, income, color, race, sex, or language" (Forest & Pearpoint, p. 3).

Dissatisfaction with Pull-out Programs

Another rationale used by inclusion proponents is the dissatisfaction with the efficacy of "pull-out" programs (Hunt et al., 1986; Lilly, 1970). Lipsky and Gartner (1989) claim that the current system of special education does not work and needs to be changed. It should be noted that many of these claims are refuted by other researchers.

Labeling Practices

Another rationale for inclusion is based on criticisms of identification and labeling practices for students with disabilities. There are similar characteristics across disability categories that may lead to inaccurate identification. A student's label could change as a result of moving across state boundaries. The label a student receives may also be the result of an administrative decision based on services and programs available in that district. Similarly, how a child is labeled often depends on the professional background of the person proposing the label (Hobbs, 1975). Further, many students are mislabeled due to language or cultural differences. Ysseldyke et al. (2000) stated that at one time or another, 80% of all American children could be identified as learning disabled based on varying criteria used across the United States.

Parent Attitudes

Another rationale used by inclusion proponents is the views of parents. Many parents want their children with disabilities to have opportunities to interact with peers without disabilities (O'Neil, 1995). Additionally, parents report that inclusion benefits their children with severe disabilities (Giangreco et al., 1993b). Overall, in a recent research review of parent perceptions of inclusion for their children with disabilities, Garrick Duhaney and Salend (2000), report that perceptions are generally positive. A majority of parents (based on the reviewed research) believe that inclusion promotes social acceptance and helps their child with disabilities improve both socially and academically (Garrick Duhaney & Salend, 2000). Furthermore, the researchers report that parents believe their children with disabilities in inclusive classrooms have better role models, are happier, and are better prepared for the real world.

Teacher Attitudes

Finally, there are also reports of teachers' positive attitudes toward inclusion in the literature. For example, in Gibb et al. (1999) study, junior high school teachers were positive regarding students with behavioral disorders receiving their education in general education classrooms. It should be noted that in this study, general education teachers had support from special educators and special assistance from "trackers." Additionally, Villa et al. (1996) reported that a majority of 680 general and special educators were positive in their responses regarding their beliefs on inclusion. These teachers believed that general and special educators can work together as partners. Also, in a qualitative study of inclusion of students with severe disabilities, teachers who were initially negative, after gaining experience with inclusion, "transformed" their attitudes and became more positive (Giangreco et al., 1993a). Finally, in a research synthesis of mainstreaming/inclusion literature from 1958 to 1995, Scruggs and Mastropieri (1996) reported that approximately two thirds of general education teachers in 28 studies support the concept of inclusion.

RATIONALE AGAINST INCLUSION

Within this section are various perspectives of those who are against inclusion. Rationales include opposition to full inclusion, the focus of general education, and attitudes of teachers, students, and parents.

Full Inclusion

The term full inclusion is used by some authors to mean, all students, regardless of disabilities, attend their neighborhood schools with supports and services provided in general education classrooms (e.g. Rogers, 1993). However, not all inclusion proponents support "full inclusion." Skrtic (1991) describes three categories of inclusion proponents: (a) fully including students with mild disabilities while maintaining separate programs for students with moderate and severe disabilities; (b) fully including students with mild and moderate disabilities while providing separate programs for only those students with the most severe disabilities; and (c) fully including students with all disabilities.

Various professional organizations refute the philosophy of full inclusion. The Learning Disabilities Association (LDA), the Council for Learning Disabilities (CLD), and The National Joint Committee for Learning Disabilities (NJCLD) (1993) do not support policies that mandate the same placement for all students with learning disabilities. Similarly, the Council for Children with Behavioral Disorders (CCBD, 1994) is concerned with the loss of placement options for students with behavioral disorders who may need specialized instruction. Further, other professional organizations seem supportive of the overall philosophy of inclusion but express a concern for maintaining a full continuum of placements (CEC, 1993; National Association of State Boards of Education, 1992).

Perhaps Fuchs and Fuchs (1994) developed the best interpretation in their summary of the various inclusion definitions present in the literature, ". . . inclusion means different things to people who wish different things from it. For the group that wants the least . . . maintain the status quo. To those who want more, it means . . . a fundamental reorganization of the teaching and learning process . . . But to yet a third group, those who currently lead the inclusive schools movement, . . . no meaningful transformation can occur unless and until special education and its continuum of placements are eliminated altogether" (p. 299).

General Education Classroom Instruction

Another rationale used against inclusion is the lack of readiness in general education to educate students with disabilities. It has been noted within the literature that the current focus in general education is on outcomes and academic achievement and that inclusion advocates for students with severe disabilities mainly focus on social behaviors (Macmillan et al., 1996). This difference in educational focus between the two groups appears to be grounds for controversy.

Attitudes Regarding Inclusion

A third rationale against inclusive classrooms is teacher, student, and parent attitudes toward inclusion. For example, Vaughn et al. (1994) conducted focus group interviews with teachers. They found that the majority of teachers interviewed held strong negative feelings regarding inclusion. Further, Monahan et al. (1996) conducted a survey of 342 teachers in rural South Carolina and reported that over 60% of those teachers stated that inclusion would not succeed. In this study, there was a general feeling of resistance from general education teachers due to a reported lack of skills and a preference for sending students with disabilities to separate special education classrooms. Overall, many general education teachers prefer "pull-out" programs for special education (e.g. Coates, 1989; Semmel et al., 1991).

Earlier researchers examining teachers' attitudes also found that teachers displayed negative attitudes toward students with disabilities because the teachers believed students with disabilities would slow down the progress of general education students (Alexander & Strain, 1978; Graham et al., 1980). Also, in a review of earlier research, Hannah (1988) concluded that general education teachers tend to have more positive feelings towards certain types of disabilities. Students who were emotionally disturbed or mentally retarded were perceived more negatively than other students. Students who were gifted were perceived more positively. Guralnik (1980) found that students with mild disabilities were reacted to more positively than those who had more severe disabilities. Finally, some parents are opposed to inclusion. Carr (1993), a mother of a student with learning disabilities, reports that her son's needs were not met in general education classrooms.

OUTCOMES OF INCLUSION

It is important to note that the majority of studies on inclusive practices are descriptive studies or qualitative studies. Currently, there is little "true experimental" research. Thus, this section is a review of the current state of the literature.

EVIDENCE FOR INCLUSION

Social Benefits of Inclusion

One benefit of inclusion is the increased opportunity in inclusive classrooms for students to develop or improve social skills. Students with and without disabilities learn to work with one another in classrooms; advocates claim this prepares them to work together in the real world. Most studies that have been conducted on the benefits of inclusion focus on social outcomes (rather than academic) for students with disabilities, particularly those with severe disabilities. In a review of earlier research, Sailor and Halvorsen (1990) reviewed 261 studies comparing integrated and segregated placements. They concluded that students in integrated settings displayed lower levels of inappropriate behaviors and improved communication skills. It has also been established that students with disabilities interact more frequently with peers without disabilities in inclusive settings than in self-contained settings. This occurs for students at all grade levels, preschool (Hanline, 1993), elementary (Fryxell & Kennedy, 1995), and secondary (Kennedy et al., 1997).

Cole and Meyer (1991) conducted comparisons of social behaviors of students with disabilities in integrated vs. segregated settings over a two year span. Students with disabilities who were in integrated classrooms made progress on a measure of social competence including communication, initiation, self-regulation, choice, and terminating contacts. Students who were placed in segregated settings showed decreases in their social competence skills.

Various researchers study social skills of students with severe disabilities in inclusive classrooms. For example, Hunt et al. (1994a) reported that students' with severe disabilities social interactions with both peers and adults were improved in inclusion classrooms. In another study, Fryxell and Kennedy (1995) studied 18 elementary students with severe disabilities. The students had higher levels of social contact and a larger friendship network in inclusive classrooms. Hanline (1993) studied an inclusive preschool program that focused on social interaction and play. Hanline reported that students with profound disabilities engaged in interactions with peers for a majority of the times of observation. Finally, Kennedy et al. (1997) conducted a study of social skills in a middle school. In this study, eight students with severe disabilities who were included were compared to eight students who were in self-contained classrooms. The social benefits of the inclusive placement were that the students with disabilities interacted more frequently with peers without disabilities. However, it should be noted that the majority of the interactions were less than 10 seconds and were described as "social amenities."

Gibb et al. (1999) studied inclusion of 14 students with EBD in a junior high school. Qualitative interviews were conducted and students with EBD reported that they perceived that their social and academic skills had improved. Similarly, general education students stated that the inclusion program was worthwhile. Further, the general education teachers perceived that the inclusion program had a positive impact on social skills of students with EBD; the special education teachers reported that the behaviors of students with EBD were more appropriate in general education classrooms than in special education classrooms. Finally, in studies of inclusion in middle and high schools, researchers reported that students without disabilities had positive attitudes toward students with severe disabilities (Peck et al., 1990; York et al., 1992).

Students without disabilities also report on the social benefits of inclusion. High school students reported on inclusion benefits during interviews. These students reported that they had improved self concepts and less fear of differences of students with severe disabilities (Peck et al., 1990). Similarly, students in middle and high schools indicated that inclusion had a positive effect on them, however, these students felt that they should initiate friendships but indicated that they might not know how to do this (Hendrickson et al., 1996). Finally, Helmstetter et al. (1994) distributed surveys to 166 high school students in 45 different high schools in Washington. The students reported positive attitudes toward students with severe disabilities. These researchers reported that the amount of contact the two groups of students had with each other was positively associated with outcomes. Thus, the increased opportunity for students with disabilities to interact with students without disabilities in inclusive classrooms is a benefit of inclusion.

Academic Instruction

Another rationale contained within the pro-inclusion literature is that instruction in inclusive classrooms will meet all students' needs (i.e. not only students with disabilities) (Sailor, 1991; Villa et al., 1992). There is support for academic achievement for specific instructional techniques used in inclusion classrooms that work for students with and without disabilities. For example cooperative learning (Johnson & Johnson, 1999; Slavin, 1995), and peer tutoring (Arreaga-Mayer, 1998; McDonnell & Fister, 2001) are effective techniques that can be used in inclusive classrooms. Hunt et al. (1994b) conducted a study in which three elementary students with multiple severe disabilities participated in cooperative learning groups in general education classrooms. The students with disabilities improved their basic communication and motor skills. Additionally, in this study it was reported that general education students' academic skills increased.

Researchers also examine IEPs in relation to inclusion programs. One example of a study with an examination of IEPs was conducted by Hunt, Farron-Davis, Beckstead, Curtis and Goetz (1994a). These researchers found that IEPs of students with severe disabilities who were included contained more objectives for basic skills (i.e. communication, academic) than those in segregated classrooms.

Additionally, Hunt et al. reported that students with disabilities had higher levels of engaged time and the IEPs had more relevance to the general curriculum than IEPs of students in special education settings.

Further, researchers indicate no negative effects on peers without disabilities when students are included in general education classrooms. Again, most research to date has focused on the inclusion of students with severe disabilities. Many researchers report that there are no significant negative academic or behavioral effects on peers when students with severe disabilities are included in general education (e.g. Hollowood et al., 1994/1995; Sharpe et al., 1994). Some researchers focus on instructional opportunities for students without disabilities in inclusive classrooms. These researchers report that there is no negative impact on instructional opportunities in classrooms when students with severe disabilities are included (Hollowood et al., 1994/1995; McDonnell et al., 1997).

EVIDENCE AGAINST INCLUSION

General Education Classroom Instruction

The instruction in general education classrooms does not always seem conducive for students with disabilities. The general education curriculum often is not individualized for students with disabilities (Schumm & Vaughn, 1991). Teachers rely on large group instruction (Baker & Zigmond, 1990). Teachers tend to plan for a "whole class" rather than individual students (Vaughn & Schumm, 1994). Thus, instruction in general education is often not related to students' IEP goals (Lynch & Beare, 1990). Similarly, Scruggs and Mastropieri (1996) conducted a research synthesis and found that overall most teachers report that they do not have enough time to implement inclusion properly.

Additionally, general education teachers report that they do not have the skills required to teach in inclusive classrooms. For example, Schumm and Vaughn (1995) conducted a summary of studies over a five year span and concluded that overall teachers did not feel prepared to make adaptations for students with disabilities in inclusive classrooms. Additionally, teachers did not feel ready to teach a broad range of students (i.e. academic and cultural). Other researchers have reported similar claims by general education teachers reflecting a lack of expertise to teach students with disabilities in general education classrooms (Kearney & Durand, 1992; Merrow, 1996). Some teachers even resist inclusion because of the extra work necessary to individualize instruction (Gersten et al., 1988; Munson, 1986). Researchers also report that teachers perceive that their preservice preparation is not adequate to teach in inclusive classrooms. General education teachers often leave college unprepared to teach students with a wide range of abilities (Rosjewski & Pollard, 1990; Williams, 1990).

Lack of Specialized Instruction

A second rationale against inclusion is related to the first rationale, a loss of specialized instruction for students with disabilities. First, it should be noted that the efficacy studies cited by inclusion advocates in favor of general education classrooms (e.g. Gartner & Lipsky, 1987) were conducted between 1950 and 1980. Comparing the instruction in these studies to instruction in today's classrooms may be misleading. Also, the often cited studies in support of inclusion were flawed (Hallahan & Kauffman, 1994). For example, the efficacy studies do not include random assignment of students to classrooms (Hallahan & Kauffman). In studies with actual random assignment of students (e.g. Goldstein et al., 1965), the results favor special education placements (Hallahan & Kauffman). Additionally, Hallahan and Kauffman noted that the flaws in the efficacy studies were noted by other researchers (e.g. Macmillan & Becker, 1977). Finally, placing all students with disabilities (i.e. full inclusion) in general education classrooms denies students' rights to an individualized education (Lieberman, 1992).

Outcomes for Students with Disabilities

A final rationale against inclusion is the lack of data on positive student academic and/or social outcomes. Proponents of inclusion have relied strongly on anecdotal reports and small numbers of participants (Macmillan et al., 1996). Scruggs and Mastropieri (1996) in a synthesis of 28 studies found that only a minority of general education teachers believes that general education is the best environment for students with disabilities or that full time inclusion will produce social or academic benefits comparable to special education. Further, social acceptance may not occur for some students with disabilities (Baker & Zigmond, 1990; Gersten et al., 1988). Students with learning disabilities are often rated as unpopular in general education classrooms (Gresham, 1982; Schumaker & Hazel, 1984). Further, Gresham (1982) conducted a review of mainstreaming literature and found that mainstreamed students with disabilities are less accepted by peers, and that there is little evidence that integration had positive modeling effects. Placement in a mainstreamed class does not ensure that favorable attitudes will develop toward students with disabilities. In fact, it was reported by Gottlieb (1981) that the more students became familiar with students with disabilities, the less they liked them.

Further, some researchers have reported that inclusion is not superior to special education settings. For example, Zigmond and Baker (1990) examined the impact of mainstreaming on the achievement of 13 elementary students with learning disabilities. The students were placed in general education classrooms on a full-time basis. After two years, student progress was examined. The students with learning disabilities made no significant progress in reading or math and also earned lower grades.

In more recent research, Klinger et al. (1998) studied the academic progress of students with and without LD in general education classrooms in grades 3–6. Twenty-five students with LD were studied. The inclusive classrooms had additional in-class support of special education teachers, and inservice training on four instructional practices for literacy instruction. Results of the study indicated that some students with LD achieved gains in reading, however other students with LD achieved little or no gains. Additionally, it was reported that some students who were low-average did not improve their skills. The students who made no progress in the inclusion classrooms were nonreaders or low readers. Further, Manset and Semmel (1997) reviewed eight different "model" inclusive programs in elementary schools for students with mild disabilities (most had LD). Only in two out of eight model programs did students with disabilities make any significant gains in reading. Finally, Carlberg and Kavale (1980) conducted a meta-analysis of 50 experimental studies. Results indicated that special class placements had better outcomes (even though a relatively small difference) than general education placements for students with specific disabilities (i.e. learning disabilities, behavioral disorders, and emotional disorders). It should be noted that this study is often cited in the pro-inclusion literature as support for general education. However, it is often misinterpreted throughout the pro-inclusion literature (e.g. Gartner & Lipsky, 1987).

Further, Zigmond et al. (1995) reported on findings from three research projects conducted at the University of Pittsburgh, the University of Washington, and Vanderbilt University on programs serving students with LD in general education. These authors concluded that general education settings do not produce acceptable achievement outcomes for students with LD. Further support for special education was reported by Fuchs et al. (1994). These authors found that instructional gains for LD were greater in separate special education classrooms than in general education.

Similarly, not all researchers report positive effects of socialization in inclusive classrooms. For example, Schnorr (1997) studied student relationships in middle and high schools. He found that students' relationships depend on an affiliation with a subgroup within the class at this age level. In this study, only some students with disabilities connected with subgroups and then were considered as class members; others were not as accepted.

Other researchers examined social acceptance in combination with classroom composition. Cook et al. (1999) studied the effects of the severity of students' disabilities and classroom composition on peers' acceptance of included students. They examined 285 students (44 had a disability) in 14 elementary classrooms. Their results indicated that included students with severe disabilities in nonheterogeneous classrooms were better accepted than students in classrooms with greater heterogeneity. Also, students with mild disabilities were better accepted in heterogeneous classrooms. Overall, Cook, Semmel, and Gerber reported that students with disabilities were less socially desired in academic work situations but were better accepted in play situations. Similarly, Ferguson (1999) reported that a majority (i.e. 67% of 196) of high school general education students in an inclusive school did not want to be in the same class as a student with a disability.

SUMMARY OF INCLUSION RESEARCH

Overall, there are few studies on the efficacy of inclusion. Those that do exist are generally conducted in elementary classrooms and focus on students with severe disabilities and the social benefits that exist. Additionally, most studies have small sample sizes, are qualitative studies or descriptive research. Much more research needs to be conducted at the secondary level and with students of all specific disability categories. In order to make comparisons between inclusion and separate special education, each must be clearly defined. Research should be in place before inclusion is adopted for students with all disabilities at various grade levels.

There is limited research thus far on academic benefits of inclusion for students with disabilities. Most inclusion researchers are focusing their efforts on the effects of inclusion on students with severe disabilities. Those who do study students with mild disabilities have reported varying results with some researchers finding positive effects in inclusive classrooms and others finding that students perform better academically in special education classrooms. Many schools in the U.S. are implementing inclusion for all students with disabilities but the current research base is not conclusive.

Overall, regarding the research on inclusion, the most consistent outcome is academic gains for students without disabilities (Manset & Semmel, 1997). In conclusion, the literature contains various rationales both for and against inclusion. Perhaps Hocutt (1996) summarized this literature in an insightful way. There is no concrete evidence to demonstrate that placement is the critical factor in a student's academic or social success (Hocutt). Perhaps the most important factor is the specific instruction that is occurring and the available resources to support effective instruction.

RESOURCES FOR INCLUSION

If a school district or classroom is implementing inclusion, there are a variety of supplementary resources to enhance the program. In fact, within the literature, resources are often mentioned as a critical component of inclusion. For example, in Knoster et al. (2000) model of change for inclusive schools, resources are a crucial component. In fact, Fullan and Miles (1992) described school change (i.e. inclusion) as "resource hungry" (p. 750). Further, in a research synthesis on mainstreaming/inclusion, Scruggs and Mastropieri (1996) reported that overall, elementary teachers did not receive sufficient resources for their inclusive classrooms. These authors also found that the success of inclusion programs may depend on the extent to which resources are available to teachers. Similarly, in focus group interviews with elementary and secondary teachers, Vaughn, Schumm et al. (1994) found that most teachers stated that decision makers (i.e. administrators, policy makers, and university personnel) were unaware of daily classroom realities. Teachers in this study reported inadequate resources and lack of teacher preparation as influences on the success of inclusion. Research by Schumaker and Deshler (1988) indicates that the differences between the organization and curricula in elementary and secondary classrooms can result in additional barriers for inclusion. Teaching students with disabilities in inclusive secondary settings is impeded by: (a) a large gap between students' skill levels and classroom demands; (b) intensive instruction required to improve student skill deficits; and (c) the context of secondary settings (Schumaker & Deshler).

Various researchers list resources as important sources of support for teachers in inclusive classrooms. For example, Scruggs and Mastropieri (1994) conducted a qualitative study of three inclusive science classrooms. They identified seven variables that were common to all three settings without regard for grade level or disability: (a) administrative support; (b) support from special education personnel; (c) a positive classroom atmosphere; (d) appropriate curriculum; (e) effective general teaching skills; (f) peer assistance; and (g) disability-specific teaching skills. Similarly, a national forum on inclusive schools (CEC, 1994) examined twelve schools throughout the United States and Canada and subsequently formed a list of twelve important features of inclusive schools: (a) a sense of community; (b) leadership; (c) high standards; (d) collaboration and cooperation; (e) changing roles and responsibilities; (f) an array of services (e.g. mental health, social services); (g) partnerships with parents; (h) flexible learning environments; (i) strategies based on research (e.g. cooperative learning, peer tutoring); (j) accountability; (k) access (e.g. building modifications); and (l) professional development.

The research conducted by this author was based on a subset of the aforementioned components of inclusive schools, the resources provided by local school districts to general education classroom teachers. A study was conducted to determine if the resources reported in the literature as necessary for elementary inclusion (i.e. organizational climate, personnel, time, inservice training, supplementary materials) are the same resources perceived to be needed by teachers and administrators in rural secondary schools. Additionally, this researcher examined the perceptions of general education teachers, special education teachers, and administrators to determine if there were differences among the three groups' perceptions of resources necessary for inclusion. A summary of the methods used and specific results for this study can be reviewed in Harriott (2005, in preparation). Each of these five resource areas considered necessary for inclusion classrooms is outlined in the following section.

ORGANIZATIONAL CLIMATE

The general resource areas included within the category of organizational climate are various forms of administrative support, use of collaboration and teams, consideration of class size, and consideration of the appropriateness of resources for the severity of students' disabilities. The following paragraphs include a description of each type of resource.

Administrative Support

It is crucial for programs such as inclusion to have the support and interest of the administration in order to sustain employee morale and to implement change. Various researchers (e.g. Scruggs & Mastropieri, 1994; Vaughn & Schumm, 1995) stress the importance of the building principal's role in assisting a school's efforts in the implementation of inclusive programs. The principal can model and emphasize the importance of an inclusive philosophy and provide emotional, personnel, and materials resources for teachers who are attempting to implement inclusion. Praisner (2003) conducted a survey of 408 elementary principals. She found that principals with positive attitudes and experiences with special education students were more likely to place students in less restrictive settings (and thus more inclusive classrooms). Therefore, the building principal is a key element in the adoption and development of any program (Siu-Runyan, 1990).

Collaboration

Collaboration and teaming among staff are viewed as another main resource for successful inclusion (Stainback & Stainback, 1992; Williams et al., 1990). Collaboration consists of all team members contributing their individual expertise to brainstorm and implement creative solutions for problems encountered in inclusive settings. Cross and Villa (1992) conducted research with teachers who had been working in inclusion classrooms for five years. Educators in this study attributed their ability to educate all students within one classroom to ongoing teaming and collaboration. Further, Giangreco et al. (1993a) conducted interviews and found that teachers who were working in teams reported feeling productive and supported. The teams, according to the teachers, provided sources of technical, resource, evaluation, and moral support.

Class Size

The general educator's class size must be considered before placing students with disabilities in the general education classroom. Class size should be reduced to fewer than 20 students in inclusive classrooms (Scruggs & Mastropieri, 1996). East (1992) surveyed 202 Iowa elementary teachers educating students with severe disabilities. These teachers reported that a class size of 19 or less was necessary for inclusion. Pearman et al. (1997) surveyed various personnel (e.g. teachers, administration, paraprofessionals, central office staff) K-12 within one school district. Ninety-eight percent of these participants recognized the importance of reduced class size for inclusion.

Appropriateness of Resources for Severity of Disability

The number of students included as well as the severity of their disabilities must be considered in providing appropriate resources to teachers. Teachers are more willing to include students with mild disabilities than those with more severe disabilities (Scruggs & Mastropieri, 1996). Further, students with disabilities should be placed in general education classrooms in "natural proportions." Brown et al. (1989) describes natural proportions for students with severe disabilities. Students with disabilities will achieve more when the classroom population is in the range of natural proportions (Brown et al.). Thus, students with disabilities should be placed somewhat evenly throughout the general education classrooms in a school building. For example, if there are three students with severe disabilities, they might be placed in three different general education classrooms. Or if there are 20 students with learning disabilities in one school, perhaps they could be placed evenly among five different classrooms.

PERSONNEL RESOURCES

In a national research study, one of the key elements of successful inclusion reported by school districts was personnel (NCERI, 1995). Further, teachers report a need for additional assistance for inclusive programs. This support could be the help of a paraprofessional or support from special education teachers (Scruggs & Mastropieri, 1996). In a synthesis of twelve inclusion studies, teachers reported that personnel such as special education teachers and reading specialists were valuable in helping with planning and making adaptations (Schumm & Vaughn, 1995).

Several researchers examining inclusion in elementary schools report on the importance of personnel resources. East's (1992) elementary teachers reported that the services of a paraprofessional for the entire school day are necessary to include students with severe disabilities. Similarly, Gessler Werts et al.'s (1996) elementary participants perceived that personnel assistance is important in inclusive classrooms. Further, Giangreco et al. (1993a) conducted interviews with 19 general education teachers in grades K-9. These teachers reported that support from various personnel (i.e. paraprofessionals, specialists, special education teachers) is important for inclusion of students with severe disabilities.

A variety of staffing models are utilized to support inclusion. The most frequently used model is co-teaching (NCERI, 1995). Cooperative teaching (a term used for co-teaching) has been described as a process that involves "a restructuring of teaching procedures in which two or more educators possessing distinct sets of skills work in a co-active and coordinated fashion to jointly teach academically and behaviorally heterogeneous groups of students in educationally integrated settings, that is, in general classrooms" (Bauwens & Hourcade, 1995, p. 46). More recently, co-teaching has been described as "two or more professionals delivering substantive instruction to a diverse, or blended, group of students in a single physical space" (Cook & Friend, 1998, p. 454).

Regardless of the definition of co-teaching used, a variety of models or roles for teachers are described in the literature. Cook and Friend (1995) describe one model of co-teaching that differentiates among five instructional variations: (a) one teacher and one assistant; (b) station teaching; (c) parallel teaching; (d) alternative teaching; and (e) team teaching. Cook and Friend describe the one teacher and one assistant model as one teacher assuming the major teaching role, and one teacher assisting and monitoring students who need extra help. Station teaching is described as students being divided into smaller groups and then rotating around the classroom. During station teaching, the two teachers (and possibly other personnel) teach at different locations independently. During parallel teaching, the two teachers teach the same information simultaneously to two smaller mixed-ability groups. The alternative teaching model incorporates both teachers delivering instruction, but the groups are more flexible. For example, a small group may be formed for more intensive instruction or additional practice while a larger group learns the same information in a more traditional fashion. The last model, team teaching, is described as both teachers assuming an equal partnership, sharing responsibility for the instruction of the whole class (Cook & Friend).

TIME

Williams et al. (1990) found that the majority of teachers surveyed stated that lack of time is the major barrier to best practices in inclusion. Similarly, teachers report a need for at least one hour daily in order to plan for students with disabilities (Scruggs & Mastropieri, 1996). Additionally, in CEC's (1996) and NCERI's (1995) best inclusive practice lists, common planning time is cited as one of the important elements. NEA (1994) describes various strategies to find time for collaboration: (a) "freed-up time" (release teachers from class); (b) "restructured time" (altering the traditional calendar); (c) "common time" (scheduling so teachers can meet); (d) "better-used time" (using available time for effective professional development); and (e) "purchased time" (hiring additional staff). Further, results of a survey of various professionals in one school district reported that the issue of time is a primary concern for teachers in grades K-12 in inclusive classrooms (Pearman et al., 1997). However, it was also noted that in this study, additional time was more important for elementary teachers than for secondary teachers.

INSERVICE TRAINING

Kearney and Durand (1992) conducted surveys of postsecondary institutions and found that over 50% of those institutions required only one or fewer courses in special education for preservice teachers. Similarly, Reiff et al. (1991) reviewed certification requirements for general education teachers and found that most states required only one course in special education for state certification in general education.

Many teachers in general classrooms have been trained at the preservice level to work with "typical" students and thus are unprepared to meet the challenges of teaching in an inclusive setting. Practitioners also report a lack of necessary skills to teach students with disabilities (e.g. Schumm & Vaughn, 1995; Scruggs & Mastropieri, 1996).

Therefore, teachers need intensive training at the preservice and inservice levels in order to teach in inclusive classrooms (Scruggs & Mastropieri, 1996). This training should be on-going and conducted at the local school site (CEC, 1996; Vaughn & Schumm, 1995). Training programs should be provided for special and general education teachers, parents, and paraprofessionals involved in inclusive programs (CEC, 1996; NCERI, 1995). Common inclusion training topics across the nation include curriculum adaptations, collaboration, strategies, disability awareness, behavior management, friendships, teaming, and organizational topics (Katsiyannis et al., 1995). Other topic areas such as instructional methods, communication skills, assessment, technology use, vocational and transition issues, and the benefits of inclusion to students should also be considered as inclusion training topics (Harriott, 2004, in press). Further, researchers indicate that proper training is one of educators' primary concerns for instruction in inclusive classrooms (e.g. Gessler Werts et al., 1996; Pearman et al., 1997). A high percentage of Wolery et al.'s (1995) 158 PA elementary teachers perceived a need for training. Additionally, Pankake and Palmer (1996) conducted a qualitative case study in three inclusive kindergarten classrooms. These participants recognized the importance of "useful" staff development (i.e. appropriate content delivered at the appropriate time). These participants stated that they wanted training to incorporate practical strategies for use in the classroom.

SUPPLEMENTARY MATERIALS

A final necessary resource for inclusive programs is adapting the curriculum and/or environment to meet the needs of students with disabilities. Teachers need appropriate curriculum materials and adaptive equipment to meet the needs of students with disabilities (Vaughn & Schumm, 1995). Adaptations can be defined as "any adjustments or modifications in the environment, instruction or materials used for learning that enhances the person's performance or allows at least partial participation in an activity" (Udvari-Solner, 1992, p. 3). These adaptations must be made to allow students to participate as much as possible in general education classroom activities.

Examples of "low-tech" adaptations for students with disabilities include calculators, pencil grips, visual cues or charts, mnemonic strategies, audiotaped books, and using alternative texts on lower reading levels. Examples of technological adaptations used for students with physical disabilities include keyboard adaptations such as key guards, alternative keyboards, and switches (Langone, 2000). Other students may need augmentative communication devices. Students with learning disabilities may need word processors with spelling and grammar checks, word processors with word prediction software such as Co-Write, or word processors with speech synthesis (Zhang, 2000).

There are numerous adaptations available for students with disabilities. Each student may need different adaptations in order to meet their unique needs. The adaptations listed above are only examples and are not meant to be an all-inclusive list.

SUMMARY AND IMPLICATIONS

Within this chapter, the reader has been introduced to an overview of the literature on inclusion of students with disabilities in general education classrooms. As this research base is ongoing, students are already being included across the United States. Even in the absence of a great deal of research on academic benefits of inclusion for students with disabilities, the "wave" is spreading. If inclusion is being implemented, resources must be provided for teachers in order to provide effective instruction to the diversity of learners in today's classrooms. After several years of research on this topic, the author has many more questions than answers. Following are implications and remaining questions based on this research.

- More research on the effects of inclusion for all disabilities at all age levels is needed. What are the social and academic benefits? Much more research on the implementation of inclusion is needed at the secondary education level.
- If the five resource areas identified as necessary are provided, does this lead to better outcomes for students? Or does this only lead to more satisfied teachers? Which resources lead to improved student outcomes?
- Much more research on co-teaching is needed. What are the effects of co-teaching on student performance? Is using co-teaching in inclusive classrooms beneficial for students with disabilities? Is co-teaching effective at all grade levels? Are there differences in the implementation of co-teaching at the elementary, middle, and secondary levels? Does co-teaching work for all types and severities of disabilities? Which specific models of co-teaching are used for various grade levels, subject areas, and/or types of students? Will one model work better for a particular age/disability? Does training (i.e. preservice and inservice) affect the implementation of co-teaching?

- Is inclusion a current bandwagon? Will the pendulum swing back the other way with the increased demands for accountability (in the form of standardized tests)?
- Are general education teachers prepared and trained to meet the needs of all students in today's increasingly diverse classrooms?
- Is separate special education intensive instruction more beneficial than inclusive instruction for some individuals with disabilities?

REFERENCES

Alexander, C., & Strain, P. S. (1978). A review of educator's attitudes toward handicapped children and the concept of mainstreaming. *Psychology in the Schools, 15*, 390–396.

Arreaga-Mayer, C. (1998). Increasing active student responding and improving academic performance through classwide peer tutoring. *Intervention in School and Clinic, 34*(2), 89–94.

The Association for Persons with Severe Handicaps (TASH) (1993, February). *Resolution on inclusive education* (Position paper). Baltimore: Author.

Baker, J. M., & Zigmond, N. (1990). Are regular education classes equipped to accommodate students with learning disabilities? *Exceptional Children, 56*, 515–526.

Bauwens, J., & Hourcade, J. J. (1995). *Cooperative teaching: Rebuilding the schoolhouse for all students.* Austin, TX: Pro Ed.

Biklen, D. (Ed.) (1985). *The complete school: Integrating special and general education.* New York: Teachers College Press.

Brown v. Board of Education, 347 U.S. 483; 74 S. Ct. 686 (1954).

Brown, L., Long, E., Udvari-Solner, A., VanDeventer, P., Ahlgren, C., Johnson, F., Gruenewald, L., & Jorgenson, J. (1989). The home school: Why students with severe intellectual disabilities must attend the schools of their brothers, sisters, friends, and neighbors. *Journal of the Association for Persons with Severe Handicaps, 14*(1), 1–7.

Calfapietra, E. A. (1996). Accommodating diversity in the regular classroom: Perceptions of secondary teachers in the Catholic high schools of New York City (Doctoral dissertation, Columbia University, 1997). *Dissertation Abstracts International, 57*(7), 2955A.

Carlberg, C., & Kavale, K. (1980). The efficacy of special vs. regular class placement for exceptional children: A meta-analysis. *Journal of Special Education, 14*, 295–309.

Carr, M. N. (1993). A mother's thoughts on inclusion. *Journal of Learning Disabilities, 26*(9), 590–592.

Catlett, S. M., & Osher, T. W. (1994). *What is inclusion anyway? An analysis of organizational policy statements.* (ERIC Document Reproduction Service No. ED 369 234.)

Coates, R. D. (1989). The Regular Education Initiative and opinions of regular classroom teachers. *Journal of Learning Disabilities, 22*, 532–536.

Cole, D. A., & Meyer, L. H. (1991). Social integration and severe disabilities: A longitudinal analysis of child outcomes. *Journal of Special Education, 25*, 340–351.

Cook, L., & Friend, M. (1995). Co-teaching: Guidelines for effective practices. *Focus on Exceptional Children, 28*(3), 1–16.

Cook, L., & Friend, M. (1998). Co-teaching: Guidelines for creating effective practices. In: E. L. Meyen, G. A. Vergason & R. J. Whelan (Eds), *Educating Students with Mild Disabilities: Strategies and Methods* (2nd ed., pp. 453–479). Denver: Love.

Cook, B. G., Semmel, M. I., & Gerber, M. M. (1999). Peer acceptance of included students with disabilities as a function of severity of disability and classroom composition. *Journal of Special Education, 33*(1), 50–61.

Council for Children with Behavioral Disorders (1994). Executive committee approves position statement on inclusion within a continuum of service delivery options. *Council for Children with Behavioral Disorders Newsletter, 8*(1), 1.

Council for Exceptional Children (1993). *CEC Policy on Inclusive Schools and Community Settings.* Reston, VA: Author.

Council for Exceptional Children (1994). *Creating schools for all our students: What 12 schools have to say.* Reston, VA: The Working Forum on Inclusive Schools. (ERIC Document Reproduction Service No. ED 377 633.)

Council for Exceptional Children (1996). Inclusion – Where are we today. *CEC Today, 3*(3), 1, 5, 15.

Council for Learning Disabilities (1993). Concerns about full inclusion of students with learning disabilities in regular education classrooms. *Journal of Learning Disabilities, 26*(9), 595.

Cross, G., & Villa, R. (1992). The Winooski school system: An evolutionary perspective of a school restructuring for diversity. In: R. Villa, J. Thousand, W. Stainback & S. Stainback (Eds), *Restructuring for Caring and Effective Education: An Administrative Guide to Creating Heterogeneous Schools* (pp. 219–237). Baltimore, MD: Brookes.

Daniel R. R. v. State Board of Education, 874 F.2d 1036 (5th Cir. 1989).

East, K. A. (1992). An investigation of the types of support perceived necessary by Iowa elementary classroom teachers for the integration of students identified as severely disabled (Doctoral dissertation, University of Northern Iowa, 1992). *Dissertation Abstracts International, 53*, 1866.

Education for All Handicapped Children Act of 1975, PL 94-142. Title 20, U.S.C. 1401.

Falvey, M. A., Givner, C. C., & Kimm, C. (1995a). What is an inclusive school? (pp. 1–12). In: R. A. Villa & J. S. Thousand (Ed.). *Creating an Inclusive School.* Alexandria, VA: ASCD.

Falvey, M. A., Grenot-Scheyer, M., Coots, J. J., & Bishop, K. D. (1995b). Services for students with disabilities: Past and present. In: M. A. Falvey (Ed.), *Inclusive and Heterogeneous Schooling* (pp. 23–39). Baltimore: Brookes.

Ferguson, J. M. (1999). High school students' attitudes toward inclusion of handicapped students in the regular education classroom. *The Educational Forum, 63*(2), 173–179.

Forest, M., & Pearpoint, J. (1991). Two roads: Exclusion or inclusion? *Developmental Disabilities Bulletin, 19*(1), 1–11.

Fryxell, D., & Kennedy, C. H. (1995). Placement along the continuum of services and its impact on students' social relationships. *Journal of the Association for Persons with Severe Handicaps, 20*, 259–269.

Fuchs, D., Deshler, D., & Zigmond, N. (1994, March). How expendable is general education? How expandable is special education? Paper presented at the meeting of the Learning Disabilities Association of America, Washington, DC.

Fuchs, D., & Fuchs, L. S. (1994). Inclusive schools movement and the radicalization of special education reform. *Exceptional Children, 60*, 294–309.

Fullan, M., & Miles, M. (1992). Getting reform right: What works and what doesn't. *Phi Delta Kappa, 73*(10), 744–752.

Garrick Duhaney, L. M., & Salend, S. J. (2000). Parental perceptions of inclusive educational placements. *Remedial and Special Education, 21*(2), 121–128.

Gartner, A., & Lipsky, D. K. (1987). Beyond special education: Toward a quality education for all students. *Harvard Educational Review, 57*(4), 367–395.

Gersten, R., Walker, H., & Darch, C. (1988). Relationship between teachers' effectiveness and their tolerance for handicapped students. *Exceptional Children, 54*, 433–438.

Gessler Werts, M. G., Wolery, M., Synder, E. D., & Caldwell, N. K. (1996). Teachers' perceptions of the supports critical to the success of inclusion programs. *The Journal for the Association for Persons with Severe Handicaps, 21*(1), 9–21.

Giangreco, M. F., Dennis, R., Cloninger, C., Edelman, S., & Schattman, R. (1993a). "I've counted Jon:" Transformational experiences of teachers educating students with disabilities. *Exceptional Children, 59*(4), 359–372.

Giangreco, M., Edelman, S., Cloninger, C., & Dennis, R. (1993b). My child has a classmate with severe disabilities: What parents of nondisabled children think about full inclusion. *Developmental Disabilities Bulletin, 21*(1), 77–91.

Gibb, S. A., Allred, K., Ingram, C. F., Young, J. R., & Egan, W. M. (1999). Lessons learned from the inclusion of students with emotional and behavioral disorders in one junior high school. *Behavioral Disorders, 24*(2), 122–136.

Gliedman, J., & Roth, W. (1980). *The unexpected minority: Handicapped children in America.* New York: Harcourt Brace Jovanich.

Goldstein H., Moss J. W., & Jordan, L. J. (1965). *The efficacy of special class training on the development of mentally retarded children.* Urbana: Institute for Research on Exceptional Children, University of Illinois.

Gottlieb, J. (1981). Mainstreaming: Fulfilling the promise? *American Journal on Mental Deficiency.*

Graham, S., Hudson, F., Burdg, N. B., & Carpenter, D. (1980). Education personnel's perceptions of mainstreaming and resource room effectiveness. *Psychology in the Schools, 17*, 128–134.

Gresham, F. M. (1982). Misguided mainstreaming: The case for social skills training with handicapped children. *Exceptional Children, 48*, 422–433.

Guralnik, M. J. (1980). Social interactions among preschool children. *Exceptional Children, 46*, 248–253.

Hallahan, D. P., & Kauffman, J. M. (1994). Toward a culture of disability in the aftermath of Deno and Dunn. *The Journal of Special Education, 27*(4), 496–508.

Hanline, M. F. (1993). Inclusion of preschoolers with profound disabilities: An analysis of children's interactions. *Journal of the Association for Persons with Severe Handicaps, 18*(1), 28–35.

Hannah, M. E. (1988). Teacher attitudes toward children with disabilities: An ecological analysis. In: H. E. Yuker (Ed.), *Attitudes toward persons with disabilities.* New York: Springer.

Harriott Godshall, W. A. (2001). Administrators' and teachers' perceptions of necessary resources for secondary general education inclusion classrooms in rural Pennsylvania school districts (Doctoral dissertation, The Pennsylvania State University, 2001). *Dissertation Abstracts International, 62*, 1792.

Harriott, W. A. (2004, in press). Inclusion inservice: Content and training procedures across the United States. *Journal of Special Education Leadership.*

Harriott, W. A. (2005). *Special educators', general educators', and administrators' perceptions of necessary resources for secondary general education inclusion classrooms.* Manuscript in preparation.

Helmstetter, E., Peck, C. A., & Giangreco, M. F. (1994). Outcomes of interactions with peers with moderate or severe disabilities: A statewide survey of high school students. *Journal of the Association for Persons with Severe Handicaps, 19*(4), 263–276.

Hendrickson, J. M., Shokoohi-Hekta, M., Hamre-Nietupski, S., & Gable, R. A. (1996). Middle and high school students' perceptions on being friends with peers with severe disabilities. *Exceptional Children, 63*(1), 19–28.

Hobbs, N. (1975). *The futures of children: Categories, labels, and their consequences.* (Highlights, Summary, and Recommendations for the Final Report of the Project on Classification of Exceptional Children.)

Hocutt, A. M. (1996). Effectiveness of special education: Is placement the critical factor? *Future of Children, 6*(1), 77–102.

Hollowood, T. M., Salisbury, C. L., Rainforth, B., & Palombaro, M. M. (1994/1995). Use of instructional time in classrooms serving students with and without severe disabilities. *Exceptional Children, 61*(3), 242–253.

Hunt, P., Farron-Davis, F., Beckstead, S., Curtis, D., & Goetz, L. (1994a). Evaluating the effects of placement of students with severe disabilities in general education vs. special classes. *Journal of the Association for Persons with Severe Handicaps, 19*(3), 200–214.

Hunt, P., Goetz, L., & Anderson, J. (1986). The quality of IEP objectives associates with placement in integrated vs. segregated school sites. *Journal of the Association for Persons with Severe Handicaps, 11*(2), 125–130.

Hunt, P., Staub, D., Alwell, M., & Goetz, L. (1994b). Achievement by all students within the context of cooperative learning groups. *Journal of the Association for Persons with Severe Handicaps, 19*, 290–301.

Individuals with Disabilities Education Act of 1990 (IDEA), P.L. 101-476. Title 20 U.S.C. §1400.

Individuals with Disabilities Education Act Amendments of 1997 (IDEA), P.L. 105-17, Title 20 U.S.C. §1400.

Johnson, D. W., & Johnson, R. T. (1999). *Learning together and alone: Cooperative, competitive, and individualistic learning* (5th ed.). Needham Heights, MA: Allyn & Bacon.

Katsiyannis, A., Conderman, G., & Franks, D. J. (1995). State practices on inclusion: A national review. *Remedial and Special Education, 16*(5), 279–287.

Kauffman, J. M. (1994). Places of change: Special education's power and identification in an era of educational reform. *Journal of Learning Disabilities, 27*(10), 610–618.

Kearney, C. A., & Durand, V. M. (1992). How prepared are our teachers for mainstreamed classroom settings? A survey of postsecondary schools of education in New York state. *Exceptional Children, 59*(1), 6–11.

Kennedy, C. H., Shukla, S., & Fryxell, D. (1997). Comparing the effects of educational placement on the social relationships of intermediate school students with severe disabilities. *Exceptional Children, 64*(1), 31–47.

Klinger, J. K., Vaughn, S., Hughes, M. T., Schumm, J. S., & Elbaum, B. (1998). Outcomes for students with and without learning disabilities in inclusive classrooms. *Learning Disabilities Research & Practice, 13*(3), 153–161.

Knoster, T. P., Villa, R. A., & Thousand, J. S. (2000). A framework for thinking about systems change. In: R. A. Villa & J. S. Thousand (Eds), *Restructuring for Caring and Effective Education: Piecing the Puzzle Together* (pp. 93–128). Baltimore: Brookes.

Langone, J. (2000). Technology for individuals with severe and physical disabilities. In: J. Lindsey (Ed.). *Technology and Exceptional Individuals* (3rd ed., pp. 327–351). Austin, TX: Pro Ed.

Lieberman, L. M. (1992). Preserving special education. . .for those who need it. In: W. Stainback & S. Stainback (Eds), *Controversial Issues Confronting Special Education* (pp. 13–25). Needham Heights, MA: Allyn & Bacon.

Lilly, M. S. (1970). Special education: A teapot in a tempest. *Exceptional Children, 37*, 43–49.

Lilly, M. S. (1987). Lack of focus on special education in literature on educational reform. *Exceptional Children, 53*, 325–326.

Lipsky, D. K., & Gartner, A. (Eds) (1989). *Beyond separate education: Quality education for all.* Baltimore: Brookes.

Lynch, E. C., & Beare, P. C. (1990). The quality of IEP objectives and their relevance to instruction for students with mental retardation and behavioral disorders. *Remedial and Special Education, 11*(2), 48–55.

Macmillan, D. L., & Becker, L. D. (1977). Mainstreaming the mildly handicapped learner. In: R. D. Kneedler & S. G. Tarver (Eds), *Changing Perspectives in Special Education* (pp. 208–227). Columbus, OH: Merrill.

Macmillan, D. L., Gresham, F. M., & Forness, S. K. (1996). Full inclusion: An empirical perspective. *Behavioral Disorders, 21*(2), 145–159.

Manset, G., & Semmel, M. I. (1997). Are inclusive programs for students with mild disabilities effective? A comparative review of model programs. *Journal of Special Education, 31*(2), 155–180.

McDonnell, J., & Fister, S. (2001). Supporting the inclusion of students with moderate and severe disabilities in junior high school general education classes: The effects of classwide peer tutoring, multi-element curriculum, and accommodations. *Education and Treatment of Children, 24*(2), 141–160.

McDonnell, J., Thorson, N., McQuivey, C., & Kiefer-O'Donnell, R. (1997). Academic engaged time of students with low-incidence disabilities in general education classes. *Mental Retardation, 35*, 18–26.

Merrow, J. (1996, May 8). What's so special about special education? *Education Week, 15*(33), 48, 38.

Meyen, E. L. (1990). *Exceptional children in today's schools.* Denver: Love.

Mills v. Board of Education, 348 F. Supp. 866 (D. D. C. 1972).

Monahan, R. G., Marino, S. B., & Miller, R. (1996). Rural teachers' attitudes toward inclusion. In: D. Montgomery (Ed.), *Rural Goals 2000: Building Programs that Work.* Baltimore, MD: American Council on Rural Special Education (ACRES).

Munson, S. M. (1986). Regular education teachers' modifications for mainstreamed mildly handicapped students. *The Journal of Special Education, 20*, 489–502.

National Association of State Boards of Education. (1992). *Winners all: A call for inclusive schools.* Alexandria, VA: NASBE.

National Center on Educational Restructuring and Inclusion (1995). *National study on inclusion: Overview & Summary Report, 2*(2), 1–8. New York: Graduate School and University Center, City University of New York.

National Education Association (1994). *Time strategies.* Author.

Oberti v. Board of Education of the Borough of Clementon School District, 995 F. 2d 1204 (3rd Cir. 1993).

O'Neil, J. (1995). Can inclusion work? A conversation with Jim Kauffman and Mara Sapon-Shevin. *Educational Leadership, 52*(4), 7–11.

Osborne, A. G., Jr., & Dimattia, P. (1994). The IDEA's least restrictive environment mandate: Legal implications. *Exceptional Children, 61*(1), 6–14.

Pankake, A. M., & Palmer, B. (1996). Making the connections: Linking staff development interventions to implementation of full inclusion. *Journal of Staff Development, 17*(3), 26–30.

Pearman, E. L., Huang, A. M., & Mellblom, C. I. (1997). The inclusion of all students: Concerns and incentives of educators. *Education and Training in Mental Retardation, 32*(1), 11–20.

Peck, C. A., Donaldson, J., & Pezzoli, M. (1990). Some benefits adolescents perceive for themselves from their social relationships with peers who have severe disabilities. *Journal of the Association for Persons with Severe Handicaps, 15*(4), 241–249.

Pennsylvania Association for Retarded Children (PARC) v. Commonwealth of Pennsylvania, 334 F. Supp. 1257 (E. D. Pa.): 343 F. Supp. 279 (E. D. Pa.) (1971, 1972).

Praisner, C. L. (2003). Attitudes of elementary school principals toward the inclusion of students with disabilities. *Exceptional Children, 69*(2), 135–145.

Reiff, H. B., Evans, E. D., & Cass, M. (1991). Special education requirements for general education certification: A national survey of current practices. *Remedial and Special Education, 12*(5), 56–60.

Reynolds, M. C. (1991). Classification and labeling. In: J. W. Lloyd, A. C. Repp, & N. N. Singh (Eds), *The Regular Education Initiative: Alternative Perspectives on Concepts, Issues, and Models* (pp. 29–41). Champaign, IL: Sycamore.

Reynolds, M. C., Wang, M. C., & Walberg, H. J. (1987). The necessary restructuring of special and regular education. *Exceptional Children, 53*, 391–398.

Rogers, J. (1993, May). The inclusion revolution. *Research Bulletin of Phi Delta Kappa, 11*, 1–6.

Rosjewski, J. W., & Pollard, R. R. (1990). A multivariate analysis of perceptions held by secondary academic teachers towards students with special needs. *Teacher Education and Special Education, 13*, 149–153.

Rothstein, L. F. (1990). *Special education law*. New York: Longman.

Sacramento City Unified School District v. Rachel Holland, 14 F.3d 1398 (9th Cir. 1994).

Sailor, W. (1991). Special education in the restructured school. *Remedial and Special Education, 12*(6), 8–22.

Sailor, W., & Halvorsen, ? (1990). *Policy implications of emergent full inclusion models for the education of students with severe disabilities*. (ERIC Document Reproduction Service No. ED365 048.)

Sapon-Shevin, M. (1988). Working towards merger together: Seeing beyond distrust and fear. *Teacher Education and Special Education, 11*, 103–110.

Schnorr, R. F. (1997). From enrollment to membership: "Belonging" in middle and high school classes. *Journal of the Association for Persons with Severe Handicaps, 22*(1), 1–15.

Schumaker, J. B., & Deshler, D. D. (1988). Implementing the regular education initiative in secondary schools: A different ballgame. *Journal of Learning Disabilities, 21*(1), 36–42.

Schumaker, L. B., & Hazel, J. S. (1984). Social skills assessment and training for the learning disabled: Who's on first and what's on second? Part II. *Journal of Learning Disabilities, 17*, 492–499.

Schumm, J. S., & Vaughn, S. (1991). Making adaptations for mainstreamed students: General classroom teachers' perspectives. *Remedial and Special Education, 12*(4), 18–27.

Schumm, J. S., & Vaughn, S. (1995). Getting ready for inclusion: Is the stage set? *Learning Disabilities Research & Practice, 10*(3), 169–179.

Scruggs, T. E., & Mastropieri, M. A. (1994). Successful mainstreaming in elementary science classes: A qualitative study of three reputational cases. *American Educational Research Journal, 31*(4), 785–811.

Scruggs, T. E., & Mastropieri, M. A. (1996). Teacher perceptions of mainstreaming/inclusion, 1958–1995: A research synthesis. *Exceptional Children, 63*(1), 59–74.

Semmel, M., Abernathy, T., Butera, G., & Lesar, S. (1991). Teacher perceptions of the regular education initiative. *Exceptional Children, 57*, 9–22.

Sharpe, M. N., York, J. L., & Knight, J. (1994). Effects of inclusion on the academic performance of classmates without disabilities. *Remedial and Special Education, 15*(5), 281–287.

Siu-Runyan, Y. (1990). Supporting principals. *Journal of Reading, 34*, 546–547.

Skrtic, T. (1991). *Behind special education*. Denver: Love.

Slavin, R. E. (1995). *Cooperative learning* (2nd ed.). Needham Heights, MA: Allyn & Bacon.

Stainback, S., & Stainback, W. (1984). A rationale for the merger of special and regular education. *Exceptional Children, 51*(2), 102–112.

Stainback, S., & Stainback, W. (1987). Facilitating merger through personnel preparation. *Teacher Education and Special Education, 10*, 185–190.

Stainback, S., & Stainback, W. (Eds) (1992). *Curriculum considerations for inclusive classrooms: Facilitating learning for all students.* Baltimore, MD: Brookes.

Taylor, S. J. (1988). Caught in the continuum: A critical analysis of the principle of the least restrictive environment. *The Journal of the Association for Persons with Severe Handicaps, 13*(1), 41–53.

Thousand, J. S., & Villa, R. A. (1990). Strategies for educating learners with severe disabilities within their local home schools and communities. *Focus on Exceptional Children, 23*(3), 1–24.

Udvari-Solner, A. (1992). *Curricular adaptations: Accommodating the instructional needs of diverse learners in the context of general education.* Topeka, KS: Kansas State Board of Education. (ERIC Document Reproduction Service No. ED 354 685.)

U.S. Department of Education. Office of Special Programs (1998). *Twentieth annual report to Congress on the implementation of The Individuals with Disabilities Education Act.* Washington, DC: Author.

U.S. Department of Education. Office of Special Programs (2001). *Twenty-third annual report to Congress on the implementation of The Individuals with Disabilities Education Act.* Washington, DC: Author.

Vaughn, S., & Schumm, J. S. (1994). Middle school teachers' planning for students with disabilities. *Remedial and Special Education, 15*, 152–161.

Vaughn, S., & Schumm, J. S. (1995). Responsible inclusion for students with learning disabilities. *Journal of Learning Disabilities, 28*(5), 264–270.

Vaughn, S., Schumm, J. S., Jallad, B., Slusher, J., & Saumell, L. (1994). Teachers' views of inclusion: "I'd rather pump gas." Paper presented at the annual meeting of the American Educational Research Association, New Orleans, LA.

Villa, R. A., & Thousand, J. S. (2000). Setting the context: History of and rationales for inclusive schooling. In: R. A. Villa & J. S. Thousand (Eds), *Restructuring for Caring and Effective Education: Piecing the Puzzle Together* (2nd ed., pp. 7–37). Baltimore: Brookes.

Villa, R. A., Thousand, J. S., Meyers, H., & Nevin, A. (1996). Teacher and administrator perceptions of heterogeneous education. *Exceptional Children, 63*(1), 29–45.

Villa, R. A., Thousand, J. S., Stainback, W., & Stainback, S. (Eds) (1992). *Restructuring for caring and effective education: An administrative guide to creating heterogeneous schools.* Baltimore: Brookes.

Wang, M. C., Reynolds, M. C., & Walberg, H. J. (1986). Rethinking special education. *Educational Leadership, 44*(1), 26–31.

Wang, M. C., & Walberg, H. J. (1988). Four fallacies of segregationism. *Exceptional Children, 55*, 128–137.

Williams, D. (1990). Listening to today's teachers: They can tell us what tomorrow's teachers should know. *Teacher Education and Special Education, 13*, 149–153.

Williams, W., Fox, T., Thousand, J., & Fox, W. (1990). Level of acceptance and implementation of best practices in the education of students with severe handicaps in Vermont. *Education and Training in Mental Retardation, 25*(2), 120–131.

Wolery, M., Gessler Werts, M., Caldwell, N. K., Snyder, E. D., & Lisowski, L. (1995). Experienced teachers' perceptions of resources and supports for inclusion. *Education and Training in Mental Retardation and Developmental Disabilities, 30*(1), 15–26.

Yell, M. L. (1998). *The law and special education.* Upper Saddle River, NJ: Merrill.

York, J. L., & Reynolds, M. C. (1996). Special education and inclusion. In: J. Sikula, T. J. Buttery & E. Guyton (Eds), *Handbook of Research on Teacher Education* (2nd ed.). New York: Simon & Schuster.

York, J., Vandercook, T., MacDonald, C., Heise-Neff, C., & Caughey, E. (1992). Feedback about integrating middle school students with severe disabilities in general education classes. *Exceptional Children, 58*, 244–258.

Ysseldyke, J. E., Algozzine, B., & Thurlow, M. L. (2000). *Critical issues in special education* (3rd ed.). Boston, MA: Houghton Mifflin.

Zhang, Y. (2000). Technology and the writing skills of students with learning disabilities. *Journal of Research on Computing in Education, 32*(4), 467–479.

Zigmond, N., & Baker, J. M. (1990). Mainstreaming experiences for learning disabled students (Project MELD): Preliminary report. *Exceptional Children, 57*, 176–185.

Zigmond, N., Jenkins, J., Fuchs, L. S., Deno, S., Fuchs, D., Baker, J. N., Jenkins, L., & Coutino, M. (1995). Special education in restructured schools: Findings from three multi-year studies. *Phi Delta Kappa, 76*, 531–540.

Zionts, P. (Ed.) (1997). *Inclusion strategies for students with learning and behavior problems: Perspectives, experiences, and best practices.* Austin, TX: Pro Ed.

USEFUL REFERENCES FOR THE IMPLEMENTATION OF INCLUSION

Beninghof, A. M., & Singer, A. L. (1995). *Ideas for inclusion: The school administrator's guide.* Longmont, CO: Sopris West.

Bradley, D. F., King-Sears, M. E., & Tessier-Switlick, D. M. (Eds) (1997). *Teaching students in inclusive settings: From theory to practice.* Needham Heights, MA: Allyn & Bacon.

Choate, J. S. (Ed.) (2000). *Successful inclusive teaching: Proven ways to detect and correct special needs* (3rd ed.). Needham Heights, MA: Allyn & Bacon.

Dieker, L. (2000). *Co-teaching lesson plan book 2000.* Reston, VA: Council for Exceptional Children.

Falvey, M. A. (Ed.) (1995). *Inclusive and heterogeneous schooling: Assessment, curriculum, and instruction.* Baltimore: Brookes.

Hammeken, P. A. (1995). *Inclusion: 450 strategies for success: A practical guide for all educators who teach students with disabilities.* Minnetonka, MN: Peytral.

Hammeken, P. A. (1996). *Inclusion: An essential guide for the paraprofessional: A practical reference tool for all paraprofessionals working in inclusionary settings.* Minnetonka, MN: Peytral.

Jorgensen, C. M. (Ed.) (1997). *Restructuring high schools for all students: Taking inclusion to the next level.* Baltimore: Brookes.

Kochhar, C. A., West, L. L., & Taymans, J. M. (2000). *Successful inclusion: Practical strategies for a shared responsibility.* Upper Saddle River, NJ: Prentice-Hall.

Male, M. (2003). *Technology for inclusion: Meeting the special needs of all students* (4th ed.) Boston, MA: Allyn & Bacon.

Mastropieri, M. A., & Scruggs, T. E. (2004). *The inclusive classroom: Strategies for effective instruction* (2nd ed.). Upper Saddle River, NJ: Prentice-Hall.

McGregor, G., & Vogelsberg, R. T. (1998). *Inclusive schooling practices: Pedagogical and research foundations* [Monograph]. Allegheny University of the Health Sciences.

Reinhiller, N. (1996). New variations on a not-so-new practice. *Teacher Education and Special Education, 19,* 34–48.

Ryndak, D. L., & Alper, S. (1996). *Curriculum content for students with moderate and severe disabilities in inclusive settings.* Needham Heights, MA: Allyn & Bacon.

Sage, D. D. (Ed.) (1997). *Inclusion in secondary schools: Bold initiatives challenging change.* Port Chester, NY: National Professional Resources.

Schmidt, M. W., & Harriman, N. E. (1998). *Teaching strategies for inclusive classrooms: Schools, students, strategies, and success.* Orlando, FL: Harcourt Brace.

Stainback, S., & Stainback, W. (Eds) (1996). *Inclusion: A guide for educators.* Baltimore: Brookes.

Vaughn, S., Bos, C. S., & Schumm, J. S. (2000). *Teaching exceptional, diverse, and at-risk students in the general education classroom* (2nd ed.). Needham Heights, MA: Allyn & Bacon.

Villa, R., & Thousand, J. (Eds) (1995). *Creating an inclusive school.* Alexandria, VA: Association for Supervision and Curriculum Development.

Villa, R., & Thousand, J. (Eds) (2000). *Restructuring for caring and effective education: Piecing the puzzle together.* Baltimore: Brookes.

Walther-Thomas, C., Bryant, M., & Land, S. (1996). Planning for effective co-teaching: The key to successful inclusion. *Remedial and Special Education, 17*(4), 255–Cover 3.

Walther-Thomas, C., Korinek, L., McLaughlin, V. L., & Toler Williams, B. (2000). *Collaboration for inclusive education: Developing successful programs.* Needham Heights, MA: Allyn & Bacon.

8. INTERNATIONAL ATTITUDES TOWARD CHILDREN WITH DISABILITIES: IDENTIFYING RISK FACTORS FOR MALTREATMENT

Andrea L. Rotzien[*]

INTRODUCTION

International rates of child maltreatment, particularly for children with disabilities are difficult to determine due to a lack of centralized data bases, a tendency to not keep consistent records of disability characteristics in cases of suspected maltreatment, and in extreme cases, because maltreatment is not acknowledged or addressed publicly (Bonner et al., 1997; Morris, 1999). Therefore, most of the data on prevalence rates of maltreatment in disabled children are from western cultures such as the U.S., Canada, and the U.K. There is some evidence to suggest that the rates internationally are probably at least equal to those in the U.S. samples (Cooke & Standen, 2002; Gringorenko, 1998). Finklehor (1994) found that the rates of sexual abuse were consistent across nations for both males and females. The nations in that study included most European countries, Canada, Dominican Republic, Australia, New Zealand, and South Africa. On the other hand, Forrester and Harwin (2000) note that measuring child maltreatment internationally is nearly impossible due to the varying cultural norms, national resources, and the

[*] Andrea Rotzien is Assistant Professor at Grand Valley State University, Michigan.

Administering Special Education: In Pursuit of Dignity and Autonomy
Advances in Educational Administration, Volume 7, 167–188
Copyright © 2004 by Elsevier Ltd.
All rights of reproduction in any form reserved
ISSN: 1479-3660/doi:10.1016/S1479-3660(04)07008-8

tendency for many forms of maltreatment to go unnoticed. They suggest that an alternative to measuring maltreatment internationally may be to evaluate each nation's willingness to both address issues regarding the rights of children and to provide services to children who are maltreated.

Recent U.S. studies have confirmed a relationship between disabled children and maltreatment risk. Sullivan and Knutson (1998, 2000) compared maltreatment rates between disabled and non-disabled children and found strong correlations between behavioral disorders and maltreatment and cognitive impairment and maltreatment. They reported that special education students were 3.4 times as likely to be maltreated as general education students. This is likely an underestimation of the seriousness of this problem, since many cases of maltreatment go unreported (Nunnelley & Fields, 1999). Neglect was the most common form of maltreatment across disabled and non-disabled groups, but many of the children experienced more than one kind of maltreatment. The disabled children were more likely to experience more than one kind of maltreatment and multiple episodes of maltreatment. The reality of this risk has been substantiated by many other studies (Cowen & Reed, 2002; Embry, 2001; Hassouneh-Phillips & Curry, 2002; Orelove et al., 2000; Sobsey, 2002; Verdugo et al., 1995; Westat, 1993).

A number of risk factors for maltreatment have been identified. Children with disabilities are more vulnerable to maltreatment because of issues such as gullibility, powerlessness, dependency, a desire to please, and the exposure to multiple caregivers or professionals. Problems with communication or inappropriate behaviors may impede the attachment process and increase the likelihood that the parent will use corporal punishment. As a result of difficulties the family of origin may face in relation to a child's disability, these kids are more likely to live in residential schools, institutions, and foster homes, all of which increase the risk for maltreatment (American Academy of Pediatrics, 2001; Prevent Child Abuse America, n.d.; Tharinger et al., 1990; U.S. Department of Health and Human Services, 2001; Vig & Kaminer, 2002; Walker, 2002).

Children with disabilities are also vulnerable due to societal attitudes. Many cultures still actively engage in stereotyping and marginalizing of the disabled. Examples of risky attitudes include distancing or isolating disabled individuals, blaming the disabled person or his/her family for the problems or behaviors he/she exhibits, minimizing the impact of maltreatment on this population or denying the existence of a problem, assuming the quality of life for these individuals will be sub par, and denying educational opportunities (Goldson, 1998; Sobsey, 2002; The U.S. Department of Health and Human Services, 2001).

Finally, parental factors such as substance abuse, low education, poor parenting skills, and single parenthood increase the likelihood of child maltreatment. Parents with mental health issues, other disabilities, and a personal history of abuse may also resort to inappropriate discipline. Parental perceptions of the disability and the amount of support the parent or caregiver receives can influence the relationship with the disabled child (Burrell et al., 1994; Gaudin, 1993; Heiman, 2002; Sobsey, 2002; Sullivan & Knutson, 2000; U.S. Department of Health and Human Services, 2001; Verdugo et al., 1995; Vig & Kaminer, 2002). These factors in addition to large families, poor knowledge of or access to prenatal care and other resources, when paired with negative societal attitudes, leads to a sad situation indeed.

In the following section, a brief summary of representative research is offered for several international areas. Studies reported may represent only a sample of what is available and frequently attitudes have to be determined by the availability of services. Furthermore, what follows are general representations of attitudes and behaviors toward individuals with disabilities for the various cultures. Individual differences do exist and often depend on a number of factors such as disability type, disability severity, educational background of the family members, religious beliefs, support available, and psychological health and coping of the caregivers. Finally, at times the only information reported pertains to risk factors for maltreatment evident in a particular culture. The presence of risk factors does not necessarily mean a child will be maltreated and conversely, the absence of risk factors does not necessarily mean a child is safe.

Europe

The European Opinion Research Group for the Education and Culture Directorate recently conducted a study of Europeans regarding their awareness, contact, comfort level, and attitudes toward individuals with disabilities (2001). Results indicate that most of the 16,014 Europeans surveyed know someone with a disability, 8 out of 10 Europeans report feeling comfortable around individuals with disabilities, and 40% think others feel uncomfortable around individuals with disabilities. All surveyed Europeans see public access difficulties as an issue for all forms of disability and many noted a desire to see more integration. Differences exist between countries in this area as well.

For example, Sweden and Finland had the lowest reported rates of familiarity with a person with a disability. Germany and Greece had the lowest reported rates of comfort with individuals with disabilities. These data are further supported by research comparing Greek Americans to Greek nationals on attitudes toward the disabled that revealed more negative attitudes in Greek nationals (Zarometidis et al., 1999). While Italy has higher ratings overall regarding attitudes toward individuals with disabilities, the Italians tended to perceive others as uncomfortable around the disabled (i.e. I am comfortable around these individuals, but I think many other people are not). A similar finding was reported by Manetti et al. (2001) who interviewed Italian children about their willingness to accept a child with disabilities. Although the children vocalized a willingness to interact, sociometric ratings of severely disabled children in the school indicated they were rejected socially. Access issues were particularly high in France and Greece whereas, Sweden had the best access for individuals with disabilities. A number of interesting attitudes emerged among the countries. Most reported feeling sad when seeing a person with a disability, which seems counter to the belief that individuals with disabilities are just like everyone else. Most Europeans reported a tendency to see mental disabilities as more difficult to deal with than physical disabilities. Finally, attitudes about inclusion differ somewhat in relation to education. While a majority of Europeans want more integration of individuals with disabilities, some countries reported less support for educating children with learning problems in the same schools as children without learning problems. Portugal, Netherlands, Greece, and Belgium were the least likely to support inclusion. Although this study does not specifically address maltreatment concerns with the disabled population, it provides insight into the attitudes that can inadvertently support or hide maltreatment.

Cooke and Standen (2002) surveyed 73 chairs of the Area Child Protection Committee in the United Kingdom and found that while 50% reported identifying disability status in reports of child maltreatment, only 10% could specifically note how many disabled children had been abused. The authors state that given the high risk of maltreatment, it is critical to discern not only prevalence rates but also outcomes for victims and perpetrators. Another issue is that the source of reports for disabled children differs significantly from those of non-disabled children. For non-disabled children, social workers and health care workers were as likely to make a report as parents. On the other hand, for disabled children, social workers and health care workers were the least likely to make a report. Perhaps training for these professionals is necessary to improve the identification of maltreatment in disabled children. In this study, disabled children were less likely to be placed on the child protection register and less likely to receive a family support package. Cooke and Standen attempted to estimate prevalence rates of disabled children who are abused. They note that 0.42–0.45% of children in the population were placed on the register in the study time period. If the rate of maltreatment in children with disabilities is presumed to be at least equal to those of non-disabled children, then 59 children with disabilities should have been on the register during the given time period. However, only 35 were identified which leads one to conclude that they are either at lower risk (counter to all previous research), or that cases of maltreatment in this population are being overlooked.

Oosterhoorn and Kendrick (2001) state that there have been a number of issues that have led to a tendency to overlook maltreatment in the disabled population. These include social myths such as: no one could or would abuse this population, disabled individuals are not sexual beings or not sexually desirable, and disabled individuals are not integrated enough to be exposed to abusers. To the contrary, there are a number of factors that make disabled individuals more vulnerable to maltreatment. Dependency in the form of long-term intimate care from family members or strangers places them at risk. Dependency is also encouraged through the emphasis on compliance with this group. In some countries, institutionalization is still highly employed, particularly for severe impairments. The rates of maltreatment in these settings are notoriously high. Communication deficits are another commonly noted barrier to detecting maltreatment in this population. Persons with disabilities may be fearful, guilty, ashamed, or feel emotional ties to their abuser, which can inhibit their desire to report abuse incidents. A primary concern is the lack of verbal skills or language particularly for sexual issues. In this study, the authors interviewed 20 staff from 8 different facilities in Scotland about communication methods used with the disabled population. Unfortunately, the most frequently used methods did not include icons or language to report sexual abuse. The staff interviewed stated that they were unsure if the children could understand the concepts of sexuality well enough to know they are being abused, or use the communication methods available to them to report it. The staff also voiced concerns about false allegations. For example, if a child was attempting to communicate about a sexual issue with his/her new icons, it is possible a staff member could "read too much" into these statements and make a false allegation.

Kvam (2000) surveyed doctors at medical hospitals in Norway where children are evaluated when sexual abuse is suspected. She attempted to determine if the rate of sexual abuse for disabled children was the same in Norway as in other countries (1.7–2 times that of non-disabled children). She noted that the rate of disability matched those in other countries (11% of population) and that the rate of sexual abuse in the general population matched that of other countries (13% females and 7% males), so the assumption would be that the rate of sexual abuse in the disabled population would match other countries. She found that from 1994 to 1996, the number of cases of confirmed sexual abuse in disabled children did not match expected odds. She further noted that of the cases examined, doctors were more likely to doubt the reports of disabled children than those of normal children. Kvam indicated that the lower rates are due to underreporting and communication difficulties. She cited a number of previous studies that indicate that parents who know their disabled child has been abused may actually decide not to report it to avoid further trauma (i.e. child not believed), or because they think the child doesn't recall the abuse or wasn't affected by the abuse. Furthermore, for children living in residential settings, there is a tendency not to report abuse to protect the institutional reputation and avoid litigation.

Hintermair (2000) surveyed 317 parents of hearing impaired children. He compared the parents of children with only hearing impairments to parents of children with hearing impairments and an additional disability (physical disability was the most common). As can be expected, the latter group of parents had significantly higher reported stress scores in relation to their child. Specifically, parents of children with multiple disabilities reported that their children were less adaptable, more demanding, and created more parental role strain than the average child. According to Hintermair, Germany has had difficulty fulfilling the emotional and social needs of parents with disabled children. This study is important because it is the first step in acknowledging maltreatment risk. Awareness of this stress can open the door to ideas for alleviating the stress and hopefully the potential for maltreatment.

Olsson and Hwang (2001) evaluated parental depression in 216 families with children with autism and/or intellectual disability and 214 control families from Sweden. Mothers with autistic children had higher depression scores than mothers with children with intellectual disabilities. Both groups were higher than control mothers. Fathers had lower depression scores than mothers in all three groups. Single mothers had the highest risk for depression.

Gonzalez and Valle (1999) summarized the history of special education in Spain. Reviewing this history can help the reader better understand attitudes toward the disabled. The article revealed a history similar to many westernized cultures in that special education began for those who were deaf and blind. The cognitively impaired populations were first addressed in the 1940s and 1950s, when society accepted the idea that their functioning could be improved. Educational rights for all of the disabled were in the forefront during the late 1960s and laws passed in the 1980s and late 1990s have emphasized integration. The focus on integration may decrease the isolation of these populations and hence, decrease the risk for maltreatment. Verdugo et al. (1995) studied maltreatment rates in a sample of 445 cognitively impaired children and adolescents living in institutions in Spain and found 11.5% of the sample had experienced maltreatment compared to 1.5% of controls.

Israel/Jordan

Israeli attitudes and practices in relation to individuals with disabilities are complex. The research coming out of academic institutions and hospitals in

Jerusalem is comprehensive and advanced. For example, numerous articles have been published examining the issues of children with a variety of disabilities and their families (Brook & Galili, 2000; Galil et al., 2001; Goldman, 2000; Gross-Tsur et al., 2001; Heiman, 2001, 2002; Katz et al., 2000; Merrick et al., 2001; Mizrachi, 2001; Pencovici, 2001; Rimmerman et al., 2000; Schwartz & Rabinovitz, 2001). Israeli researchers have produced premiere studies on educational practices and inclusion concerns for children with cognitive impairment and other serious disabilities (Faust et al., 2003; Gumpel & Nativ-Ari-Am, 2001; Heiman & Precel, 2003; Hetzroni & Boaz, 2002; Hetzroni & Shavit, 2002; Hutzler et al., 2002; Liftshitz & Glaubman, 2002; Schwartz & Armony-Sivan, 2001). Furthermore, data on child maltreatment in both Jewish and Arab settlements is available (Benbenishty et al., 2002; Haj et al., 2002; Khamis, 2000; Shor, 1997, 1998, 2000; Shor & Haj-Yahia, 1996), and indicates that primary school students report high levels of psychological and physical maltreatment, particularly if they are male, Arab and from low income and low education families. A study by Benbenishty et al. (2002) found that 8.2% of their sample of school children reported sexually inappropriate behavior perpetrated by a school staff member. Khamis (2000) found that Palestinian families were more likely to psychologically abuse their children if they are in refugee camps and have financial concerns. In addition, psychological maltreatment was often accompanied by physical maltreatment and child labor. Shor (1997, 1998) reported that Israeli teachers and pediatricians miss indicators of neglect and psychological maltreatment and are reluctant to report even blatant forms of maltreatment to the appropriate authorities. Shor and Haj-Yahia (1996) found significant differences between Arab and Jewish college students regarding perceptions, awareness, and reporting of child maltreatment. Thus, there seems to be a high risk for maltreatment of children in general, most of the aforementioned studies did not include disabled children in the samples.

A recent study by Schwartz et al. (2002) found that services to families of children with disabilities vary significantly in Israel, depending on where the families live. Social workers in Arab sectors reported poorer service availability than in the Jewish sectors with 21% of the Jewish sector social workers reporting poor availability. The authors note that in areas of Israel where inhabitants are uneducated, attitudes toward individuals with disabilities remain negative.

A study of northern Jordanian families with handicapped children found that caregiving falls solely on the mother, leading to problems if she is dies or is otherwise unable to provide care. The father of the disabled child, or his family, bears the cost of therapy and medical treatment. Consequently, female siblings of handicapped children often have difficulty finding suitors due to fears of transmitting a handicap and incurring expenses (Young, 1997). This leads to an additional strain on the family of a disabled child.

Pakistan/Afghanistan/India/Turkey/Saudi Arabia

According to Miles (1998), rural families who have children with disabilities in Pakistan receive very few services. The programs that are in place have little research to support them. There has been very little research on the mentally impaired population, which leads to a lack of information on their daily life, needs, support, and problems. One study found that Pakistani parents of children with disabilities may be more accepting of children who had visible disabilities (e.g. blind, deaf, physical impairments), and mothers may be more rejecting of disabled children than fathers (Ansari, 2002). The president of the Pakistani disability group noted in 2001 that although 10% of the Pakistani population is disabled, there are very few services in place. He noted problems with transportation, accessibility, programming, jobs, and tax breaks and economic assistance. Afghani children with disabilities face similar problems. Very few formal services are available although some for children with physical and visual impairments are being developed (Miles, 1997). Children with cognitive impairments or hearing impairments are the least likely to receive support. Educational integration is casually adopted in some areas and neglected in others and there is a desperate need for family support services using indigenous counselors.

Datta et al. (2002) studied risk factors for burden among Indian caregivers of children with cognitive impairment. The two major risk factors noted were expressed emotion in the family and low income. Expressed emotion is the level of criticism and hostility voiced in a family that is often coupled with an over-involvement of family members. It has been associated with negative outcomes for a number of mental illnesses. Another factor related to higher levels of stress was the age of the child; the younger the child, the more stressed the family. The most prevalent form of maltreatment noted in India is child labor. Recent estimates indicate that 14.4% of children aged 10–14 are economically active in India. Females are at particular risk. These children are often employed in high-risk industries such as tobacco, cement making, match making, explosive or fireworks companies, and glass making. Many are employed in domestic services and prostitution. Child labor is related to high rates of poverty, the displacement of rural peoples due to lack of agricultural development, societal biases that children are better workers, and that employing children keeps families from starving. The reality is that child laborers provide cheap labor, experience delays in physical and cognitive development, and are more vulnerable to job related injuries that result in a permanent disability status. These children often work in lieu of an education which traps them in low paying, unskilled labor. Although legislation has been passed to alleviate this problem, it has not been well enforced (Caesar-Leo, 1999).

Akkok (2000) noted a number of problems with special education services in Turkey. Information is not well disseminated in the country leading to problems linking research and policy. The methodology used in research is weak which leads to problems with validity and applicability. Attitudes towards individuals with disabilities are still rather negative in areas of Turkey, which inhibits policy changes.

The prevalence rate of cognitive impairment or developmental delay in Saudi Arabia is estimated to be from 4 to 30% (Kearney et al., 2002). Like many other countries, there is a lack of national or cross-cultural research. In addition, there is no consistent diagnostic or assessment process, which can also lead to problems with achieving accurate estimates. Furthermore, Kearney et al. (2002) report that there is a shortage of services for developmentally disabled children, so consistent follow-up and treatment is rare.

Australia

While Australia is highly visible in major research journals, a number of authors have noted that information specific to the problems of the disabled are limited (Chenowith, 2002; Stehlik, 2001). Chenowith (2002) reported that the Australian Institute of Health and Welfare does not include any data on children with disabilities in child protection reports; therefore, accurate prevalence rates for maltreatment with this population are difficult to determine. Stehlik (2001) expressed concern that a number of troubling attitudes are still evident. For example, the Australian government has openly discussed offering private health care for families with disabled children to "remove this burden from the tax payers." Allegations of euthanasia have arisen in institutions housing folks with severe disabilities. Sterilization is still in practice in disabled children as young as four. Brady (2001) posits that the cognitively impaired population is the most likely to be sterilized. She notes that although the government passed laws in 1992 that prevent the parents from deciding on sterilization without the involvement of family court, only 17 cases have appeared before the court since the law was passed. However, in the same time period, some estimate that as many as 1,000 hysterectomies have been completed on minors. Brady (2001) summarized the reasons given by professionals for this practice. These include to decrease sexual misconduct, improve personality during menstruation, make the patient more agreeable, remove the necessity for birth control and/or education on menstruation, avoid the trauma of pregnancy and childbirth, prevent sexual abuse, and because it is in the best interest of the patient. Many of these goals may be supportable, yet it seems as though other alternatives exist for improving personality. In addition, sterilizing a person does make him/her invulnerable to sexual abuse.

Unfortunately, these attitudes and beliefs are not uncommon. The issues noted here are evident in most westernized countries, as many of these countries have proceeded through the same history in regard to dealing with the disabled. An initial pattern of rejection, isolation, institutionalization, parental blame, gene pool fears, and egregious rights violations, has been followed by a long struggle to better understand disabled populations and address the rights violations and quality of life for various groups. The first groups identified are those with visual, hearing, and physical impairments. Those with cognitive impairments are typically the next group identified as needing services, but the transition into mainstream culture is much more difficult. Individuals with less visible disabilities such as emotional or behavioral disorders are typically the last to be identified, yet perhaps the most at risk for maltreatment (Sullivan & Knutson, 2000).

Africa

Due to a significant lack of national data sources and the diverse cultures present, determining the rates of disability, much less maltreatment is difficult. Christianson et al. (2002) found high prevalence rates of intellectual disability in South Africa (i.e. 35.6 in 1000). May et al. (2000) studied the epidemiology of Fetal Alcohol Syndrome (FAS) in South Africa and found very high rates, particularly in mixed race groups (39.2–42.9 per 1000). These rates exceed the highest reported rates of FAS in disenfranchised Native American tribes. The authors note that these rates are likely the result of racial bias, low socioeconomic status, rural living, and residing on grape farms where workers are routinely paid in wine. Akande (2000) also reported high rates of violence and poverty in South Africa. He linked these problems to poor cognitive, emotional, and behavioral development in young children in South Africa, and expressed concern about the elevated risk for physical, sexual, and psychological maltreatment.

Balogi (1998) studied 70 Africans from Venda Pedi, Tsonga, and Ndeble tribes to assess attitudes toward the disabled. He found individuals with cerebral palsy and other physical impairments, or who were blind or deaf, were more likely to be seen as undesirable and problematic. This is counter to many westernized cultures where intellectual, behavioral and emotional problems are often implicated as more difficult to address (European Opinion Research Group, 2001). It is possible that these biases are rooted in beliefs about the causes of disabilities (e.g. witchcraft). Education about disabilities is needed in these groups. Madu (2000) measured parental attitudes in 126 Nigerian parents with disabled children. He found that parents of handicapped children had more negative attitudes than parents of non-handicapped children. Parents of children with cognitive impairments were the most negative. Most of the parents prefer institutionalization to the child living at home. He concluded that these attitudes increase the risk for maltreatment and neglect, correlate with a poor response to interventions, and increase the risks for maltreatment through institutionalization. Tanzanian cultural attitudes toward the disabled appear to be positive; however, there is little involvement of the family or community in education, which has led to a lack of organized intervention (Kisanji, 1995).

Gresson et al. (2001) studied the perceptions of disability in a small sample of Somali immigrants and found that cognitive impairment was perceived as more severe than physical impairment; the family is responsible for care of disabled individuals; Somali views of treatment differ significantly from U.S. views, and prevention is impossible as Allah determines disability status. Reproduction is perceived to be more important than prevention, which further complicates disability prevention efforts.

Hispanic Culture

This is a very broad group, represented by many cultures. Research on this population is limited. Bailey et al. (1999) studied Latinos in the U.S. with young disabled children. Common stressors included: poor access to health care and community services, language barriers, a lack of information about the disability or services available, distrust of the "system," discrimination, and lack of social networks. The highest need reported from their sample of 100 Latino couples was information.

Magana (1999) surveyed 72 Puerto Rican families with cognitively impaired children about the role of the family, role strain, and depression in the parents. The participants valued the concept of "La Familia" in that the families were very important in care giving and in supporting the mothers. Mothers with the highest support had the lowest rates of depression. Emotional support was more influential than direct care assistance. In this culture, motherhood is the central role of the woman and perceived to offer the greatest satisfaction, which is perhaps why the level of impairment in the child was not related to the level of caregiver burden. Unmet service needs and lack of information were related to caregiver burden in this sample. One major concern was the poor physical health reported by the mothers. As the level of physical health decreased, the reported well being of the mothers decreased. Magana postulated that the poor health might represent either extreme self sacrifice in the mother, or perhaps a channeling of depressive symptoms into physical problems.

As aforementioned, research from South American countries is limited. However, Block (2002) summarized Brazilian attitudes toward sexuality and cognitive disability. Human service professionals she interviewed stated that

Brazil is "20 years behind the United States" a belief Block challenges in her article. The previous statement implies that Brazil is following the same developmental projection as the U.S. only slower. She argues that while some biases and stereotypes existed about sexuality and cognitively impaired individuals in Brazil, these issues never reached the epic proportions evident in the U.S. in the early 20th century. The larger issue for Brazil has been the tendency to de-sexualize the cognitively impaired female population, which leads to ignoring sexuality (and consequently sexual maltreatment) altogether. At the same time, Brazilian society has treated cognitively impaired males as if they have the same developmental timeline for sexuality as non-impaired males. In the article, Block shares a story about a young man with cognitive impairments who was traumatized by an incident where his father forced him to visit a prostitute, which is not uncommon in this culture. Another source of sexual exploitation has been in the residential institutions where incidents of maltreatment were silenced well into the 1990s. The silence has carried over into Brazilian literature where mention of sexual abuse in disabled populations is rare. The only acknowledgement of or solution for sexual exploitation of the disabled population has been sterilization.

Russia

Although special education began in Russia around 1917, the prevalent tendency has been to isolate special needs kids by removing defective individuals. This practice is called defectology (Korkunov et al., 1998). Children were typically removed from their families and placed in institutions at very young ages. In fact, the government forbade contact between "normals and abnormals" and consequently, individuals with disabilities were relegated to a life of poverty and rejection. With the fall of the communist regime, the government has been attempting to decentralize the delivery of education, take a more humanitarian approach, and increase integration. According to Korkunov et al. (1998), a majority of children with disabilities are still institutionalized because there are very few public schools equipped to offer special education programs. In addition, Russian society is not prepared to integrate individuals with limited job and social skills. Parents who have children with disabilities still have little say or power in what happens to their children because, because in reality the options are extremely limited and many families are struggling financially. Assessment is also problematic. There is only one assessment center for every 120,000 children. Each center is responsible for approximately 10,000–11,000 placements. Under those conditions, it is highly unlikely that abuse evaluation is of primary concern.

Gringorenko (1998) estimates that 20–30% of students under the age of 18 in Russia have some type of disability or developmental delay. Disabilities have received little public attention, and the primary focus has been on those with a loss of natural functioning (e.g. deaf, blind). Children with mild disabilities are completely overlooked, which often leads to an early departure from school. She links this to the increasing behavioral problems of Russia's youth and the rising crime rates in the adolescent population. This is supported by data cited by Pervova (1998) that indicate crimes by youth increased 21% from 1991 to 1995. Unfortunately, this growth is largely in violent crimes and drug use. According to her, disabled youth are at high risk to become "social orphans." Social orphans are children who have a family, but do not live with them due to emotional problems, violence in the home, or maltreatment. It is estimated that 50,000 children leave home each year for these reasons. Many enter children's houses (orphanages) initially, but end up homeless after turning 17–18. Recent research indicates that 30% of social orphans end up homeless, 20% commit crimes, and 10% commit suicide. Not all of the news is bad. Pervova mentions that the 1990s brought special preschools for children with disabilities, research on prevalence rates (cognitive impairment the most prevalent, with learning disability diagnoses increasing rapidly), autism classrooms, and classes for cognitively impaired children in regular schools.

Korea/China/Japan/Vietnam

Cho et al. (2000) report that most children with disabilities are served in special schools. Early intervention services are essentially nonexistent. Cho et al. interviewed Korean parents on their experiences raising a disabled child. Children ranged from mildly to severely disabled. Reactions to the diagnosis were similar to what has been noted in previous literature (i.e. guilt, sadness, blame, denial). One exception was that 44% of the sample considered suicide, with accompanying filicide of the exceptional child, in order to protect the extended family from disgrace. Generally, all of the parents developed loving feelings toward the child, but periods of despair were not uncommon. The Korean parents also had a tendency to interpret the cause of the disability as relating to their own behavior and mistakes. The parents also reported a number of stressors including: public embarrassment, challenging behaviors, lack of information about the disability, lack of resources, comparisons between the disabled child and normal children, worry about the impact of the disability on the siblings or other family members, and lack of respite care. Cho et al. conclude that the lack of public awareness of disabilities in Korea make the situation more stressful for the parents and the children. Education of this population is very expensive, most reports indicate it is 15–20% of the family income and many of the mothers did not work. These factors certainly increase the risk for resentment and maltreatment.

By the year 2000, there could be as many as 60 million disabled persons in China (Stratford & Hannah, 2000). More than half of the disabled individuals in China cannot read or write and school attendance is rare even for the blind and deaf populations. Stratford and Hannah (2000) report that hearing and speech impairments are the most common category of disabilities (34.3%) followed by cognitive impairment (19.7%), visual (14.6%), physical (14.6) impairments, multiple disabilities (13%), and psychiatric impairment (3.8%). Due to the lack of education and literacy, individuals with disabilities often remain dependent on their families. Societal attitudes are gradually shifting. The most significant change has been in the area of physical disabilities.

In Japan, education for disabled children has been compulsory since 1979. In 1990, only 366 children were not in school because of significant physical or cognitive disabilities (Mitchell, 1995). There are 5 types of schools (blind, deaf, cognitively impaired, physically impaired, and health impaired) and 7 types of special classes offered in regular schools (i.e. cognitively, physically, health, partial sight, hard of hearing, language disordered, and emotionally disturbed). The Ministry of Education has voiced a commitment to improving the education of special needs children through teacher training and alternative programs. While efforts have been made to improve social attitudes toward persons with disabilities (Misawa, 1994; cited in Mitchell, 1995), through international campaigns by disability associations, new laws, information from other nations and an improving economy, Iwakuma and Nussbaum (2000), noted that societal views in Japan still involve a strong sense of shame and a fear of genetic pollution associated with disability. In addition, the school system is still quite competitive and rigidly structured. Early intervention and transition services, in addition to long-term care and follow-up, have been rather limited. Recent research has revealed that Asian American adults aged 18–61 were more likely to stigmatize and less likely to differentiate between physical and mental disabilities than African American, Latin American and European American counterparts (Saetermoe et al., 2001). This finding appeared to be modulated by nativity, as individuals with Asian ancestry who were born in the U.S. were less likely to have negative attitudes toward the disabled than Asian born participants (Saetermoe et al., 2001). Thus, professionals must not only consider cultural background, but also level of assimilation.

Huer et al. (2001) stated that the rate of disabilities in Asian cultures is underreported due to religious beliefs, medical practices, fear, shame and stigma. Estimates indicate 10% of Vietnamese have disabilities, with half of those being severe. The authors studied 43 Vietnamese American families to determine their attitudes toward children with disabilities. They found that the families did not feel shame when faced with a disability and did not feel that disabilities were a punishment from God. However, they did report high levels of hopelessness in the face of a disability, particularly as the level of acculturation decreased. This attitude can lead to a tendency not to seek services for a disabled child. The authors note that this belief may be related to the scarcity of services in Vietnam and limited English proficiency. However, the authors caution professionals not to overgeneralize Vietnamese attitudes. Acculturation, religious practices, and comfort with the professional involved can influence expressed concerns and perceptions.

Summary

It is evident from these studies that societal attitudes are extremely influential in the education and treatment of individuals with disabilities. One can see a continuum that ranges from complete exclusion, which is usually related to political and economic oppression to a gradual understanding of the importance of prevalence rates, education, access, diagnosis and early intervention, and civil rights/maltreatment. Many of the countries exhibit a phenomenon described by Goldson (1998) as a *hierarchy of acceptability*.

> The least acceptable groups are those with mental retardation, cerebral palsy, and dysmorphic characteristics. Those with medium acceptability include individuals with blindness, deafness, speech defects, seizures, and those with psychiatric problems are learning disorders. The final group typically gains acceptance the earliest and is comprised of amputees, and those who are wheel chair bound, or chronically ill (p. 665).

It is possible that the research in these nations will follow the history outlined by Wescott and Jones (1999) on maltreatment and disability. There is some evidence of awareness of the issue in the 1930s and 1940s, but the 1960s and 1970s represent the first time period where numerous articles are evident. These studies were often compromised by small samples and a limited focus. During the 1980s, the research on maltreatment was often restricted to the occurrence in institutions or residential schools. The 1990s brought the most progress in that all forms of maltreatment were studied, in multiple settings, with varying disability populations. The current emphasis is on risk factors, treatment, and prevention. One can already see similar patterns in other countries and pinpoint the progression of various nations on a timeline anchored by the 1930s to the present day by the data collected in the U.S. and other westernized countries.

CONCLUSION

From an international perspective, intervention is complicated due to poor availability of resources, a lack of awareness or knowledge of maltreatment in the disabled population, long standing cultural attitudes regarding the disabled or help seeking behaviors outside of the family (Choi & Wynne, 2000), and the number of stressors faced by these individuals and their families on a daily basis (e.g. famine, war, etc.). Nevertheless, awareness of the seriousness of this problem and confronting the societal attitudes that allow it to occur are key factors in creating change. Many countries do not track disability rates or maltreatment rates, much the less the combination of the two. This includes countries that are westernized. Even in the U.S., the most recent source of data on national maltreatment rates did not track disability status (Kendall-Tackett, 2002). Keeping these records would provide insight and aide in prevention. Perceptions of the disabled and their loved ones need to be examined. These individuals can be contributing members of society, but they need skills and education to self-advocate and protect themselves from harm. Blaming the family or viewing the disability as a punishment or curse often arises from a lack of understanding about the causes of disability. At a minimum, each nation should know which disability group appears to be at the highest risk for ongoing problems. Current research in this area has revealed differences between cultures regarding acceptance of various types of disabilities (Grinde, 1999; Wang, 1999).

Intervention and prevention should occur at multiple levels. Primary prevention efforts should target poverty, poor health and prenatal care, substance use and abuse and violence (Gaudin, 1993). Educating the public about maltreatment using data from epidemiological studies can increase the likelihood that maltreatment will be identified and reported. Raising the awareness about disabilities including causes, treatments, common issues, and prognosis may facilitate a decrease in stereotyping this group.

Secondary prevention should concentrate on at risk groups. At risk groups may vary from culture to culture. These programs should increase the support for parents in a culturally sensitive manner, challenge negative parental views of the child or the disability, provide respite care, improve parenting skills, and educate the parent and the child about his/her disability and the risk for maltreatment (American Academy of Pediatrics, 2001; Prevent Child Abuse America, n.d.; U.S. Department of Health and Human Services, 2001). Sexual education is critical for this population, as the threat of sexual abuse is life long in many cases (Patterson & Kratz, 2002; Strickler, 2001; U.S. Department of Health and Human Services, 2001; Wescott & Jones, 1999).

Given that a majority of maltreatment occurs in the home and is perpetrated by individuals known to the child, tertiary prevention should focus on a systemic approach to the treatment of abuse in order to reduce the likelihood of repeated offenses. There is a tendency to minimize the impact of maltreatment on children with disabilities and to discount the usefulness of therapy, particularly as the level of impairment increases (Strickler, 2001). These stereotypes must be confronted in order to prevent revictimization. Offenders should be actively pursued and prosecuted. This means that there is a need for better communication between government agencies, treatment providers, school personnel, and the families (Buchele-Ash et al., 1995). Recent research indicates that even Child Protective Service (CPS) workers report lacking knowledge in recognizing and responding to maltreatment in children with disabilities (Orelove et al., 2000). Therefore, parents and professionals should be trained on the indicators of maltreatment and appropriate intervention (Manders, 1998; U.S. Department of Health and Human Services, 2001; Wescott & Jones, 1999; Zeanah & Hamilton, 1998).

REFERENCES

Akande, A. (2000). Effects of exposure to violence and poverty on young children: The Southern African context. *Early Child Development & Care, 163*, 61–78.

Akkok, F. (2000). Special education research: A Turkish perspective. *Exceptionality, 8*(4), 273–279.

American Academy of Pediatrics (2001). Assessment of maltreatment of children with disabilities. *Pediatrics, 108*(2), 508–512.

Ansari, Z. A. (2002). Parental acceptance-rejection of disabled children in non-urban Pakistan. *North American Journal of Psychology, 4*(1), 121–128.

Bailey, D. B., Skinner, D., & Correa, V. I. (1999). Needs and supports reported by Latino families of young children with developmental disabilities. *American Journal on Mental Retardation, 104*(5), 437–451.

Balogi, B. H. (1998). Black community attitudes towards the disabled: Educational implications. *Dissertation Abstracts International, 59*, 0080.

Benbenishty, R., Zeira, A., & Astor, R. A. (2002). Children's reports of emotional, physical and sexual maltreatment by educational staff in Israel. *Child Abuse & Neglect, 26*(8), 763–782.

Benbenishty, R., Zeira, A., Astor, R. A., & Khoury-Kassabri, M. (2002). Maltreatment of primary school students by educational staff in Israel. *Child Abuse & Neglect, 26*(12), 1291–1309.

Block, P. (2002). Sexuality, parenthood, and cognitive disability in Brazil. *Sexuality & Disability, 20*(1), 7–28.

Bonner, B. L., Crow, S. M., & Hensley, L. D. (1997). State efforts to identify maltreated children with disabilities: A follow-up study. *Child Maltreatment, 2*, 52–60.

Brady, S. M. (2001). Sterilization of girls and women with intellectual disabilities. *Violence Against Women, 7*(4), 432–461.

Brook, U., & Galili, A. (2000). Knowledge and attitudes of high school pupils towards children with special health care needs: An Israeli exploration. *Patient Education & Counseling, 40*(1), 5–10.

Buchele-Ash, A., Turnbull, H. R., & Mitchell, L. (1995). Forensic and law enforcement issues in the abuse and neglect of children with disabilities. *Mental & Physical Disability Law Reporter*, *19*(1), 115–121.

Burrell, B., Thompson, B., & Sexton, D. (1994). Predicting child abuse potential across family types. *Child Abuse & Neglect*, *18*(12), 1039–1049.

Caesar-Leo, M. (1999). Child labour: The most visible type of child abuse and neglect in India. *Child Abuse Review*, *8*, 75–86.

Chenowith, L. (2002, September). Children with disabilities: What evidence do we have for better practice? Paper presentation at the ACWA Conference in Sydney, Australia.

Cho, S., Singer, G. H. S., & Brenner, M. E. (2000). Adaptation and accommodation to young children with disabilities: A comparison of Korean and Korean American parents. *Topics in Early Childhood Special Education*, *20*(4), 235–249.

Choi, K. H., & Wynne, M. E. (2000). Providing services to Asian Americans with developmental disabilities and their families: Mainstream service providers' perspective. *Community Mental Health Journal*, *36*(6), 589–595.

Christianson, A. J., Zwane, M. E., Manga, P., Rosen, E., Venter, A., Downs, D., & Kromberg, J. G. R. (2002). Children with intellectual disability in rural South Africa: Prevalence and associated disability. *Journal of Intellectual Disability Research*, *46*(2), 179–186.

Cooke, P., & Standen, P. J. (2002). Abuse and disabled children: Hidden needs . . .? *Child Abuse Review*, *11*(1), 1–18.

Cowen, P. S., & Reed, D. A. (2002). Effects of respite care for children with developmental disabilities: Evaluation of an intervention for at risk families. *Public Health Nursing*, *19*(4), 272–283.

Datta, S. S., Russell, P. S. S., & Gopalakrishna, S. C. (2002). Burden among the caregivers of children with intellectual disability: Associations and risk factors. *Journal of Learning Disabilities*, *6*(4), 337–350.

Embry, R. A. (2001, July). Examination of risk factors for maltreatment of deaf children. Findings from a national survey. Paper presented at the 7th International Family Violence Research Conference, Portsmouth, NH.

European Opinion Research Group (2001). *Attitudes of Europeans to Disabilities*. Retrieved March 7, 2003 from www.gesis.org/en/data_service/eurobarometer/standard_eb_profiles/data/eb_54_2.htm.

Faust, M., Dimitrovsky, L., & Schacht, T. (2003). Naming difficulties in children with dyslexia: Application of the tip of the tongue paradigm. *Journal of Learning Disabilities*, *36*(3), 203–215.

Finklehor, D. (1994). The international epidemiology of child sexual abuse. *Child Abuse & Neglect*, *18*(5), 409–417.

Forrester, D., & Harwin, J. (2000). Monitoring children's rights globally: Can child abuse be measured internationally? *Child Abuse Review*, *9*, 427–438.

Galil, A., Carmel, S., Lubetzky, H., Vered, S., & Heiman, N. (2001). Compliance with home rehabilitation therapy by the parents of children with disabilities in Jews and Bedouin Israel. *Developmental Medicine & Child Neurology*, *43*(4), 261–268.

Gaudin, J. M., (1993). Child neglect: A guide for intervention (HHS Publication No. 105-89-1730, pp. 12–380). Washington, DC: U.S. Department of Health and Human Services.

Goldman, T. (2000). AVHA: A self-help organization for the improvement of quality of life of people with disabilities. In: K. D. Keith & R. L. Schalock (Eds), *Cross-cultural Perspectives on Quality of Life* (pp. 45–54). Washington, DC: American Association of Mental Retardation.

Goldson, E. (1998). Children with disabilities and maltreatment. *Child Abuse & Neglect*, *22*(7), 663–667.

Gonzalez, J. E., & Valle, I. H. (1999). A Spanish perspective on LD. *Journal of Learning Disabilities, 32*(3), 267–275.

Gresson, C. J., Veach, P. M., & LeRoy, B. S. (2001). A qualitative investigation of Somali immigrant perceptions of disability: Implications for genetic counseling. *Journal of Genetic Counseling, 1*(5), 359–378.

Grinde, L. R. (1999). A cross-cultural, qualitative study of childhood physical disability in Finland, Haiti and Latvia: Views from parents, professionals, and the community. *Dissertation Abstracts International, 60,* 2984.

Gringorenko, E. L. (1998). Russian "defectology": Anticipating perestroika in the field. *Journal of Learning Disabilities, 31*(2), 193–207.

Gross-Tsur, V., Landau, Y. E., Benarroch, F., Wertman-Elad, R., & Shalev, R. S. (2001). Cognition, attention, and behavior in Prader-Willi syndrome. *Journal of Child Neurology, 16*(4), 288–290.

Gumpel, T. P., & Nativ-Ari-Am, H. (2001). Evaluation of technology for teaching complex social skills to young adults with visual and cognitive impairments. *Journal of Visual Impairment & Blindness, 95*(2), 95–107.

Haj-Yahia, M. M., Musleh, K., & Haj-Yahia, Y. (2002). The incidence of adolescent maltreatment in Arab society and some of its psychological effects. *Journal of Family Issues, 23*(8), 1032–1064.

Hassouneh-Phillips, D., & Curry, M. A. (2002). Abuse of women with disabilities. *Rehabilitation Counseling Bulletin, 45,* 96–104.

Heiman, T. (2001). Depressive mood in students with mild intellectual disability: Students' reports and teachers' evaluations. *Journal of Intellectual Disability Research, 45*(6), 526–534.

Heiman, T. (2002). Parents of children with disabilities: Resilience, Coping, and Future Expectations. *Journal of Developmental and Physical Disabilities, 14*(2), 159–171.

Heiman, T., & Precel, K. (2003). Students with learning disabilities in higher education: Academic strategies profile. *Journal of Learning Disabilities, 36*(3), 246–256.

Hetzroni, O., & Boaz, O. (2002). Effects of intelligence level and place of residence on the ability of individuals with mental retardation to identify facial expressions. *Research in Developmental Disabilities, 23*(6), 369–378.

Hetzroni, O., & Shavit, P. (2002). Comparison of two instructional strategies for acquiring form and sound of Hebrew letters by students with mild mental retardation. *Education & Training in Mental Retardation & Developmental Disabilities, 37*(3), 273–282.

Hintermair, M. (2000). Children who are hearing impaired with additional disabilities and related aspects of parental stress. *Exceptional Children, 66*(3), 327–332.

Huer, M. B., Saenz, T. I., & Doan, J. H. D. (2001). Understanding the Vietnamese American Community: Implications for training educational personnel providing services to children with disabilities. *Communication Disorders Quarterly, 23*(1), 27–39.

Hutzler, Y., Fliess, O., Chacham, A., & Van den Auweele, Y. (2002). Perspectives of children with physical disabilities on inclusion and empowerment: Supporting and limiting factors. *Adapted Physical Activity Quarterly, 19*(3), 300–317.

Iwakuma, M., & Nussbaum, J. F. (2000). Intercultural views of people with disabilities in Asia and Africa. In: D. O. Braithwaite & T. L. Thompson (Eds), *Handbook of Communication and People with Disabilities: Research and Application* (pp. 239–255). New Jersey: Lawrence Erlbaum.

Katz, S., Shemesh, T., & Bizman, A. (2000). Attitudes of university students towards the sexuality of person with mental retardation and persons with paraplegia. *British Journal of Developmental Disabilities, 46*(91), 109–117.

Kearney, C. A., Smith, P. A., & Tillotson, C. A. (2002). Assessment and prediction of mental retardation in Saudi children. *Journal of Developmental and Physical Disabilities, 14*(1), 77–85.

Kendall-Tackett, K. (2002). Abuse and neglect of children with disabilities. *Rehabilitation Psychology News, 29,* 12–13.

Khamis, V. (2000). Child psychological maltreatment in Palestinian families. *Child Abuse & Neglect, 24*(8), 1047–1059.

Kisanji, J. (1995). Interface between culture and disability in the Tanzanian context. *International Journal of Disability, Development & Education, 42*(2), 93–108.

Korkunov, V. V., Nigayev, A. S., Reynolds, L. D., & Lerner, J. W. (1998). Special education in Russia: History, reality, and prospects. *Journal of Learning Disabilities, 31*(2), 2–12.

Kvam, M. H. (2000). Is sexual abuse of children with disabilities disclosed? A retrospective analysis of child disability and the likelihood of sexual abuse among those attending Norwegian hospitals. *Child Abuse & Neglect, 24*(8), 1073–1084.

Liftshitz, H., & Glaubman, R. (2002). Religious and secular students' sense of self-efficacy and attitudes towards inclusion of pupils with intellectual disability and other types of needs. *Journal of Intellectual Disability Research, 46*(5), 405–418.

Madu, S. N. (2000). Nigerian parental attitude towards their handicapped children and suggestions for proper rehabilitation. In: S. N. Madu et al. (Eds), *Psychotherapy and African Reality* (pp. 183–195). Sovenga, South Africa: UNIN press.

Magana, S. M. (1999). Puerto Rican families caring for an adult with mental retardation: Role of familism. *American Journal on Mental Retardation, 104*(5), 466–482.

Manders, J. (1998). Inclusive families and communities minimize risk factors of child abuse. In: *Institute on Human Development and Disability Update* (pp. 1–3). Retrieved March 7, 2003 from http://www.uap.uga.edu/news98-inclus.html.

Manetti, M., Schneider, B. H., & Siperstein, G. (2001). Social acceptance of children with mental retardation: Testing the contact hypothesis with an Italian sample. *International Journal of Behavioral Development, 25*(3), 279–286.

May, P. A., Brooke, L., & Gossage, J. P. (2000). Epidemiology of fetal alcohol syndrome in a South African community in the western cape province. *American Journal of Public Health, 90*(12), 1905–1912.

Merrick, J., Morad, M., & Levy, U. (2001). Spiritual health in residential centers for persons with intellectual disability in Israel: A national survey. *International Journal of Adolescent Medicine& Health, 13*(3), 245–251.

Miles, M. (1997). Afghan children and mental retardation: Information, advocacy and prospects. *Disability & Rehabilitation: An International Multidisciplinary Journal, 9*(11), 496–500.

Miles, M. (1998). Development of community based rehabilitation in Pakistan: Bringing mental handicap into focus. *International Journal of Disability, 45*(4), 431–448.

Mitchell, D. R. (1995, April). Special education policies and practices in the pacific rim region. Paper presented at the 73rd Annual International Convention of the Council for Exceptional Children, Indianapolis, IN.

Mizrachi, N. (2001). When the hospital becomes home. *Journal of Contemporary Ethnography, 30*(2), 203–239.

Morris, J. (1999). Disabled children, child protection systems and the Children Act 1989. *Child Abuse Review, 8,* 91–108.

Nunnelley, J., & Fields, T. (1999). Anger, dismay, guilt, anxiety – The realities and roles in reporting child abuse. *Young Children, 17,* 111–116.

Olsson, M. B., & Hwang, C. P. (2001). Depression in mothers and fathers of children with intellectual disability. *Journal of Intellectual Disability Research, 45*(6), 535–543.

Oosterhoorn, R., & Kendrick, A. (2001). No sign of harm: Issues for disabled children communicating about abuse. *Child Abuse Review, 10*(4), 243–253.

Orelove, F. P., Hollahan, D. J., & Myles, K. T. (2000). Maltreatment of children with disabilities: Training needs for a collaborative response. *Child Abuse & Neglect, 24*(2), 185–194.

Patterson, J. M., & Kratz, B. (2002). *Child maltreatment among children with chronic illnesses and disabilities.* Retrieved February 20, 2003 from http://www.mincava.umn.edu/CAPS/Seminars/Patterson.ppt.

Pencovici, A. (2001). Kfar-Tikva – Therapeutic concept for people with special needs: Knock, knock, knock . . . is someone out there? *Child & Youth Services, 22*(1–2), 23–36.

Pervova, I. (1998). Children and youth with special needs in Russia, and educational services to meet them. *Education and Treatment of Children, 21*(3), 412–423.

Prevent Child Abuse America (n.d.). *Fact sheet: Maltreatment of children with disabilities.* Retrieved March 7, 2003 from http://www.preventchildabuse.org.

Rimmerman, A., Hozmi, B., & Duvdevany, I. (2000). Contact and attitudes toward individuals with disabilities among students tutoring children with developmental disabilities. *Journal of Intellectual & Developmental Disability, 25*(1), 13–18.

Saetermoe, C. L., Scattone, D., & Kim, K. H. (2001). Ethnicity and the stigma of disabilities. *Psychology & Health, 16*(6), 699–714.

Schwartz, C., & Armony-Sivan, R. (2001). Students' attitudes to the inclusion of people with disabilities in the community. *Disability & Society, 16*(3), 403–413.

Schwartz, C., Duvdevany, I., & Azaiza, F. (2002). Working families whose children have disabilities: Service provision by Jewish and Arab Israeli social workers. *International Social Work, 45,* 353–373.

Schwartz, C., & Rabinovitz, S. (2001). Residential facilities in the community for people with intellectual disabilities: How neighbours' perceptions are affected by the interaction of facility and neighbour variables. *Journal of Applied Research in Intellectual Disabilities, 14*(2), 100–109.

Shor, R. (1997). Identification and reporting of maltreated children by teachers in Israel. *Early Child Development & Care, 134,* 61–73.

Shor, R. (1998). Pediatricians in Israel: Factors which effect the diagnosis and reporting of maltreated children. *Child Abuse & Neglect, 22*(2), 143–153.

Shor, R. (2000). Child maltreatment: Differences in perceptions between parents in low income and middle income neighborhoods. *British Journal of Social Work, 30*(2), 165–178.

Shor, R., & Haj-Yahia, M. M. (1996). A cross-cultural study of attitudes toward child maltreatment: Arab vs. Jewish students of mental health professions. *Journal of Applied Social Sciences, 20*(2), 135–145.

Sobsey, D. (2002). Exceptionality, education, and maltreatment. *Exceptionality, 10*(1), 29–46.

Stehlik, D. (2001). A brave new world? *Violence Against Women, 7*(4), 370–392.

Stratford, B., & Hannah, Ng. (2000). People with disabilities in China: Changing outlook, new solutions, growing problems. *International Journal of Disability, 47*(1), 7–14.

Strickler, H. (2001). Interaction between family violence and mental retardation. *Mental Retardation, 39,* 461–471.

Sullivan, P. M., & Knutson, J. F. (1998). The association between childhood maltreatment and disabilities in a hospital based pediatric sample and a residential treatment sample. *Child Abuse & Neglect, 22,* 271–288.

Sullivan, P. M., & Knutson, J. F. (2000). Maltreatment and disabilities: A population-based epidemiological study. *Child Abuse & Neglect, 24*(10), 1257–1273.

Tharinger, D., Burrows-Horton, C., & Millea, S. (1990). Sexual abuse and exploitation of children and adults with mental retardation and other handicaps. *Child Abuse & Neglect, 14,* 301–312.

U.S. Department of Health and Human Services (2001, February). *The risk and prevention of maltreatment of children with disabilities.* Retrieved on March 7, 2003 from http://www.calib.com/nccanch/prevmnth/actions/risk.cfm.

Verdugo, M. A., Bermejo, B., & Fuertes, J. (1995). The maltreatment of intellectually handicapped children and adolescents. *Child Abuse & Neglect, 19*(2), 205–215.

Vig, S., & Kaminer, R. (2002). Maltreatment and developmental disabilities in children. *Journal of Developmental and Physical Disabilities, 14*(4), 371–386.

Walker, A. P. (2002). Parenting stress: A comparison of mothers and fathers of disabled and non-disabled children. (Doctoral dissertation: University of North Texas, 2002). *Dissertation Abstracts International, 62,* 3393.

Wang, M. H. (1999). Factors influencing preferences for persons with disabilities: A conjoint analysis and cross-cultural comparison. *Dissertation Abstracts International, 60,* 0414.

Wescott, H. L., & Jones, D. (1999). Annotation: The abuse of disabled children. *Journal of Child Psychology & Psychiatry & Allied Disciplines, 40*(4), 497–506.

Westat, Inc. (1993). *A report on the maltreatment of children with disabilities.* Washington, DC: National Center on Child Abuse and Neglect.

Young, W. C. (1997). Families and the handicapped in northern Jordan. *Journal of Comparative Family Studies, 28*(2), 151–169.

Zarometidis, K., Papadaki, A., & Gilde, A. (1999). A cross-cultural comparison of attitudes toward persons with disabilities: Greeks and Greek-Americans. *Psychological Reports, 84*(3), 1189–1196.

Zeanah, P. D., & Hamilton, M. L. (1998). Staff perceptions of sexuality-related problems and behaviors of psychiatrically hospitalized children and adolescents. *Child Psychiatry & Human Development, 29*(1), 49–64.

9. A META-ANALYSIS OF COMPARATIVE STUDIES OF DEPRESSIVE SYMPTOMS IN MOTHERS OF CHILDREN WITH AND WITHOUT DISABILITIES

George H. S. Singer[*]

INTRODUCTION

This chapter addresses the question of how we might best characterize the morale of mothers of children with disabilities. Views of this question have undergone substantial evolution over the past quarter century (Turnbull & Turnbull, 2002). Early writers on the topic emphasized negative impacts on the family. Farber (1959) characterized the birth of a mentally retarded child as a tragic crisis that over time impeded the family from developing normally. Olshansky (1962) described the typical reaction of parents to a child with mental retardation as long-term demoralization, which he termed "chronic sorrow." These assertions were then followed by empirical studies suggesting high levels of depression in mothers of children with disabilities (Cummings et al., 1966; Gath, 1977). Gath (1977), for example, compared two groups of parents with and without children with disabilities on a researcher developed measure of psychological distress and found significantly higher levels in parents of children with disabilities. She titled her

[*]George Singer is Professor at the University of California at Santa Barbara, California.

Administering Special Education: In Pursuit of Dignity and Autonomy
Advances in Educational Administration, Volume 7, 189–221
© 2004 Published by Elsevier Ltd.
ISSN: 1479-3660/doi:10.1016/S1479-3660(04)07009-X

report, "The impact of an abnormal child upon the parents," seeming to imply that emotional distress, perhaps even mental illness, was the most characteristic impact. This literature also appeared to imply that the cause of parental distress was univariate, that is, the child's disability uniquely caused it. Early studies of parental distress selected child variables as the sole predictors of emotional distress (e.g. Beckman, 1983). Turnbull and Turnbull (2002) reviewed this literature and described this historical phase as pathogenic.

This point of view began to change in the mid 1980s when authors began to challenge the monolithic pessimistic model (Allen & Affleck, 1985; Turnbull et al., 1986; Wikler et al., 1986). In an influential essay Turnbull and her colleagues argued that the received view of families ignored evidence of effective coping, of families that were strengthened by their experience, and by positive attributions that family members held about their relatives with disabilities (Turnbull et al., 1986). They argued that researchers appeared to hold a negative bias and they over generalized based on limited data. Wikler et al. (1981) similarly described the differing perspectives of professionals and parents and argued that the negative emphasis prevalent among professionals ignored the more diverse and often more positive views of parents.

A number of newer studies have painted a much more complex picture of the impact of childhood disability on families. Evidence for a wide range of maternal responses has emerged regarding maternal depression, marital satisfaction, divorce, and sibling adaptation. Studies of marital satisfaction have been mixed, varying with type of disability as well as within specific disabilities (Hodapp & Krasner, 1995). Studies of siblings have found varied evidence for elevated risk of problem behaviors (Breslau & Prabucki, 1987), no unusual risk (Mates, 1982) and evidence of positive effects such as altruism and cooperativeness (Simeonson & Bailey, 1986). As discussed in this paper, some studies have found no significant differences in rates of depressive symptoms in parents of children with and without disabilities whereas others have reported significant differences. Thus there is considerable variability in findings contrary to the pathogenic hypothesis. Given the recognition of extensive variability, researchers have developed new models emphasizing parental and family adaptation. Singer and Irvin (1991) presented a stress and coping model based on Hill's ABCX model of family adjustment and research literature on adaptation to stress in individuals. The model allows for positive as well as maladaptive outcomes and they reviewed evidence for positive adaptation. Since then researchers have developed multivariate models attempting to account for the wide range of differences in how family members respond to a family member's disability (Orr, Cameron & Day, 1991).

Recently, a few studies have reported on parents who positively appraise their child with a disability and their children's impacts on the family (Barakat & Linney,

1995; Behr & Murphy, 1993; Hastings & Trute, 2003; Trute et al., 1980). The general consensus in this literature is that family *adaptation* should be the guiding construct for studying these families and the process of adaptation often involves creativity, resourcefulness, and effective coping. These effective responses, in turn, are associated with positive appraisals of children's contributions to their families (e.g. Gallimore et al., 1996; Hastings & Trute, 2002; Hodapp, 1995). Furthermore, several studies have presented multivariate models of parental response to a child's disability, showing that it is multiply determined by personal, social, and economic variables more so than characteristics of children (Smith et al., 2001).

Although researchers' views have evolved away from the pathogenic model, the question of whether or not children with disabilities meaningfully contribute to maternal depression is still an open one. Some studies show significantly higher levels of depression (Dumas et al., 1991) others have nonsignficant results (Walker et al., 1989). Despite the fact that the pathogenic model is outmoded, researchers continue to conduct comparative studies of levels of depressive symptoms in parents of children with and without disabilities (Blacher et al., 1997).

PARENTAL DEPRESSION

Parental depression is a topic of major contemporary concern in the literature on public mental health (Hays et al., 1995; Lin et al., 1986) and developmental psychology (Coyne & Downey, 1990). People who experience elevated levels of depressive symptoms report feelings of hopelessness, low self-esteem, fatigue, sleep disruption, difficulty in experiencing pleasure, and somatic complaints. It not only constitutes suffering in its own right but it has serious consequence for other members of the family, particularly young children. Downey and Coyne (1990), in reviewing the literature in which depressed and non depressed mothers of infants and toddlers were directly observed, concluded that elevated levels of depressive symptoms disrupt normal parenting of typically developing infants and young children. When contrasted with non-depressed parents, those who experience affective problems show consistent differences in their behavioral and emotional responsiveness to their children. Depressed parents interact less with their children and their interactions are marked by more negative affect and less positive affect. They are less contingently responsive to children, and are more likely to use explosive or harsh discipline. In turn, young children of depressed parents are less likely to direct their behavior toward their parents, smile and less likely to express positive affect. These children are also more irritable and fussy. The disrupted parent-child relationship places children at risk for social and emotional problems. When compared with children of non-depressed parents, children of depressed parents show, on average, three times the rate of affective disorders (Downey & Coyne, 1990).

It should be noted that this connection between depressive symptoms and maternal interaction with young children with disabilities has not been supported by research. Smith et al. (1991) conducted direct observations of 48 mothers with their infants with disabilities and correlated depressive symptoms and mother/infant interaction. They found *no meaningful relationship* between maternal depressive symptoms and parent/child interactions. It is possible that early intervention services help distressed mothers to interact positively. Nothing is known about the connection between depressive symptoms and mother/child interactions in older children and youth with disabilities. Even with this finding, the topic of elevated depressive symptoms is important in its own right. For example, Breslau and Prabucki (1987) reported that maternal stress and depressive symptoms were predictive of emotional and behavioral problems in siblings of children with chronic illness and disability. Kobe and Hammer (1994) reported a strong association between parental depressive symptoms and depression in children with mental retardation. And, as described below, elevated depressive symptoms indicate daily living problems for the women who experience them.

ELEVATED DEPRESSIVE SYMPTOMS
VS. DEPRESSION

Before examining the studies on depressive symptoms and depression in parents of children with and without disabilities, a brief discussion of the construct, depression, is necessary. In the psychological and psychiatric literature a distinction is made between *depressive symptoms*, *subclinical depression*, and *clinical depression* (Breslau et al., 1982). Depressive symptoms are measured by self-report inventories such as the Center for Epidemiological Studies Depression Scale (CES-D) (Radloff, 1975) and the Beck Depression Inventory (BDI) (Beck et al., 1963). These questionnaires ask people to report on common symptoms of depression. The most commonly used self-report measures of depressive symptoms have been analyzed in clinical diagnostic studies to determine cut-off scores that predict a clinical diagnosis via an interview with a trained diagnostician. The person so identified is said to manifest a psychological malady, major depressive disorder (MDD) or a related affective disorder. Typically, the self-report measures such as the CES-D over identify clinical cases (Lin et al., 1988). For example, the commonly used cut-off score for the CES-D is 16. Studies that compare the CES-D with clinical diagnoses indicate that this cut-off point over identifies case of depression by 36.4% (Hisaini et al., 1979). Despite this fact a custom has grown in the literature of labeling scores over clinical cut-offs as depression or sub-clinical depression. In this meta-analysis a distinction is made between depressive symptoms as measured by self-report instruments and major depression as measured by structured clinical interview.

Traditional clinical cut-off scores are used but solely as indicators of elevated depressive symptoms, not as indicators of major depression.

Evidence about the social significance of symptoms, however, blurs somewhat the functional distinction between elevated depressive symptoms and clinical depression (Hays et al., 1995; Klerman, 1989). People with elevated depressive symptoms have shown considerable limitation and distress in social, work, and physical functioning. Further, elevated depressive symptoms may have important consequences for young children. In some of the studies reviewed by Downey and Coyne (1990), levels of depressive symptoms that were only slightly above the cut-off scores but were strongly associated with disrupted parent-child interactions. Hays et al. (1995) reported that elevated but subclinical levels of depressive symptoms were associated with lowered well-being, impaired role function, impaired social function, and poor general health. In their longitudinal study of 1,790 persons they found that people with depressive symptoms but without current major depression had lower levels of functioning than people with serious chronic illnesses including congestive heart failure and other heart disease. Thus elevated levels of depressive symptoms are an important set of phenomena in themselves when considering parental functioning. In this review, we discuss self-reported symptoms as measured by commonly used short depression instruments. Scores above clinical cut-off scores indicate elevated depressive symptoms. The term "major depression" is only used in reference to the one study using structured clinical interviews for determining "caseness."

META-ANALYSIS AS A TEST OF THE PATHOGENIC MODEL

The purpose of this paper is to consider the accumulated evidence regarding the pathogenic model for mothers of children with disabilities. In order to address this issue, methods from meta-analysis and traditional literature review are employed to summarize the published studies on comparisons of elevated depressive symptoms in mothers of children with disabilities and typically developing children. Meta analysis affords a statistical synthesis of a quantitative body of research.

When a group of studies utilize the similar measures, it is possible to mathematically combine them as if they represent one large investigation of a much larger sample than any one study can muster. Meta analysis overcomes problems that are inherent in typical inferential statistics. These problems relate to the impact of the size of the sample on statistical significance. Meta analysis is particularly useful for summarizing a literature characterized by mixed findings.

The pathogenic model implies at least three assumptions that can be treated as hypotheses for a meta analysis. The pathogenic model would predict the following:

(1) The effect size for the difference between average depressive symptom levels in parents of children with disabilities and parents of typically developing children will be moderate to large. The pathogenic hypothesis would predict a large effect size, d, of 0.80 and above based on Cohen's suggested definition of a large effect size (Cohen, 1977).

(2) The pathogenic model suggests little variability in parental emotional response to their children with disabilities because it assumes that all parents are negatively impacted. Thus a second hypothesis is the variability in depressive symptom scores of parents of children with disabilities will be lower than the variability in parents of children without disabilities.

(3) When comparing the percentage of mothers who score above the clinical cut-off scores on the BDI and CES-D the effect size will be moderate to large, $d > 0.35$.

METHODS

Sampling Procedure

Studies were identified for this review through computer searches of several large databases: PsychInfo, PubMed, Eric, and Dissertation Abstracts. Four different researchers mounted the searches. They were instructed to use the following descriptors for their search: children and disabilities, or children and mental retardation, or children and chronic illness, or children and developmental disabilities, or parents and the above disability labels, mothers and the above disability label, fathers and the above disabilities, and depression or stress or distress. Keyword and titles searches were conducted. In addition to the general computer searches we examined titles of every article in 64 journals and searched for the above terms. When an article was located it was reviewed and reference citations were examined to find any articles that had not been found through the computer search. We also contacted authors who have published on the topic and requested unpublished data or further information about published studies.

In order to be included in the study, research reports had to meet specific criteria: (a) the study must have completed between 1975 and 2003, (b) utilized published standardized measures of depressive symptoms or standardized methods of making a clinical diagnosis, (c) included one or more comparison groups of parents of children with developmental disabilities and parents of typically developing children or presented multiple regression models of predictors of parental depressive symptoms, (d) recruited subjects in the United States or Canada; and (e) provided sufficient statistical information for a meta analysis. In regard to dependent measures, we excluded studies using the Questionnaire on Resources and Stress because it has been convincingly challenged as a measure of depressive symptoms (Masters, 1997). Once all articles were evaluated for adherence to the inclusion criteria, 19 studies were included in the meta-analysis. We included unpublished doctoral dissertations. Table 1 lists all studies.

When studies presented means and standard deviations for more than one disability group, they were averaged so that there was only one effect size per study.

Similarly, when longitudinal data was reported the combined average across each time was calculated.

Analyses

For purposes of conducting meta analyses we report a weighted effect size, d, recommended by Hedges and Olkin (1985). The effect size is a standardized index of the difference between levels of a phenomenon in two populations. The effect size was calculated by subtracting the mean for mothers of typically developing children from the mean for mothers of children with disabilities, and dividing by the pooled standard deviation. The d statistic is usually reported as a single number ranging from 0 to 2.

As a general rule of thumb Cohen (1977) suggested that effect size from 0 to 0.29 are low, 0.3 to 0.79, moderate and above 0.8, large. It should be noted that, while convenient, this rule of thumb gives only a rough interpretation. A way to refine the interpretation of an effect sizes is by comparing findings from one meta analysis with other related findings. In this chapter, the d statistic from maternal depressive symptoms is compared to effect sizes from research on elevated depressive symptoms in divorced vs. married women and in employed vs. unemployed men and women.

QUALITY OF STUDIES

Before presenting the meta analysis, it is important to examine the quality of the studies under review. Meta analysis has been criticized when authors have grouped

Table 1. Meta Analysis of Group Comparison Studies of Depressive Symptoms in Mothers of Children with Developmental Disabilities.

Authors/Date	N Subjects		Disability Category			Mean (S.D.)		Effect Size d
	Dis	ND	Sample Dis. Group	Child Age, Mean (S.D.)	Measure	Disability	Typical	
Barakat and Linney (1992)	29	28	Mean age: 34.9 (8.13) Yrs. education: 12.38 (1.61) 8 single SES: 34.8 (12.73)	Spina Bifida 8.45 years (1.74)	BSI	1.88 (0.13)	1.84 (0.15)	0.29
Beckman (1991)	27	27	Mean age: 32 (4.9) Yrs. education: 15.3 (3.3)	Moderate/Severe developmental disability 3.83 years (1.26)	PSI-D	25 (7.8)	20.5 (6.6)	0.61
Blacher, Lopez, Shapiro and Fusco (1997)	148	101	Latina immigrants Low SES Single: 21.5% 88.5 married	Mental retardation 3–19 years	CES-D	Percent >16 50%	33%	0.36
Breslau, Glenn and Davis (1988)	319	360	Mean age: 41 (7.9)	Cerebral palsy	CES-D	11.76 (9.87)	8.31 (8.25)	0.38

Study								
Breslau, Staruch and Mortimer (1982)	369	456	White: 79% Black: 21% Married: 68% Single: 32% Income Low: 33% Middle: 25% Upper middle: 42%	Mylodysplasia Cystic fibrosis Multiple disabilities 8–23 years	Four questions from Langer	1.8 (1.5)	1.4 (1.3)	0.28
Bristol, Gallagher and Schopler (1988)	31	25	White: 76% African-American: 24% Age: 30.47 (4.86) SES: 41.63 (13.59)	Autism 3.82 years (1.04)	CES-D	14.39 (10.66)	9.12 (7.93)	0.54

Mean age: 37 (8.3) Married: 75% Single: 25% Middle class Mean yrs. education: 11.9 (2.4)

Cerebral palsy Mylodysplasia Cystic fibrosis Multiple disabilities Median age: 10.5 years

Table 1. (*Continued*)

Authors/Date	N Subjects		Sample Dis. Group	Disability Category Child Age, Mean (S.D.)	Measure	Mean (S.D.)		Effect Size d
	Dis	ND				Disability	Typical	
Cameron, Dobson and Day (1991)	39	40	Yrs. education[a]: 5.0	Developmental delay 3.99 years	PSI Depression Scale	19.92 (6.06)	21.20 (5.84)	−0.21
Capelli (1990)	46	46	Canadian occupation Housewife: 30% Skilled labor: 19% Unskilled: 17% Semi-professional: 11% Professional: 11% Other: 10% Years married: 12.8 (5.4) High school: 56% Some jr. College: 13% Jr. College: 6%	Spina Bifida 7.25 years (4.35)	CES-D	10.6 (9.1)	9.0 (7.2)	0.19

Study			Sample characteristics	Disability group	Measure	M (SD)	M (SD)	d
Gowen, Johnson, Martin and Applebaum (1989)	21	20	Some university: 4% University: 17% Graduate: 2%; Mean age: 31.15 (6.64); 20 married; 1 single; Education 6 post high school, 6 college, 7 graduate	7 down syndrome; 2 developmental delay; 4 cerebral palsy; 8 developmental disabilities; Age: 0.5–2.25 months	CES-D	10.2 (9.26)	8.0 (6.5)	0.26
Guess (1996)	35	18	Mothers[b]: 75% Father: 25% Married: 77% Black: 45% Other: 3% White: 62%	Mental retardation Autism Age: 5.25 years	PSI depression subscale	20.7 (6.39)	22.4 (5.68)	−0.27
Harris and McHale (1989)	30	30	Married: 34.1 years (7.93) Mean income: $18[c] ($12.5)	Mental retardation Age: 7.7 years	BDI[c]	5.77 (5.0)	3.87 (4.24)	0.40
Kazak (1987)	125	127	All married	36 mental retardation	Langer	4.21 (3.19)	3.16 (2.1)	0.39

Table 1. (*Continued*)

Authors/Date	N Subjects		Disability Category			Mean (S.D.)		Effect Size d
	Dis	ND	Sample Dis. Group	Child Age, Mean (S.D.)	Measure	Disability	Typical	
			Mean age: 21 years (9–30) 43 PKU Mean age: 3 years (1–8) 46 Spina Bifida Mean age: 7 years (1–16)					
Kazak and Marvin (1984)	53	53		Spina Bifida	Langer			0.49[c]
Miller, Gordon, Daniele and Diller (1992)	69	63	Married: 83% Single: 17% Median age: 32 Employed: 42% <$25[c]: 21% $25–39.9: 13% $40–59.9: 24% $60–above: 42%	31 cerebral palsy 16 paraplegia 9 developmental delay 4 orthopedic 4 quadriplegia 3 spina bifida 2 TBI	Depression scale of BSI	54.6 (10.74)	51 (8.68)	0.37
Roach, Orsmond and Barrat 1999	41	58	Mean age: 35.8	Down syndrome 3 years	PSI depression scale	18.88 (4.5)	16.84 (4.1)	0.47

Study							
Selzer, Greenberg, Floyd, Pettee and Hong (1998)	92	126	Developmental disability Adults >30 years	SES: 50.51	CES-D	10.1 (8.8)	9.1 (7.1)	0.11
Scott, Atkinson, Minton and Bowman (1997)	46	46	Down syndrome 1.18 years	Canadian middle class	BDI	7.61	5.66	0.38
Walker, Ortiz-Valdes and Newbrough (1989)	24	24	24 mental retardation 8–19 years	Married: 71% Single: 29%	CES-D	9.67 (9.75)	10.12 (10.08)	−0.05
Wolf, Noh and Speechly (1989)	61	62	30 autism 31 down syndrome: 8.9 (4.0)	Mean age: 35.5 (10.4) Yrs. education: 13.7 (4.7) Income mean: $22.4[c] ($5.8)	BDI	9.24 (7.27)	6.05 (5.88)	0.47

[a] Median Hollingshead category.
[b] Fathers and mothers' scores were not disaggregated.
[c] Data averaged across time periods.

together studies with varying quality in their design, implementation, or analysis. There are many threats to the quality of a study and its report. After examining the studies under review carefully, two issues appear to deserve particular attention: the equivalence of comparison groups and the quality of the dependent measures.

Equivalence of Comparison Groups. Equivalence of the comparison groups on demographic variables is important because some of these variables have been shown to correlate with depression in the general population (Kessler et al., 1994; Lin et al., 1986). Specifically, gender, employment status, marital status, age, SES, minority ethnic status and low educational achievement systematically co-vary with depression. Eaton and Kessler (1981) studied 2,867 persons in a national survey and found that married people had consistently lower depression scores on the CES-D (Mean = 14.5) than single (Mean = 17.1) and divorced persons (Mean = 28.2). Similarly, years of education correlate with depression in such a way that people with 0–7 years of education had average CES-D scores of 25.3, those with 12 years; 15.6, and those with 13+ years; 8.8 (Eaton & Kessler, 1981). These findings were replicated in subsequent large scale studies (Lin et al., 1986). Finally, depression scores varied systematically with employment such that unemployed persons had average scores of 28.1 compared to 13.1 for employed persons (Eaton & Kessler, 1981). Other studies have found a similar pattern in regard to social class with lower SES persons more vulnerable than persons from higher SES groups (Myers et al., 1974). A recent national prevalence study again found that income, gender, ethnicity and education are demographic correlates of depression (Kessler et al., 1994). This study, the largest to date, found that Hispanic and African American ethnicity increased risk of depression.

Although equivalence of samples in any group comparison study is important, there is a need for added vigilance in comparative research involving families of children with disabilities because there is reason to believe that the distribution of childhood disability is skewed toward lower SES groups because of environmental and social circumstances that increase risk of disability (Hodapp & Krasner, 1995).

Most of the studies under review dealt effectively with the issue of group equivalence by either demonstrating no significant differences on *t*-tests of differences between group means on key demographic variables, or by controlling for differences by using analysis of covariance methods. Three studies did not report the demographic characteristics of their samples (Brown & Pacini, 1989; Kazak, 1987; Walker et al., 1989) and information was not available for another (Glidden, 1998) and so it is not possible to determine if groups were equivalent or if differences were controlled.

Sampling procedure. With one exception all parents of children with disabilities appear to be convenience samples recruited from clinics and early intervention programs. Given the low prevalence of developmental disabilities, convenience samples are the norm in research on parents and families. Selzer et al. (1998) drew their sample of mothers of children with disabilities from a larger population study conducted in Minnesota. It may be a more representative of parents of children with disabilities. It, however, is the only study I found that reports on depressive symptoms in mothers of *adult* children. Other research has suggested that by the time children with developmental disabilities reach adulthood, most parents have adapted and do not an perceive increased burden of care. Thus the effect size in the Selzer et al. (1998) study is likely low because of the age of the children. In all of the other studies under review the age of the children with disabilities ranged from infancy to age 21. In three studies, comparison groups were drawn from large randomized samples (Breslau et al., 1986, 1988; Selzer et al., 1998). These three present the most representative data for mothers on children who do not experience disabilities. Representativeness is also likely to be a function of sample size. The studies by Breslau et al. (1986, 1988), Blacher et al. (1997), Kazak (1987), Masters (1998), and Selzer et al. (1998) had the largest samples.

Measures. The studies identified for this review utilized five different measures of depression. The following catalogue of these measures presents their psychometric properties and evidence for validity.

The Beck Depression Inventory (BDI) (Beck et al., 1963) is the most frequently used measure in the depression literature (Shaw et al., 1985). It is a 21-item self-report measure of cognitive, mood, and physiological symptoms that are characteristic of depression (e.g. self-dislike, hopelessness, fatigue). Each symptom is rated by choosing among five responses per item ordered by incremental increases in the severity of the symptom. Over a twenty-five year period a substantial body of evidence has accumulated regarding its psychometric properties and validity (Beck et al., 1988). The split-half reliability for the instrument was reported at 0.93 (Beck et al., 1961). Internal consistency has been established at adequate levels (Gallagher et al., 1982). Evidence for concurrent validity with the Research Diagnostic Criteria and psychiatric interview has also been published (Gallagher et al., 1983). It correlates highly with other depression measures, but unlike several depression measures it discriminates well between depression and anxiety. Clinical cut-off scores have been developed for the BDI. Based upon a meta-analysis of 28 studies, Nietzel et al. (1987) support a score of 10 as a cut-off for mild depression. Three studies reviewed here used the BDI (Dumas et al., 1991; Harris & McHale, 1989; Glidden, 1988).

The Center for Epidemiological Studies Depression Scale (CES-D) (Radloff, 1975) is comprised of 20 items that were selected from five previously published depression measures in order to assess five major components of depression: (1) depressed mood; (2) feelings of guilt and worthlessness; (3) feelings of helplessness and hopelessness; (4) loss of appetite; (5) sleep disturbance; and (6) psycho-motor retardation. Respondents are asked to indicate on a four-point scale how often they have experienced a depressive symptom during the past week. The CES-D has been reported as having high internal consistency with an alpha of 0.89 and 0.90 in two large studies (Lin et al., 1986) and test-retest reliability ratings ranging from 0.70 to 0.45 depending upon the length of time between assessments (Radloff, 1977). The scale correlates highly with other measures of depression such as the Beck, Zung, and Minnesota Multiphasic Personality Inventory (Radloff, 1977) and it has discriminated between groups exposed to major life stressors compared to groups in more stable circumstances (Lin et al., 1986). The CES-D has been used in at least four large epidemiological studies with a total combined sample size of over 5,500 respondents (Lin et al., 1986). Clinical cut-off scores have been empirically established with a score of 16 and above as the most commonly used indicator of possible depression (Meyers & Weisman, 1980). Seven studies under review used the CES-D (Blacher et al., 1997; Breslau & Davis, 1988; Bristol et al., 1988; Capelli; Gowen et al., 1989; Selzer et al., 1998; Walker et al., 1989).

The CES-D and the BDI are the two most commonly used measures of depressive symptoms and deserve high weighting in respect to instrumentation.

The Langer Symptom Inventory (Langer, 1962) was developed as a instrument for large epidemiological survey studies in order to detect the incidence and prevalence of mental illness. It consists of 22 closed ended questions which ask about whether or not respondents experience psychological, psycho-physiological, and physiological complaints. Items were selected by their ability to discriminate between some groups of people who were known to have a mental illness from people who were known not to have mental illness. Prior to the development of more focused depression-specific measures, it was one of the most widely used measures of mental distress and was employed in several large-scale studies (e.g. Billings & Moos, 1984; Dohrenwend et al., 1980). Based upon a conceptual and empirical review, Seiler (1973) recommended that the instrument was best interpreted as a measure of psychological and physiological stress. Subsequently, the instrument has been refined by reducing the number of its items to the psychological symptoms items alone. A scale composed of these items was shown to be highly predictive of a current psychiatric diagnosis in the category of depression-anxiety disorders (Wheaton, 1980). Six of the twenty-two items ask about symptoms that are commonly associated with depression and anxiety. They inquire about nervousness, low spirits, feelings of isolation, restlessness, worry, and inability to take care of things because "you can't get going." When internal reliability of this subscale was analyzed it yielded a Cronbach alpha of 0.67. The instrument does not identify clinical cut-off scores. One study under review here used the smaller subset of depression questions from the Langer Inventory (Brelau et al., 1988) whereas Kazak (1987) used the entire 22 item instrument.

The study by Breslau et al. (1988) should not be given as much weight as those employing the full depression scales.

Parent Stress Inventory-Depression Scale (Abidin, 1995) is a 9 item scale, one of 13 scales that make-up the Parent Stress Inventory. It intends to measure symptoms that suggest significant depression in a parent (Abidin, 1995) with particular reference to parenting. That is, high scores on this scale are meant to indicate that a parent finds it difficult to mobilize the energy, both psychic and physical, to carry out parenting responsibilities (Abidin, 1995). The items were developed by referencing items from widely used depression measures. They differ from items on the most widely used measures such as the BDI and CES-D in that, with a few exceptions, they refer specifically to depressive cognitions and feelings *as they pertain to parenting*. For example, one item of the CES-D reads, "I thought my life had been a failure." An item about a sense of failure on the PSI-Depression scale reads, "When my child misbehaves or fusses too much, I feel responsible, as if I didn't do the right thing." Similarly an item about guilt on the BDI reads, "I feel guilty most of the time." compared with "I feel guilty about the way I feel about my child" on the PSI-D.

Evidence for the internal consistency of the scale was established with a normative sample of 2,633 parents and an additional validation sample with coefficient alphas of 0.84 and 0.78. Test-retest reliability studies carried out over a three month period found correlations of 0.91 for the Parent Domain, a group of scales of which the Depression scale is one. A principal components analysis yielded evidence suggesting that the nine items on the Depression scale measures a "moderately distinct source of stress" (Abidin, 1995, p. 32).

Because the focus of the PSI Depression scale is on parent's depressive reactions to their child, there is a question of the content validity of the PSI-Depression scale as a measure of the broader construct of psychological depression. Abidin (1993) reports on one study with evidence for convergent and divergent validity. It is probable that the PSI-Depression measure may assess a constellation of attitudes and feelings concerning depressive responses about parenting rather than the broader construct of depression. No clinical cut off scores have been reported for the PSI Depression subscale as a predictor of clinical depression. The author does recommend that people with high scores on this domain should be provided with counseling aimed at enhancing self-esteem and assessing the significance of the depressive symptoms. The question of whether or not the PSI Depression scale is a measure of depressive symptoms, *per se*, is unresolved at present. Conservatively, it is best considered an indicator of difficulties that have a depressive tone in the parent-child relationship rather than a more pervasive depression syndrome. However, depression in regard to child rearing is an important variable in the study of families of children with disabilities so two studies that used the PSI-D is included in this review (Beckman, 1991).

The PSI Depression subscale, nonetheless, should be regarded with caution as an indicator of depressive symptoms. Thus the two studies under review that used this measure should be given less weight (Beckman, 1991; Guess, 1996).

The National Institute of Mental Health Diagnostic Interview Schedule (DIS) (Robins et al., 1981) is a structured interview that has been used by trained lay people in research studies of depression and other mental illness. It generates psychiatric diagnoses according to the DSM-III and the Research Diagnostic Criteria. The DIS is a structured interview that is administered in person, or by telephone. In addition to a series of questions about common symptoms of depression (e.g. lost appetite, insomnia, hypersomnia, excessive guilt, trouble concentrating, suicidal thoughts), it includes questions about history of the emotional problem, duration, and present functioning. Consequently, in addition to a diagnosis it also yields lifetime prevalence of depressive episodes, age of first on-set, and the duration of episodes. Evidence for the validity of the DIS has been provided in several psychiatric patient and nonpatient populations (Helzer et al., 1985). The DIS and other structured interview methods are generally considered to be more accurate than self-report questionnaires in assigning a clinical diagnosis of a mental disorder as they adhere more closely to the diagnostic practices of mental health care providers. Breslau et al. (1988) reported a comparison of DIS lay interviewer's ratings and psychiatrist's ratings of patients and found reasonably high levels of agreement: kappa was 0.68, sensitivity was 0.93 and specificity was 0.77. The DIS was used in one of the studies under review here (Breslau & Davis, 1988).

The DIS is the only measure in this report capable of determining whether or not a person has clinical depression. Thus it contributes uniquely to this study.

In summary, all of the measures in the studies under review meet traditional psychometric standards for reliability and all have evidence for validity. The clinical cut-off scores on the BDI and CES-D, when compared to clinical evaluation tend to over estimate clinical depression. However, these scores predict problems in daily functioning and have social significance as indicators of stress. The one measure that has questionable validity as a measure of general depressive symptoms is the PSI Depression subscale. The DIS provides the only evidence for major depression as measured by clinicians because it is administered by interview and asks questions regarding duration of symptoms, a key variable in determining whether or not a person meets the DSM IV criteria for Major Depression.

RESULTS

Hypothesis 1 *(Overall effect size).* When pooled these 15 studies have a combined sample size of 1,669 mothers of children with disabilities and 1,706 mothers of typically developing children. The overall weighted effect size was 0.28, a small effect according to Cohen's (1977) rule of thumb. The pathogenic hypothesis, consequently, is rejected.

Hypothesis 2 *(Less variability in mothers of children with disabilities).* In every case the variability in the samples of mothers of children with disabilities was greater than that in mothers of children without disabilities. Contrary to the pathogenic model, children with disabilities do not uniformly impact their mothers.

Hypothesis 3 *(Percentage of parents with elevated levels of depressive symptoms).* Twelve of the studies under review utilized measures that have well established clinical cut-off scores indicating high risk for clinical depression. Table 2 shows the percentage of parents in the studies under review with scores of 16 and above on the CES-D. These percentages were determined by converting clinical cut-off scores to standardized z-scores, using the observed means and standard deviations. Across nine studies using the CES-D, an average of 30% of mothers of children with disabilities compared to 18% of mothers of children without disabilities had scores above the cut-off, a difference of 12%. Table 3 presents similar findings from studies that utilized the BDI. The overall percentage for mothers of children with disabilities was 34% vs. 17%, a difference of 17%. As a result, having a child with a disability raises the incidence of elevated depressive symptoms by 14.5%. The effect size difference is small $d = 0.28$. Once again the pathogenic hypothesis is rejected.

Hypothesis 4 *(Difference in prevalence of clinical depression).* The pathogenic model implied that there would be more clinical depression in mothers of children with disabilities. Only one study was available that used clinical interview methods to determine "caseness." Breslau and Davis (1988) utilized the DIS (Robins et al., 1981) to interview the mothers in their study. There were only small differences in the percentages of mothers who were diagnosed as having clinical depression. Both lifetime and six month rates of clinical depression were only slightly higher among mothers of children with disabilities, 18.4% vs. 16.6%, an effect size of $d = 0.04$. Because this finding is based on only one study, the pathogenic hypothesis can be provisionally rejected.

Table 2. Percentage of Mothers Scoring 16 or Above on CES-D Based on Z Scores.

Authors/Date	Mean (S.D.)		z score		Percent at or >16		Difference (%)
	Dis	ND	Dis	ND	Dis	ND	
Blacher, Lopez, Shapiro and Fusco (1997)					50	30	20
Breslau and Davis (1986)	11.76 (9.87)	8.31 (8.25)	0.42	0.93	33	17	16
Bristol, Gallagher and Schopler (1988)	14.39 (10.66)	9.12 (8.25)	0.15	0.83	44	20	24
Capelli (1990)	10.6 (9.1)	9.00 (7.20)	0.59	0.97	27	16	11
Gowen, Johnson, Marine, Goldman and Applebaum (1989)	10.20 (8.00)	9.26 (6.5)	0.63	1.23	26	11	15
Ortiz-Valdes (1987)	29.7 (9.8)	29.0 (9.1)	−1.39	−1.42	8	7	−1
Selzer, Greenberg, Floyd, Pettee and Hong (1989)	10.1 (8.8)	9.1 (7.1)	0.68	0.97	24	17	7
Walker, Ortiz-Valdes and Newbrough (1989)	10.46 (8.83)	10.12 (10.08)	0.66	0.58	25	28	−3
Wolf, Noh, Fishman and Speechley (1991)	9.24 (7.27)	6.05 (5.88)	0.92	1.69	17	4	13
Mean					28.4	16.8	11.6

Table 3. Comparison of Percentage of Mothers Scoring at or Above 10 on the BDI.

Study	Mean (S.D.)		Z score		Percentage >10	Difference (%)
	Dis	ND	Dis.	ND		
Dumas et al. (1991)	9.24 (7.27)	6.05 (5.88)	0.10	0.67	46	25	28
Harris and McHale (1989)	5.77 (5.0)	3.87 (4.24)	0.84	1.44	20	7	13
Mean					34	17	17

There were other ways in which the two groups differed. When the authors examined the time of onset of the first episode of MDD, they found that mothers of children with disabilities were much more likely to have experienced onset following the birth of their child with disability than were mothers after the birth of a typically developing child. Secondly, when women were asked about the number of lifetime episodes of MDD that they had experienced, mothers of children with disabilities reported significantly more episodes (mean of 16 vs. mean of 6.5, $t = 2.3$, $p = 0.02$). When the women with MDD were compared on a list of 16 symptoms of depression, mothers of children with disabilities were significantly more likely to experience excessive guilt and suicidal thoughts. For the small percentage of mothers of children with disabilities who require intensive treatment, therapists should be aware of increased vulnerability to repeated episodes.

Hypothesis 5 *(The child with a disability as the univariate cause of depressive symptoms).* This hypothesis cannot be tested via meta analysis and instead was examined through more traditional review methods. Studies that reported multivariate predictors of parental depressive symptoms were selected for review. Table 4 summarizes eight multivariate studies.

Bristol (1987) tested the Double ABCX theory of family adjustment to stress (Hill, 1958; McCubbin & Patterson, 1981). It holds that family response to a major stressful event or condition is determined by an interaction of background stress and the severity of the specific major stressor, family resources including social support, and routine coping skills as well a coping skills marshaled specifically in response to the target stressor. Hill originally developed the theory to explain the variability in family responses to wartime separation. Bristol (1987) employed this theory to try to account for variability in how parents adapt to young children with autism and other communication disorders. To assess stressors she used a measure of life events and one of severity of the child's symptoms. Family resources were measured with an assessment of informal and formal social support and an

Table 4. Multiple Regression Studies of Parental Depressive Symptoms: Significant Contributing Variables.

Author & Date	Subjects	N	Dependent Variable & Measure	Analysis	Predictive Variables	Parameter	Variance Accounted for by Full Model R^{2a}
Bristol (1987)	Mothers of children with autism & communicative disorders	45	Depression CES-D, Marital adjustment, Family adaptation	Canonical Correlation	Severity of disability, pile-up of other stressors,* family cohesion, informal social support, formal support, self blame, catastrophic beliefs, coping		0.33
Bristol, Gallagher and Schopler (1988)	Mothers and fathers of children with autism & communicative disorders	28 mothers	Depression CES-D	Multiple regression	Severity of disability, childcare, household work, disharmony re childcare*, disharmony house work,*** expressive support,** expressive disharmony**		0.43
Gill and Harris (1991)	Mothers children with autism ages 2–18	60	BDI	Multiple regression	Hardiness, social support		0.78****
Gowen et al. (1989)	Mothers of infants with disabilities	18	CES-D	multiple regression	*Child* Level of functioning, irritability, caregiving difficulty, sociability *Social Support* Number of sources, helpfulness, family, respite		0.53*** 0.13
McKinney and Peterson (1987)	Mothers children with disabilities ages 7 to 41 months	67	PSI depression scale	Multiple regression	Child characteristics Perceived control Spouse support control × support	Beta 0.32c – 0.70c 1.04c	0.36b
Trute (1995)	Children birth-8, developmental disabilities	88 couples, fathers & mothers	BDI	Multiple regression	Child related stress***, child's temperament, child's age, SES, self-esteem****, marital satisfaction****, respite***, social support		0.27

Study	Sample	N	Instrument	Analysis	Variables	Beta	R^2
Walker, Ortiz-Valdes and Newbrough (1989)	Diabetes, cystic fibrosis, mental retardation, well	95 mothers		Multiple regression	Child diagnosis, SES, employment		0.17
Wolf, Noh, Fisman and Speechly (1989)	Mothers and fathers of children with Downs Syndrome, and Austism	61 mothers	BDI	Multiple regression	Parenting stress[****] social support, interaction of social support & parenting stress[****]		0.29
Walker, Ortiz-Valdes and Newbrough (1989)	95 mothers of children ages 8–10 Mental retardation, diabetes, cystic fibrosis, well	24 m.r. 24 diabetes 23 cystic fibrosis 24 well	CES-D	Multiple regression	Child diagnosis m.r. c.f. diabetes SES employment	Beta −0.03 0.00 −0.09 −0.28 −0.21	0.17
Wolf, Noh, Fisman and Speechly (1989)	Mothers and fathers of children with Downs Syndrome, and Austism	61 mothers	Depression Beck Depression Inventory	Multiple regression	Parenting stress Social support Interaction support & stress	Beta 1.05[****] 0.43 −0.95[****]	0.29

[a] Absence of an asterisks indicates that p was not reported.
[b] $F = 11.85$, $p < 0.000$.
[c] $F = 3.67$, $p < 0.01$.
[*] $p = 0.10$
[**] $p = 0.05$
[***] $p = 0.01$
[****] $p = 0.001$

instrument that examines family coping strategies. The family definition of the stressor, a cognitive variable, was measured using a scale that asked about the ways the parents thought about the causes and meanings of the disability. In order to measure adaptation, Bristol employed three measures: one of Depression (CES-D), a measure of marital satisfaction (Marital Adjustment Test) and a measure of the harmony of the home and quality of parenting. For purposes of this review, only findings pertaining to depression are included. Bristol used canonical correlation techniques to test the model. Variables were entered into the equation in an order determined by the theory. The model accounted for 33% of the variance in maternal depressive symptoms. Table 4 shows the significant for the predictive variables. When shared variance with other predictors was accounted for, the pile-up of stressors made a statistically significant contribution to the prediction suggesting that on-going life stressors are a particularly important contextual variable that contributed to maternal depressive symptoms. It also shows that parent morale is multiply determined.

Bristol et al. (1988) focused on the contribution of child-centered variables and spousal support to parental depressive symptoms. Examining mothers and fathers of young children with autism and communication disorders, they used multiple regression analyses to predict depressive symptoms with a model consisting of childcare and household demands and disharmony between spouses about childcare and household work, expressiveness between spouses, and disharmony regarding expressive support. For mothers, the model accounted for 43% of the variance in CES-D scores. Disharmony between spouses contributed most to the prediction. For mothers, contextual variables – mainly spousal disharmony over household work roles, was the most significant predictor.

Gill and Harris (1991) investigated hardiness and social support as predictors of maternal depression in a group of 60 mothers of children with autism, ages 2–18. They used the Beck Depression Inventory as the measure of depressive symptoms. The construct of hardiness is a personality variable that has identified individuals who are able to withstand high levels of stress without negative effects (Kobasa, 1979). When scores from a measure of hardiness and combined scores from three measures of social support were regressed on the BDI scores, the two variables accounted for 60% of the variance with both social support and hardiness negatively correlated with depressive symptoms. Thus a combination of personality variables and social support predicted maternal distress.

Gowen et al. (1989) compared mothers of infants with disabilities compared to mothers of typically developing infants at four time intervals. For purposes of this review, only data from the observations at 27 months are included. They carried out two separate regression analyses using backward stepwise procedures to predict maternal scores on the CES-D. Child centered variables such as level of functioning, irritability, caregiving difficulty, and sociability accounted for 39% of the variance ($F = 3.62, p < 0.04$). A second analysis of social support regressed on the CES-D scores accounted for 13% of the variance and did not reach significance. They did not examine other contextual variables that mediated maternal distress in the other studies under review. This study does indicate that infant characteristics do predict depressive symptoms.

McKinney and Petersen (1987) studied 67 mothers of children with disabilities served in early intervention programs. Like Bristol (1987) they examined the contributions of child characteristics; a cognitive variable, perceived control; spousal support; and the interaction of perceived control and spousal support. Together they accounted for 36% of the variance in the depression scores ($R^2 = 0.37, F = 12.68, p < 0.000$). The interaction term was the most important predictor followed by child characteristics, and spousal support. All three made significant contributions to the prediction. Their use of an interactional term that examines the connection between a personality variable and marital variable is unique in the studies under review.

Trute (1995) studied predictors of depression in 88 Canadian mothers and fathers of young children with developmental disabilities. A six stage hierarchical regression model tested the contribution of child related stress, child temperament and characteristics, SES, parental self-esteem, marital satisfaction, respite care, and social support. In addition to the child related stress, spousal support and informal respite assistance along with self-esteem accounted for significant portions of the variance. They buffered child related stress. Overall the model accounted for 42% of the variance ($R^2 = 0.42, F = 3.70, p = 0.001$). Once again maternal distress was multiply determined.

Walker et al. (1989) examined a different contextual variable in addition to child diagnosis and SES, maternal employment status. Based upon earlier findings that mothers in the general population who are employed are less vulnerable to depression than mothers who are not, they studied the association of these variables with depressive symptoms in 95 mothers of children from four diagnostic groups: mental retardation, diabetes, cystic fibrosis, and children with out a disability or chronic illness. When they regressed the three variables on maternal scores on the CES-D, they accounted for 17% of the variance with SES being the most important predictor followed by employment status ($R^2 = 0.17, F = 3.67, p = 0.01$).

Wolf et al. (1989) studied 61 mothers and an equal number of fathers of children with Downs Syndrome. Their analysis proceeded in three stages. In the first they established that mothers of children with autism had elevated levels of depressive symptoms as did, to a lesser extent, mothers of children with Downs Syndrome. In the second step they regressed demographic variables and parenting stress on maternal depression scores and found that parenting stress was the only significant predictor. In a third step, they tested a model of parenting stress and social support and found that, for mothers, parenting stress is mediated by social support such that the more support, the less distress. For mothers the final model accounted for 27% of the variance in depression scores on the Beck Depression Inventory with social support making a significant contribution to the prediction when shared variance was taken into account. Thus contextual variables contribute to the prediction along with the child-centered variables.

Eight studies under review reported on predictive models of parental depression. Seven of these found that contextual and parental personality variables were important predictors of distress in addition to child related factors. Every study that included a measure of social support suggests that it mediates child related stress alone or in interaction with parental personality variables. The kind of social support that appears to be most important is spousal support in two parent heterosexual families. Disharmony between spouses appears to amplify stress related to caring for the child whereas a positive spousal relationship buffers this stress. In addition to social support and such personality variables as hardiness, self-esteem, and perceived control, other situational characteristics such as SES and employment were also significant predictors of parental symptoms in some studies. While child characteristics play a role, parental distress is multiply determined. The hypothesis that a child's disability is the univariate predictor of maternal distress is rejected.

DISCUSSION

The question of parental distress and its social significance is a controversial one because of the recent history of a seeming bias in the literature and its subsequent critique. For heuristic purposes, I posited a set of hypotheses based on the strong pathogenic theory which still has a hold on many professionals. These views are necessarily simplistic but provide a useful way to assemble and examine the extent research. Clearly, the picture that emerges from testing these hypotheses leads to a rejection of the outdated view that having a child with a disability causes most mothers to experience psychological distress. The pathogenic model should be laid to rest. It is probably not a good use of research resources to keep running comparative studies unless they are designed to ask much more sophisticated questions. In addition to rejecting the pathogenic model, the data also paint a more complex picture.

It is quite clear that parents of children with disabilities are a diverse population characterized by more variability on measures of depressive symptoms than the general population. In most cases the variability in parents of children with disabilities was higher than the comparison groups and this difference was significant. Thus there is a great deal of variability in how mothers respond to parenting a child with a disability. The multivariate studies indicate that a combination of community, familial, and personality variables are important sources of this variability.

An effect size of 0.28 suggests that the difference in levels of depressive symptoms between mothers of children with and without disability is small, much smaller than would be expected if the pessimistic tradition was correct. But the studies reviewed here do not mean that there is not a social problem. Effect size statistics are best understood in relationship to findings from the same or related areas of research (Cooper, 1989). For example, the percentage increase associated with unemployment and with divorce or separation can help put the findings in perspective for the purposes of judging their social significance. Four studies of large samples of people in the general population used the CES-D and reported the percentage of people who scored over 16 (cited by Lin et al., 1986). They found that unemployment for men and women combined raised the percentage of people with elevated depressive symptoms from 15 to 30% a difference of 15%. These same studies examined the difference between women who were married and women who were divorced or separated and found an average of 15 and 29% respectively, a difference of 14%. In this meta-analysis 18% mothers of typically developing children and 32% mothers of children with disabilities scored over the cut-off for minor depression on the CES-D, a difference of 14%.

It seems that, for mothers, parenting a preschool to young adult child with a disability has roughly the same impact on psychological distress as unemployment or divorce/separation. Although the pathogenic view greatly inflates the negative impact of children with disabilities and is clearly wrong, there is evidence of a socially significant problem that deserves public resources for remediation. Roughly one out of three mothers of children with disabilities are experiencing difficulties although two-thirds of this difficulty would be there from other causes. Fortunately, there is evidence suggesting that some of these problems can be effectively addressed with supportive services. *At the same time, it is essential to emphasize that most mothers of children with disabilities are not demoralized. On average roughly 68% of mothers in these studies did not have elevated symptom levels.* Consequently, it is important that service providers do not operate out of an assumption of parental emotional distress when clearly the norm is one of effective adaptation.

Supports for mothers reduce distress. A first generation of studies suggests that maternal depressive symptoms in mothers of children with disabilities can be effectively treated in the short-term through psychosocial interventions (Bristol et al., 1993; Nixon & Singer, 1994; Singer et al., 1988, 1989, 1995, 1989, 1999).

These studies relied on parent to parent connections, psycho-educational support groups, and other family support services to help parents. None used psychotherapy or medication. My colleagues and I found that the most effective interventions connected parents to other parents, taught psycho-educational coping skills in a highly participatory way, and connected parents to other family support services (Singer et al., 1989). Supports must address the practical, day-to-day stressors, that impact the lived reality of families. They must include concrete assistance as well has social and psychological support. Based on this research we believe that a combination of supports is most effective and that parent-to-parent assistance is a key part of an effective support program. The value of parent-to-parent support has been further confirmed in a five state randomized experimental evaluation of these programs (Singer et al., 1999). Although we did not measure depressive symptoms, we found that parent to parent programs significantly raised parent's self-efficacy for parenting, sense of positive acceptance, and helped them to solve specific problems.

What about the 8% of mothers with full clinical depression? In a multi-stage intervention, my colleagues and I found that mothers with actual clinical depression required one to one therapy in addition to the psycho-educational support group and linkage to other family support services. Based on our clinical experience, the mothers described by Breslau and Davis (1988) who had clinical depression require a therapeutic and medical approach.

Predictive models of parental depressive symptoms may also help to inform intervention efforts. Most of the studies reviewed here did not base their model on an explicitly stated theory. The majority appears to be influenced by the contextual model of depression that has evolved over the past 25 years from epidemiological studies of depression in the general population. This work has focused on the influence of demographic variables, life stress, role strain, social support, and personality variables as predictors (e.g. Lin et al., 1988). As with this work on the general population, studies of parents of children with disabilities find that stress in the form of major life events and on-going role strain is modulated by social support and such personality variables as hardiness, optimism, and self-esteem. These findings help to explain why there is such a range of variability in parental response to a child's disability and show that parental depression is the result of several forces and buffers. They further undermine the earlier univariate model of parental response to a child's disability by showing the complexity and variability of the phenomena.

The data summarized in Table 4 make it clear that depressive symptoms are due to a combination of variables. Each of these variables has different implications for treatment and research. Child related stressors can sometimes be ameliorated with behavioral, educational and social support interventions such as provision of respite care. Few of the thousands of intervention studies with children with disabilities and/or chronic illness have examined the secondary effects of child treatment on parental morale. Such data would be useful in helping practitioners identify the focus of interventions and perhaps the order in which different interventions should be offered.

The efficacy of informal social support is now a well-established finding in the general research on depression as well as the studies under review. Informal support appears to play a much more important role than formal assistance in maintaining parental morale. Little is known about how to help families nurture such support or how to assist isolate parents to become part of a supportive informal network. Surprisingly little work has been published on help for conflicted networks. In two parent families the spousal subsystem emerges as a key buffer to child related stress. Although considerable knowledge has been gained regarding prevention and treatment of marital discord, little is known about the value of these methods with parents of children with disabilities.

The studies under review suggest that family centered services ought to make support of marriage or other domestic partnerships a major focus. It is to be hoped that such services would be guided by as yet to be conducted research. The findings on the importance of spousal support should also raise concern about how single parents are faring. The finding regarding the pile-up of stressors suggests that mothers of children with disabilities are most at risk when they must deal with an accumulation of unwanted life events and daily difficulties in the absence of social support. This information could be useful for identifying families that are most in need of extra supports.

Further research is called for in regard to several other questions. Research needs to reflect the dramatic demographic changes occurring in the United States. The studies under review primarily focused on Anglo, white, middle class, married parents. Research is needed on single parents of children with disabilities and on parents from the many ethnic and linguistic minorities in the United States. Blacher and her colleagues (1996) presented data on prevalence of depression in low-income Latina mothers of children with and without disability. They reported that a full 50% of mothers of children with mental retardation scored over the clinical cut-off on the CES-D. This study indicates that at least one immigrant population requires additional supports.

In summary, the field has moved well beyond the pathogenic model although it continues to have an influence. The model is simply incorrect. The reactions that mothers have to parenting a child with a disability are varied and complex. The experience does raise the level of low morale in a small percentage of mothers. When combined with the general background of stress that women experience, it means that at anytime about one in three mothers of children with disabilities are experiencing low morale compared to 20% of parents of nondisabled children. These problems are amenable by comprehensive family support including assistance from other parents of children with disabilities. Thus, in all, the research supports an optimistic view of the possibilities for this population given a sufficient level of social support. Finally, the emerging literature on the many benefits of parenting children with disabilities provides a new goal for determining the effectiveness of supports.

REFERENCES

Asterisks (*) placed before a reference indicate a study included in the meta analysis.

Abidin, R. R. (1995). *Parenting stress index professional manual* (3rd ed.). Odessa, FL: Psychological Assessment Resources.

Allen, D. A., & Affleck, G. (1985). Are we stereotyping parents? A Postscript to Blacher. *Mental Retardation, 23*(4), 200–202.

*Barakat, L. P., & Linney, J. A. (1992). Children with physical handicaps and their mothers: The interaction of social support, maternal adjustment, and child adjustment. *Journal of Pediatric Psychology, 17*(6), 725–739.

Beck, A. T., Steer, R. A., & Garbin, M. G. (1988). Psychometric properties of the Beck depression inventory: Twenty-five years of evaluation. *Clinical Psychology Review, 8*, 77–100.

Beck, A. T., Ward, C. H., Mendelson, M., Mock, J., & Erbaugh, J. (1961). An inventory for measuring depression. *Archives of General Psychiatry, 4*, 561–571.

Beckman, P. J. (1983). Influence of selected child characteristics on stress in families of handicapped infants. *American Journal of Mental Deficiency, 88*(2), 150–156.

Beckman, P. J. (1991). Comparison of mothers' and fathers' perceptions of the effect of young children with disabilities. *American Journal on Mental Retardation, 95*(5), 585–595.

Billings, A., & Moos, R. (1984). Coping, stress, and social resources among adults with unipolar depression. *Journal of Personality and Social Psychology, 96*, 877–891.

*Blacher, J., Lopez, S., Shapiro, J., & Fusco, J. (1997). Contributions to depression in latina mothers of with and without children with retardation: Implications for caregiving. *Family Relations, 46*, 325–334.

*Breslau, N., & Davis, G. C. (1988). Chronic stress and major depression. *Archives of General Psychiatry, 43*(4), 309–314.

Breslau, N., & Prabucki, K. (1987). Siblings of disabled children: Effects of chronic stress in the family. *Archives of General Psychiatry, 44*(12), 1040–1046.

*Breslau, N., Staruch, K. S., & Mortimer, E. A. (1982). Psychological distress in mothers of disabled children. *American Journal of Diseases of Children, 136*, 682–686.

Bristol, M. M. (1987). Mothers of children with autism or communication disorders: Successful adaptation and the double ABCX model. *Journal of Autism and Developmental Disorders, 17*(4), 469–486.

*Bristol, M. M., Gallagher, J. J., & Schopler, E. (1988). Mothers and fathers of young developmentally disabled and nondisabled boys: Adaptation and spousal support. *Developmental Psychology, 24*(3), 441–451.

*Cameron, S. J., Dobson, L. A., & Day, D. M. (1991, March). Stress in parents of developmentally delayed and nondelayed preschool children. *Canada's Mental Health*, 13–17.

Cohen, J. (1977). *Statistical power analysis for the behavioral sciences*. New York: Academic Press.

Cooper, H. (1989). *Integrating research: A guide for literature reviews*. Newbury Park, CA: Sage.

Cummings, S. T., Bayley, H. C., & Rie, H. E. (1966). Effects of the child's deficiency on the mother: A study of mentally retarded, chronically ill, and neurotic children. *American Journal of Orthopsychiatry*, *36*, 395–408.

Dohrenwend, B., Shrout, P., Egri, G., & Medelson, F. (1980). Nonspecific psychological distress and other dimensions of psychopathology. *Archives of General Psychiatry*, *37*, 1129–1238.

Downey, G., & Coyne, J. C. (1990). Children of depressed parents: An integrative review. *Psychological Bulletin*, *108*(1), 50–76.

*Dumas, J. E., Wolf, L. C., Fisman, S. N., & Culligan, A. (1991). Parenting stress, child behavior problems, and dysphoria in parents of children with autism, down syndrome, behavior disorders, and normal development. *Exceptionality*, *2*, 97–100.

Eaton, W. W., & Kessler, L. G. (1981). Rates of depression in a national sample. *American Journal of Epidemiology*, *114*, 528–538.

Gallagher, D., Breckenridge, J., Steinmetz, J., & Thompson, L. (1983). The Beck depression inventory and research diagnostic criteria: Congruence in an older population. *Journal of Consulting and Clinical Psychology*, *51*, 945–946.

Gath, A. (1977). The impact of an abnormal child upon the parents. *British Journal of Psychiatry*, *130*, 405–410.

*Gowen, J. W., Johnson-Martin, N., Goldman, B. D., & Appelbaum, M. (1989). Feelings of depression and parenting competence of mothers of handicapped and nonhandicapped infants: A longitudinal study. *American Journal on Mental Retardation*, *94*(3), 259–271.

*Guess, P. (1996). *Parental perceptions of stress and coping: Families of preschoolers with and without disabilities*. Unpublished dissertation. Knoxville, TN: University of Tennessee at Knoxville.

Hays, R. D., Wells, K. B., Sherbourne, C., Rogers, W., & Spritzer, K. (1995). Functioning and well-being outcomes of patients with depression compared with chronic general medical illnesses. *Archives of General Psychiatry*, *52*, 11–19.

*Harris, V. S., & McHale, S. M. (1989). Family life problems, daily caregiving activities, and the psychological well-being of mothers of mentally retarded children. *American Journal on Mental Retardation*, *94*(3), 231–239.

Hedges, L. V., & Olkin, I. (1985). *Statistical methods for meta-analysis*. New York: Academic Press.

Helzer, J. E., Robin, L. N., McEvoy, L. T., Spitznagel, E. L., Stoltzman, R. K., Farmer, A., & Brockington, I. R. (1985). A comparison of clinical and diagnostic interview schedule diagnoses. *Archives of General Psychiatry*, *42*, 657–666.

Hodapp, R. M., & Krasner, D. V. (1995). Families of children with disabilities: Findings From a national sample of eighth-grade students. *Exceptionality*, *5*(2), 71–81.

*Kazak, A. E. (1987). Families with disabled children: Stress and social networks in three samples. *Journal of Abnormal Child Psychology*, *15*(1), 137–146.

*Kazak, A. E., & Marvin, R. S. (1984). Differences, difficulties and adaptation: Stress and social networks in families with a handicapped child. *Family Relations: Journal of Applied Family and Child Studies*, *33*(1), 67–77.

Kessler, R. C., McGonagle, K. A., Zhao, S., Nelson, C. B., Hughes, M., Eshleman, S., Wittchen, H., & Kendler, K. S. (1994). Lifetime and 12-month prevalence of DSM-III-R psychiatric disorders in the United States: Results from the national comorbidity study. *Archives of General Psychiatry*, *51*, 8–16.

Klerman, G. L. (1989). Depressive disorders: Further evidence for increased medical morbidity and impairment of social functioning. *Archives of General Psychiatry, 46*, 856–858.

Langer, T. S. (1962). A twenty-two item screening score of psychiatric symptoms indicating impairment. *Journal of Health and Social Behavior, 3*, 269–276.

*Miller, A. C., Gordon, R. M., Daniele, R. J., & Diller, L. (1992). Stress, appraisal, and coping in mothers of disabled and nondisabled children. *Journal of Pediatric Psychology, 17*(5), 587–605.

Myers, J. K., Lindenthal, J., & Pepper, M. (1974). Social class, life events, and psychiatric symptoms: A longitudinal study. In: B. S. Dohrenwend & B. P. Dohrenwend (Eds), *Stressful Life Events: Their Nature and Effects* (pp. 191–205). New York: Wiley.

Nietzel, M. T., Russel, R. L., Hemmings, K. A., & Getter, M. L. (1987). Clinical significance for unipolar depression: A meta analytic approach to social comparison. *Journal of Consulting and Clinical Psychology, 55*(2), 156–161.

Olshansky, S. (1962). Chronic sorrow: A response to having a mentally defective child. *Social Work, 43*, 190–193.

Orr, R. R., Cameron, S. J., & Day, D. M. (1991). Coping with stress in families with children who have mental retardation: An evaluation of the ABCX model. *American Journal on Mental Retardation, 95*(4), 444–450.

Radloff, L. (1977). The CES-D scale: A self-report depression scale for research in the general population. *Applied Psychological Measurement, 1*, 385–401.

*Roach, M. A., Orsmond, G. I., & Barratt, M. S. (1999). Mothers and fathers of children with down syndrome: Parental stress and involvement in child care. *American Journal on Mental Retardation, 104*(5), 422–436.

Seiler, L. H. (1973). The 22-item scale used in field studies of mental illness: A question of substance, and a question of theory. *Journal of Health and Social Behavior, 14*, 252–263.

*Selzer, M. M., Greenberg, J. S., Floyd, F., Pettee, Y., & Hong, J. (1998). Life course implications of parenting a child with a disability. Paper presented at the 51st Annual Scientific Meeting of the Gerontological Society of America. Philadelphia, PA.

Shaw, B. R., Vallis, T. M., & McCabe, S. B. (1985). The assessment of the severity and symptom patterns in depression. In: E. E. Beckham & W. R. Leber (Eds), *Handbook of Depression: Treatment, Assessment, and Research* (pp. 372–407). Homewood, IL: Dorsey Press.

Simeonson, R. J., & Bailey, D. B. (1986). Siblings of handicapped children. In: J. J. Gallagher & P. M. Vietze (Eds), *Families of Handicapped Persons* (pp. 67–77). Baltimore: Paul H. Brookes Publishers.

Singer, G. H. S., & Irvin, L. K. (1991). Supporting families of persons with disabilities: Emerging findings, practices, and questions. In: L. H. Meyer, C. A. Peck & L. Brown (Eds), *Critical Issues in the Lives of People with Severe Disabilities* (pp. 271–312). Baltimore: Paul H. Brookes Publishing.

Smith, T. B., Oliver, M. N. I., & Innocenti, M. S. (2001). Parenting stress in families of children with disabilities. *American Journal of Orthopsychiatry, 71*(2), 257–261.

Turnbull, A. P., Blue-Banning, M., Behr, S., & Kerns, G. (1986). Family research and intervention: A value and ethical examination. In: P. R. Dokecki & R. M. Zaner (Eds), *Ethics of Dealing with Persons with Severe Handicaps* (pp. 119–140). Baltimore: Paul H. Brookes Publishing.

*Walker, L. S., Ortiz-Valdes, J. A., & Newbrough, J. R. (1989). The role of maternal employment and depression in the psychological adjustment of chronically ill, mentally retarded, and well children. *Journal of Pediatric Psychology, 4*(3), 357–370.

Wheaton, B. (1980). The sociogenesis of psychological disorder: An attributional theory. *Journal of Health and Social Behavior, 21*, 100–124.

Wikler, L., Wasow, M., & Hatfield, E. (1981). Chronic sorrow revisited: Parent vs. professional depiction of the adjustment of parents of mentally retarded children. *American Journal of Orthopsychiatry, 51*(1), 63–70.

*Wolf, L. C., Noh, S., Fisman, S. N., & Speechley, M. (1989). Brief report: Psychological effects of parenting stress on parents of autistic children. *Journal of Austin and Developmental Disorders, 19*(1), 157–166.

10. TEACHER-OBSERVED BEHAVIORS OF POST-TRAUMATIC STRESS SYMPTOMS OF STUDENTS IN GENERAL, GIFTED, AND SPECIAL EDUCATION

Bettie Posey Bullard[*] and Donna Power Rogers[**]

Stress, disaster, and trauma are all a part of life. Seldom, however, has an entire nation been so shocked and traumatized as on September 11, 2001. According to the Council for Exceptional Children (CEC), most students recover from experiencing a disaster within a few days to a few weeks. However, "for some, the aftershock of a tragedy may last for years," (CEC, 2002, para 1). Petersen and Straub (1992) (as cited in Obiakor et al., 1997), emphasize that it is important for educators to recognize the symptoms of post-traumatic stress disorder (PTSD) and become aware of interventions that may assist an individual to overcome this disorder (CEC, 2002, para 1). Concern about the impact of September 11 on students prompted this study.

---

[*] Bettie Posey Bullard, Ph.D., is Assistant Professor and Director of the Gifted Program, at the University of South Alabama.
[**] Donna Power Rogers, Ed.D., is Undergraduate Program Coordinator at the University of South Alabama.

Administering Special Education: In Pursuit of Dignity and Autonomy
Advances in Educational Administration, Volume 7, 223–237
Copyright © 2004 by Elsevier Ltd.
All rights of reproduction in any form reserved
ISSN: 1479-3660/doi:10.1016/S1479-3660(04)07010-6

Daniel DeNoon, expert on terror, suggests that America should prepare for a mental-health crisis (2001, para 1). He predicts that witnessing a life-threatening event will trigger the need in millions of American for help with PTSD. "Seventeen percent of the U.S. population outside of New York City reported symptoms of September 11-related post-traumatic stress 2 months after the attacks" (Silver et al., p. 1235). Even before September 11, 2001, according to the National Institute of Mental Health (NIMH), there was a large increase in persons affected by PTSD. "The number of Americans treated for depression [one of the characteristics of PTSD] soared from 1.7 million to 6.3 million between 1987 and 1997" (NIMH, para 7). Yet, there are no clear plans for screening, identifying and treating people who need help (DeNoon, 2001). A structure to screen, identify, and treat children on a large scale does not exist.

PTSD is diagnosed when a significant stressor leads to symptoms in each of three categories. The American Psychiatric Association (APA) explains that these categories include: (1) re-experiencing the trauma – which may be implied from observation of children who repeatedly act out trauma-related themes in play; (2) suppression or attempts to avoid reminders of the trauma (general numbing of emotions); and (3) increased arousal, defined as effects exhibited in behaviors that are recognizable, such as increased irritability and sleep disturbance (APA, 1994). To make a PTSD diagnosis, there must be a specified number of symptoms in each of these categories that last for at least a month and interfere with everyday functioning. These behaviors may vary according to the age of the child. "Very young children may become clingy, cry often, or regress in some of their behaviors. . . . Older children may withdraw, act out or become irritable. Schoolwork may suffer as well. Adolescents may respond by experiencing nightmares, using alcohol or drugs or arguing with peers" (McPherson, 2002, p. 4).

Other common characteristics include unwarranted fears, anxiety, sleep disorders, and increased physical complaints. Because fear has assumed a greater role in the lives of many Americans, worry about our personal safety or our loved ones and anxiety about unknown dangers have changed our lives. "Our children know it. They sense the concern, the anxiety" (McPherson, 2002, p. 4).

When anxiety and fear are present, children may engage in behaviors that are not usual for them. "Tens of thousands of New York City schoolchildren were suffering from depression, severe anxiety, and other mental-health disorders six months after the September 11 terrorist attack on the World Trade Center," according to Bowman (2002, p. 3). The large study, evaluating approximately 8,300 students (grades 4–12) in the 1.1 million-student New York City district six months after the disaster, estimates that 10.5% of those students, or 75,000 youngsters, suffered identifiable symptoms of post-traumatic stress disorder after the attack. Researchers projected that more than "60,000 students are estimated to have suffered from serious depression, nearly 74,000 from anxiety, and 107,000 from agoraphobia, the fear of being in or near public places" (Bowman, p. 3).

Another national study included parents' observations of their children's behaviors following September 11. Gill et al. (2002) concluded that "the effect of the terrorist attacks on children seems to be negligible" (13); however, their study indicated that of Americans with children, 9% indicated their children had an increase in headaches or stomach aches, 5% indicated their children had an increase in emotional problems, 6% indicated their children had an increase in behavioral problems, and 15% indicated their children had more difficulty sleeping since the attacks. When those numbers are projected to actual children, it does, however, seem highly significant.

After disasters, children frequently have shown symptoms associated with PTSD even if they did not live near the area of impact. Neither distance nor personal experience can predict the degree of response (Silver et al., 2002). For example, "Two years after the Oklahoma City bombing, 16% of children 100 miles away reported significant post-traumatic stress symptoms related to it" (North, 2001, para 5). If the trauma involves severe life threat, up to 25 or 30% may meet criteria for PTSD.

Studies indicate that at least one in 10 people exposed to a traumatic event will develop PTSD. Severe exposure may cause symptoms to persist for more than a year. It is important to note that persons with chronic PTSD have unusually high rates of associated psychiatric disorders throughout life. Those problems include substance abuse and dependence (23%), major depression (20%), alcohol dependence (75%), and personality disorder (20%). Other documented problems include panic, agoraphobia, generalized anxiety disorder, social phobia and bipolar disorder (Khouzam & Donnelly, 2001). Identification and treatment of PTSD may help prevent more serious problems. The positive factor is that even the limited available information suggests that most children, even those affected severely, with intervention, eventually show good recovery (Vogel & Koplewicz, 1995).

Researchers agree that therapeutic intervention is needed to promote that recovery through normalization, mastery, and integration of trauma (Steele & Raider, 1991). Active treatment may help prevent an otherwise high risk of chronic PTSD and ensuing problems. If teachers are aware of the PTSD symptoms and make a conscious effort to take steps to plan and implement interventions for children who have difficulty coping with the trauma of life events, problems in later life may be averted.

Research related to young children and trauma is scanty. Kindergartners, 2nd, 3rd, and 5th graders in New York City on class trips witnessed the first World Trade Center Bombing. They were evaluated three and nine months after the disaster. Almost a year later, many of these children were still showing a moderate level of

PTSD symptoms. They expressed: (1) fears related to the disaster; (2) difficulty in getting to sleep, nightmares, or not wanting to sleep alone; and (3) behavior such as clinging to a parent or adult, indicating separation anxiety (Vogel & Koplewicz, 1995).

From the literature review, it is clear that research conducted in this field to date has been focused on general education students, the broader population. No research on the symptoms of PTSD has been reported on specific populations in gifted and special education.

The approach of the researchers in this study was to view the data from a more specific frame of reference, to determine if there were differences in student behaviors as observed by teachers of general, gifted and special education classes one month and seven months following a national disaster. The following questions were asked: (1) Was there an increase in stress-related behaviors immediately following September 11, 2001? (2) Did stress-related behaviors continue long-term after September 11, 2001, indicating post-traumatic stress disorder (PTSD)? (3) Was there an increase in altruistic behaviors immediately following September 11, 2001? (4) Did altruistic behaviors continue long-term after September 11, 2001? (5) Was there a difference in teacher-observed post-traumatic stress behaviors between gifted and special education populations when compared to the general education population? (6) What coping strategies did teachers use with students following September 11, 2001? (7) What strategies did teachers consider most effective?

PROCEDURE

Methods

Questions about the short- and long-term effects of the trauma of 9/11 on students with special needs and the coping strategies used by their teachers to deal satisfactorily with the effects prompted the creation of a survey to examine these issues. While the survey was in its inception and before its completion, a consultation was held with a counselor from the Behavioral Studies program at the University of South Alabama to ensure that the survey was thorough and relevant to post-traumatic stress.

The survey was constructed to reflect both the positive, altruistic behaviors and the negative, ineffectual behaviors evidenced by students in the 9/11 aftermath. *Positive behaviors* are defined as those behaviors and actions that promote the welfare and well-being of self or others and *negative behaviors* are defined as behaviors and actions that lead to unsatisfactory coping with the demands of daily living. Examples of positive behaviors in this study are the desire to help others, expressions of patriotism, compassion for others and service activities. Examples of negative behaviors are fear for self, fear for family, expressions of helplessness, lack of sleep due to nightmares, and sudden lack of appetite.

The survey consisted of four parts. The first section concerned the demographic characteristics of the respondents, their proximity to a disaster site, and their knowledge of first-hand experience with one of the disasters of 9/11. The second section was designed to record teacher observations of the behaviors and reactions of their students.

Teachers were presented with a list of 34 items describing behaviors that were indicative of both stress-related reactions and reactions that were positive, altruistic and outreaching. Behaviors that might be indicative of initial stress and later post-traumatic stress included such issues as increased fatigue or sleepiness in class, disinterest in activities, increased lack of concentration, a variety of fears, and irritability. Behaviors that demonstrated responses of concern, altruism, and intentions of service to others included such items as increased willingness to share, increased consideration of others, increased expressions of patriotism and compassion. The list of student reactions had the negative, stress-related behaviors and the positive, altruistic behaviors intermingled randomly so that the respondents would not immediately see a pattern to the questioning.

The third section dealt with the teachers' own reactions to the disasters of 9/11, and for purposes of this study, teachers' personal reactions and actions are not included.

The last section examined coping strategies these teachers used to effectively deal with student reaction and any behavior change teachers might have seen in the aftermath of September 11. Techniques suggested in the survey included watching or listening to media news, writing journal entries or essays, suggesting counseling for a student or students, discussing values (especially respect for diversity and tolerance), using drama, role-play or the fine arts, dramatic arts, or music as avenues for expression, and having students do service projects like writing letters of thanks to police and fire fighters.

Participants

The Survey of Student Reactions to the Disasters of September 11, 2001, was distributed to teachers in the Southeast, the Northeast, the Southwest and the Mid-south. The majority of responses came from teachers in the Southeast with small numbers of respondents from the remaining regions. Three hundred and one surveys were returned. Of those 301, thirty-five surveys had responses that were either unclear or missing. They were discarded and the remaining 266 surveys were used to provide the data. The majority of teachers responding ranged in age from 30 to 60 years old; their teaching levels were fairly evenly distributed between primary (K-4) and middle (5–6) elementary grades and junior high (7–8) and senior high (9–12) school. By ethnicity they were predominately European-Americans with African-Americans constituting the second largest group of respondents. All had bachelor's degrees and approximately half the respondents had master's degrees.

RESULTS

The first and second research questions asked whether stress-related behaviors in students showed a significant increase in the short- and long-term. The first question was answered affirmatively for the short-term in all three student populations. Long-term stress-related behaviors remained elevated in the special education and gifted students, but not in the general education students.

Research questions about the emergence of positive, altruistic behaviors were also answered affirmatively. All three groups showed marked increases in altruistic behaviors for both the short-term and the long-term.

In the month following 9/11, the most common positive attributes identified by general, gifted, and special education teachers were increased expressions of patriotism, increased expressions of desires to help others, increased expressions of compassion for others, and more openness in students sharing their feelings with others. The most common negative attributes cited by both general and special education teachers were an increased fear for family, fear for self, excessive startle reactions, and physical complaints. Gifted teachers also noted fear for family and fear for self as behaviors that significantly increased but they did not note a significant increase in startle reactions or physical complaints.

General Education Students

Of the 209 responses from general education teachers that were tallied, the positive behavior most common to this group of students was a definite increase in expressions of patriotism. In the month following the disasters of September 11, 25% of these students showed a marked increase in this behavior. The second most common positive behavioral responses were expressions of increased compassion for others. This attribute was demonstrated by 17% of general education students according to observations by their teachers. Increased patriotism and compassion were followed by two other positive attributes. Fourteen percent expressed increased desires to help others while 13.9% were observed by their teachers to be more open in sharing their feelings.

Within a relatively short period, positive altruistic behaviors seemed to recede. In the seven months between November 2001 and May 2002, increased expressions of patriotism among general education students were reduced from 25 to 19%; increased compassion for others dropped from 17 to 9%. A similar drop occurred in the categories of increased desire to help others and increased openness in sharing feelings. The former changed from a 14% increase to an 8.6% increase while the latter went from a 13.9% increase down to a 6% increase.

A similar pattern was followed in the general education student population for negative, stress-related behavioral attributes. During the first month following the disasters, negative behaviors were considerable higher than the response level demonstrated in the subsequent seven months from November 2001 through April 2002.

The most frequently expressed negative stress-related response was increased fear for family, followed by increased fear for self. The third most common negative behavior was excessive startle reactions and then physical complaints. Nineteen percent of general education students demonstrated heightened fear for family while 15% demonstrated heightened fear for self. Almost 10% (9.6%) exhibited excessive startle reactions and 8% had increased physical complaints. After October 11, 2001, these negative reactions leveled off and only a 6% increase in fear for family, a 6% fear for self, a 5% increase in physical complaints and a 2% increase in excessive startle reactions were exhibited (Tables 1 and 2).

Table 1.   Responses of Students in General Education from September 11 to mid-October, 2001 ($n = 209$).

Behavior	n	%
Negative stress-related behaviors		
Increased fear for family	39	19
Increased fear for self	32	15
Excessive startle reactions	20	9.6
Increased physical complaints	17	8
Positive, altruistic behaviors		
Increased expressions of patriotism	52	25
Increased compassion for others	35	17
Increased desire to help others	30	14
Increased openness in sharing feelings	29	13.0

Note: N = 266.

Table 2.   Responses of Students in General Education from October 2001 to
May 2002 (*n* = 209).

Behavior	*n*	%
Negative stress-related behaviors		
Increased fear for family	13	6
Increased fear for self	13	6
Excessive startle reactions	4	2
Increased physical complaints	10	5
Positive, altruistic behaviors		
Increased expressions of patriotism	39	19
Increased compassion for others	19	9
Increased desire to help others	18	8.6
Increased openness in sharing feelings	13	6

Note: N = 266.

Gifted Education Students

Teachers of gifted education students noted the greatest increase in expressions of patriotism and the desire to help others in the month following the disasters. There was almost a 50% decline in the expressions of patriotism at the seven-month period, but the desire to help others remained significantly high. Other positive behaviors noted by teachers of gifted education students were openness in sharing feelings, consideration for others, compassion for others, tolerance for others, and willingness to share belongings.

Responses from teachers of gifted students showed mostly positive behavior increases among their students. Expressing fear for family, expressing fear for self, and art involving traumatic themes were the only significant negative responses recorded by teachers of gifted students in the first month after September 11. However, while those behaviors diminished in the ensuing six-month period, teachers reported an increase in behaviors indicative of appearing sad or depressed (15% in October 2001 to 40% in May 2002). It is important to note that there was a marked difference in physical complaints between gifted and special education students. In fact, the difference in physical complaints between gifted and special education students showed more marked contrast than any other measurable behavior. Special education teachers noted many more physical complaints than teachers of gifted students.

Special Education Students

Among students with learning disabilities, emotional behavioral disabilities, mental retardation and multiple handicaps, teacher perception of their students'

Table 3. Responses of Students in Special Education from September 11 to mid-October, 2001 (*n* = 42).

Behavior	*n*	%
Negative stress-related behaviors		
Increased fear for family	21	50
Increased fear for self	20	48
Excessive startle reactions	13	31
Increased physical complaints	9	21
Positive, altruistic behaviors		
Increased expressions of patriotism	21	50
Increased compassion for others	18	43
Increased desire to help others	18	43
Increased openness in sharing feelings	12	28.5

Note: N = 266.

reactions to the September 11 tragedies and resulting trauma paralleled the perceptions of the general education teachers concerning the rank order of both positive and negative student behaviors. The same increased expressions of patriotism, compassion for others, desire to help others and openness in sharing feelings were attributed to special education students. The difference seemed to lie in the *degree of response*. A much higher percent of special education students were reported to demonstrate both the positive and the negative attributes than the general education students did. The higher percents included reactions both within the month following 9/11 (September 11 to October 11, 2001) and reactions lasting past the initial month (November 2001 to May 2002) (Table 3).

In the month between September 11 and October 11, 50% of special education students seemed to demonstrate increased expressions of patriotism. During this same month, 43% demonstrated increased compassion for others; 43% demonstrated an increased desire to help others; and 28.5% were identified as being more open in sharing feelings.

In the seven month period following October 11 (November 2001 through May 2002), the degree of intensity of positive behavioral responses decreased as follows: 19% of special education students still showed elevated levels of both increased expressions of patriotism and a desire to help others. Twelve percent still displayed increased compassion for others and openness in sharing feelings (Table 4).

The same negative, stress-related behavioral responses that were characteristic of general education students were also characteristic of special education students. These responses, in rank order, were heightened fear for family, fear for self, excessive startle reactions and increased physical complaints. The negative behavior eliciting the greatest number of responses from students with special

Table 4.   Responses of Students in Special Education from October 2001 to
May 2002 ($n = 209$).

Behavior	n	$\%$
Negative stress-related behaviors		
Increased fear for family	5	9.5
Increased fear for self	6	14
Excessive startle reactions	6	14
Increased physical complaints	6	14
Positive, altruistic behaviors		
Increased expressions of patriotism	8	19
Increased compassion for others	5	12
Increased desire to help others	8	19
Increased openness in sharing feelings	5	12

Note: N = 266.

needs was fear for family with 50% of students identified as showing an increase in this concern during the month between September 11 and October 11. This increase reduced after the first month of the 9/11 aftermath from 50 to 9.5%. The second most commonly perceived increase in negative behaviors according to special education teachers was in the category of fear for self. Forty-eight percent of special education students reportedly showed an increase in this category during the month following 9/11. After the initial month, this response dropped off to only a 14% increase. The third most commonly elevated negative response was an escalation in excessive startle responses; teachers of special education students indicated that 31% of their students demonstrated this reaction in the month following 9/11. This elevated response rate did decline to 14% in the months after October 11. The fourth most commonly elevated negative response was in the category of physical complaints. In the initial month following September 11, 21% of special education students showed an increase in physical complaints; in the months after October 11, 2001, this negative response declined from 21 to 14%.

Coping Strategies Used by Teachers to Deal With the 9/11 Tragedies

All teachers, whether in general, gifted, or special education, had the same list of twenty-six items of coping strategies to respond to in the survey. Among these strategies were the use of discussions led by the teacher, discussions among students themselves, role-playing and drama, use of visual arts or music to express feelings, watching or listening to news, journaling or writing essays about the disasters of September 11, recommending counseling for individual students, encouraging expressions of patriotism, distracting students by changing the subject or showing movies, and using silence or meditation while reflecting.

Responses among the 209 general education teachers and the 42 special education teachers who answered the survey indicate that strategies they used to work through any trauma initiated by September 11 were direct and open and engaged their students in activities that had a positive and, often, action-oriented direction. Few teachers tried to distract students by changing the topic when the issue of September 11 was raised. Few teachers indicated the need to recommend counseling for a student or students. Relatively few teachers seemed to use drama, the visual arts or music as media for expressing concern, grief and/or trauma about September 11. These findings are true for both general education and special education teachers. Similarly the strategies that general education teachers felt were effective or highly effective were, most often, the same strategies used by special education teachers.

Among general education teachers, the strategy most commonly employed was a discussion of values (which included tolerance and respect of others). This was followed in frequency by: (1) encouraging student discussions of the tragedies; (2) encouraging expressions of patriotism; (3) generalized class discussions of September 11; and (4) encouraging service projects (sending letters of thanks to fire fighters and police).

Table 5. A Comparison of Strategies Deemed Effective by General Education Teachers and Special Education Teachers ($n = 251$).

Strategy	n	$\%$
General education teachers ($n = 209$)		
Increased explicit discussion of values	73	35
Encouraged student-led discussions	58	28
Encouraged expressions of patriotism	55	26
Teacher-led discussions of 9/11	53	25
Encouraged service projects	40	19
Watched media news in class	40	10
Special Education teachers ($n = 42$)		
Increased explicit discussion of values	18	43
Encouraged student-led discussions	14	33.3
Encouraged expressions of patriotism	21	50
Teacher-led discussions of 9/11	20	48
Encouraged service projects	10	24
Watched media news in class	11	26

Special education teachers also used these same five strategies as the preferred choices of working through the trauma, but they had somewhat different emphases. Rather than discussions of values as the most frequently used strategy, increased encouragement of expressions of patriotism was the strategy of choice by 50% of special education teachers responding. This was followed by generalized class discussions of September 11, then discussions of values *per se*, the encouragement of student discussions, watching and listening to media news, and then the encouragement of service projects.

Unlike teachers of the other groups, teachers of gifted students deemed the discussion of values, including tolerance and respect, as the most effective strategy. That technique was followed by class discussions about the tragedy, watching the news on television during class, and the incorporation of visual art in instruction. The grade level taught, not addressed in this study, would probably be a factor in determining strategy choice and effectiveness (Table 5).

CONCLUSIONS

The first research question addressed whether there were differences in teacher-observed post-traumatic stress behaviors between general and special education populations when compared to the general education population. The researchers found no differences in teacher-observed behaviors of patriotism and desire to help others between gifted and special education populations when compared to the general education population in the month immediately following 9/11. There were marked increases in all three populations.

In the longterm, altruistic behaviors in the general and special education students declined, whereas they remained elevated for gifted education students. Although the rate of change was significant for general, gifted, and special education student behaviors, reports of gifted behaviors fell within a much narrower range. It is important to note that the difference in physical complaints between general, gifted, and special education students was shown to be significant in both short- and longterm observations. Moreover, there was no report of excessive startle reaction or physical complaints of gifted students.

Teacher observations of both positive, altruistic behaviors and negative, stress-related behaviors indicate that special education students showed a greater escalation in these behaviors than their general education counterparts. Positive, altruistic behaviors are reported to have increased substantially in special education students in the month following 9/11 with almost half this population showing increases in patriotic expressions, compassionate overtures, and openness in expressing feelings. This reaction remained elevated, by comparison to reactions among general education students, for the seven months following October 2001. When the results of negative stress-related behaviors (fears, startle reactions and increased physical ailments) among general education students and special education students are compared, special education students showed a considerably higher number exhibiting these effects in *both* the short-term (the one month following 9/11) and the long-term (from October 2001 to May 2002).

One positive response, the expression of patriotism, stayed relatively elevated in both the general education and the special education populations at a 19% increase in the seven-month period after October 2001.

Negative behavioral responses should be "red flags" and teachers need to be aware that some symptoms of post-traumatic stress disorder are evidenced in some students in the long-term. Teachers should be careful not to confuse the symptoms of post-traumatic stress disorder with behavioral problems that arise with a degree of frequency in most classrooms. However, teachers should remain cognizant of PTSD symptoms and should continue to interact in a positive manner with students who still exhibit negative behavioral responses and refer students whose behavior may indicate a need for counseling.

Teachers of students in special education should be particularly sensitive to elevated responses to trauma and should continue to use coping strategies and techniques that are indicated to be effective in mitigating the aftermath of trauma. Leading students in discussions was the technique noted by the 209 general education teachers and the 42 special education teachers as being highly effective. The most effective discussions seemed to be teacher-led and dealt with the values of tolerance, respect, forgiveness, and understanding. Projects and actions that expressed patriotism and personal expressions of thanks and appreciation to public safety personnel were noted as highly effective by teacher respondents.

Overall, the data from this study shows that teacher-observed behaviors, both positive and negative, of general, gifted, and special education students increased following a national trauma. Some effects continued to be significant at seven months following the impact. Behaviors indicating stress, while declining over time, still remained elevated.

With the present unstable world situation, it may be judicious to develop a database that may help identify children at risk for subsequent difficulties. Teachers have a unique opportunity to identify potential problems and initiate help in early stages.

> The differing responses and the way students may mask them, most experts say, put teachers, principals, and school psychologists on the front lines to ensure that students are screened for psychological disorders, that they receive professional help if needed, and that they begin to heal from events that otherwise could leave lifelong scars (Hoff, 2002, p. 1).

IMPLICATIONS FOR FURTHER STUDY

The issue of proximity to a disaster site was not addressed in this study. The question of the degree of impact on students the nearer they are to the center of a disaster remains (i.e. Do students, general education and special education alike, in the New York City and the Washington, DC areas have a higher degree of continued negative and positive behavioral response to the disasters of 9/11 than do students in other parts of the country?).

Studies to determine if there are gender and age differences in the response to trauma and similar studies conducted in other countries to compare behavior patterns to identify and prevent PTSD may yield valuable information. Outcomes will help professionals who work with children or adolescents who have experienced trauma.

Research may be useful for extended traumatic events – violence, medical trauma, death of a family member, and national or man-caused catastrophic events.

ACKNOWLEDGMENTS

The authors acknowledge the contributions of Drs. Marilyn Shank, Irene McIntosh, William Gilley and Satya Mishra.

REFERENCES

American Psychiatric Association (1994). *Diagnostic and statistical manual of mental disorders* (4th ed.). Washington, DC: Author.

Bowman, D. H. (2002, May 8). N.Y.C. students suffer post-Sept. 11 trauma, study finds. *Education Week, 21*(34), 3–8.

Council for Exceptional Children (2002, January 1). What are the signs of chronic fear? Retrieved from http://www.cec.sped.org/bk/cectoday/january_2002/cectoday_01_2002_09.html.

DeNoon, D. (2001). Should America prepare for a mental health crisis? Expert says terror strikes will cause millions to need help with PTSD. Retrieved October 14, 2001 from http://www.content.health.msn.com/printing/article/1728.90613.

Gill, D. A., Paresi, D., Cosby, A. G., & Frese, W. (2002). Societal impacts of the September 11th terrorist attacks: General findings from a national survey. Paper presented at the 2002 annual meeting of the Alabama-Mississippi Sociological Association, Delta State University, Cleveland, MS.

Hoff, D. J. (2002, September 11). A year later, impact of 9/11 lingers. *Education Week, 22*(2), 1–3.

Khouzam, H., & Donnelly, N. (2001). Post-traumatic stress disorder. *Postgraduate Medicine, 110*(5), 97–98.

McPherson, R. W. (2002). How do kids cope? *Memorial Behavioral Health*. Memorial Hospital.

National Institute of Mental Health (2001, September 22*). Helping children and adolescents cope with violence and disaster*. Retrieved January 10, 2002 from www.nimh.nih.gov/publicat/depression.cfm.

North, C. (2001). *Psychological trauma caused by terrorism: Statement of Carol S. North, M.D., Professor of Psychiatry, Washington University School of Medicine Senate Committee on Health, Education, Labor and Pensions*. Retrieved February 1, 2002 from EBSCO database.

Obiakor, F., Mehring, T., & Schwenn, J. (1997). *Disruption, disaster, and death: Helping students deal with crises*. Reston, VA: Council for Exceptional Children.

Silver, R. C., Holman, E. A., McIntosh, D. N., Pulin, M., & Gil-Rivas, V. (2002, September 11). Nationwide longitudinal study of psychological responses to September 11. *JAMA, 288*(10), 1235–1244.

Steele, W., & Raider, M. (1991). *Working with families in crisis*. New York: Guilford Press.

Vogel, J., & Koplewicz, H. (1995). Trade Center bombing holds lessons for aftermath of Oklahoma tragedy. *Brown University Child & Adolescent Behavior Letter, 11*(6), 1–2.

11. PREPARING INCLUSIVE SPECIAL EDUCATORS: POLICY IMPLICATIONS FOR PARTNERSHIPS AMONG PUBLIC SCHOOLS, COLLEGES, AND UNIVERSITIES

Moira A. Fallon[*]

INTRODUCTION

Among the critical issues facing special education today is the lack of highly qualified and well trained professionals who are capable of working with the increasing numbers of students with diverse needs referred for special education supports and services. In both the popular media and the research literature, experts are attempting to delineate the numbers of schools and programs without trained, certified special educators and are attempting to predict how many more special educators will be needed in the next three to five years to come (Boe et al., 1998; Garnes et al., 2002; Goodnough, 2003; Hammond, 2003). Suffice to say, the field of special education is facing a critical shortage of teachers. There are three general goals to be achieved. As a field, we have been challenged to find high quality

*Moira A. Fallon is Associate Professor at State University of New York, College at Brockport, New York.

Administering Special Education: In Pursuit of Dignity and Autonomy
Advances in Educational Administration, Volume 7, 239–248
Copyright © 2004 by Elsevier Ltd.
All rights of reproduction in any form reserved
ISSN: 1479-3660/doi:10.1016/S1479-3660(04)07011-8

potential special educators from a variety of backgrounds and experiences. We need special educators equipped with more effective teaching strategies for a very diverse student population. We are engaged in an international pursuit to retain and improve the teacher efficacy and quality in inclusive settings given a changing educational policy context.

Developing appropriate policies that drive these three general goals is critical in implementing change and improving outcomes for all learners (Roach et al., 2002). The key to providing quality supports and services to all students with disabilities lies within collaboration. Public schools, colleges, and universities must equitably share the responsibility for recruiting, training, mentoring, and recognizing inclusive educators with the ultimate goal of increasing our pool of highly qualified teachers (Darling-Hammond & Young, 2002; Greenwood & Abbott, 2001). Interagency collaborations such as those needed to effect desired changes in policy are multidimensional and interactive in nature in order to be successful. The authors of one study on successful collaboration (Johnson et al., 2003) state that critical actions can be undertaken by committed stakeholders and can contribute to long lasting policy changes and redirections. This is unequivocally where the field of special education needs to begin.

The purpose of this chapter, therefore, is to broadly synthesize the research literature on the preparation of inclusive educators. Second is to outline the policy implications for decision making that can be a catalyst for improving quality supports and services provided world wide to students with disabilities and their families. Policy implications will be made in three general areas: recruiting and retaining inclusive educators who are new to education, those who are currently in education and wish to add special education certification, and mentoring and recognizing high professional quality and performance. The decisions facing us must be made utilizing the cooperative efforts of all critical stakeholders; K-12 public schools, colleges, and universities to improve the training preparation of inclusive educators to have success with students with disabilities and their families.

ALTERNATIVES TO TRADITIONAL TRAINING PROGRAMS

We are seeking answers in the literature that will help us to screen, select, and train, prospective inclusive educators quickly and efficiently. Darling-Hammond and Young (2002) have stated that colleges of educations have historically had an important impact on the preparation of teachers. Other studies (Rosenberg & Sindelar, 2001; Tillema & Verberg, 2002) have analyzed alternative paths to certification or licensing of new professionals as possible alternatives to traditional program in order to more quickly meet the needs of schools and districts. The implication for policy development may be in moving from the way teacher education programs have traditionally been developed towards more learner centered and needs based programs for prospective inclusive educators.

What are the characteristics of a high quality inclusive education program developed with a learning centered viewpoint and what contributions might such programs make in the preparation of new inclusive educators? Some researchers (Haworth & Conrad, 1996) state that all the stakeholders for such programs are invested in enriching learning experiences with diverse and engaged participants, participatory cultures, interactive teaching and learning, connected program requirements, and adequate resources. Such investments and connections may help new inclusive educators to better link their own dreams and goals for entering the profession to standards for high quality teaching in highly demanding inclusive environments.

The selection process for entering teaching programs in the United States has largely been dominated by the use of national, standardized scores, such as Scholastic Achievement Test (SAT), or Graduate Review Exam (GRE), and the computation of a grade point average (GPA). Some recent reports, including those by the Educational Testing Service (ETS), have emphasized the need for variables other than the traditional, standardized testing scores and grade point averages (Hagedorn & Nora, 1996) that should be used in the selection and recruitment of potential inclusive educators. These researchers, and others (Fallon et al., 2001; Morrison & Morrison, 1995), have suggested that women, minorities, and persons who are of a differing socioeconomic status may experience bias in the testing and grade computations. In order to diversify our populations of inclusive educators, we need to reach out for more inclusive entrance practices, not continue to bar the way for so many. The addition of new policies and practices for admission requirements along with or in place of the more traditional approach to selection could develop a group interview process (Brouwer et al., 2003), on demand or videotaped demonstration of teaching skills (Tillema & Verberg, 2002), documentation of a previous successful experience with children (Fallon et al., 2001), and the careful, thoughtful evaluation of a written goal statement or essay (Fallon et al., 2001).

Colleges and universities must develop "fast track" programs that, once selected, can train the best potential candidates for inclusive education, support them appropriately within public schools, and mentor these candidates in the first year placements and job experiences (Fallon et al., 2001). One example of such a "fast track" program is a Master of Arts in Teaching program with a specialized emphasis in inclusive education. In general, programs of this type may provide certification for persons who did not receive certification or who majored in general education at the undergraduate level. The result is a program with a single focus;

providing intense immersion in courses and internships centered on certification requirements, exiting graduates within a one- to two-year time span. Such programs could also place interns in public schools that have current, critical needs for inclusive educators, meeting a district need and a training need for new inclusive educators at the same time. However, caution must be taken in "fast track" programs not to simply move candidates quickly along in the process, while sacrificing quality of training. Such programs must carefully plan to evaluate candidates at the entrance, ongoing, and exit levels of the program to ensure they are "on track" with teaching standards, not merely surviving (Fallon et al., 1997).

UNIFIED PROFESSIONAL DEVELOPMENT SYSTEM

Only well trained and highly qualified teachers should work with students whose educational promise is at risk. Addressing the critical shortages of inclusive educators with attention only to new, incoming teachers is insufficient. Improving the quality of professional development for on the job inclusive educators currently in the field is a critical necessity (Boe et al., 1998). Unfortunately, many students with disabilities have teachers without any certification at all or who are teaching on emergency or otherwise limited certification in special education (Boe et al., 1998). The No Child Left Behind Act requires all teachers to be highly qualified by 2006; a deadline some school districts say they will miss (Garnes et al., 2002; Hammond, 2003). How can we measure the value of such a high quality program that is critically needed for training inclusive educators? Some researchers (Bennett, 2001) believe that measuring quality comes by looking at the outcomes of the graduates of these programs; that is, a focus on how they perform in the field of inclusive education across time.

How can colleges and universities share with K-12 schools the status of their inclusive educators as they exit a college program and enter the workplace? A possible strategy for measuring valued outcomes of exiting inclusive educators is to evaluate self reports of the participants and their engagement in the process of initial learning to the inclusive environment (Bennett, 2001). One example of such an evaluation is the National Survey of Student Engagement (NSSE) that was developed with support from the Pew Charitable Trusts and the Carnegie Foundation for the Advancement of Teachers (Bennett, 2001). This instrument asks the participants in college programs to report what they actually do while in classes and provide evidence on the extent to which they are engaged in their classes. The premise of this instrument is that the evidence provided in the self report supports long lasting change in professional behaviors and skills of the participants.

Many exiting inclusive educators have beginning professional development plans in which they map out their professional development activities (Fallon & Brown, 2002) for the first one to three years in the workplace. In a recent study, teachers who graduated from teacher education programs in Kentucky found 80% of whom felt well prepared to teach in today's diverse classrooms (Kentucky Institute for Educational Research, 1997) and who, one assumes, have plans to continue their growth. School districts could take this information and use it to plan ongoing professional development opportunities that build upon the current skills of the inclusive educators they hire to actually continue the individual growth of the professional from exit of program through the first three years of teaching. Such an evaluation system would require the joint cooperation of colleges and universities and the school districts.

Teachers of general education must be trained in special education methodology that goes beyond a simple introductory course in special education. Inclusive educators must be trained and must recognize the methods of the general educator. Both are specialists in differing ways. Working together also requires the working out of differences in philosophy, style, and culture that permeate the current general classroom and prevent the development of a truly inclusive classroom in both culture and philosophy.

Therefore, another promising possibility is a study that (Stayton & McCollum, 2002) suggests the unification of the ongoing system of professional development for general and special educators currently working in classrooms from a separate to dual system of integrated professional training for inclusive educators. Roach et al. (2002) strongly suggest that prior to changing policy, a framework based on a clearly articulated philosophy or set of values is in place while undertaking such an evaluation or unification of professional development systems. Their project, The Consortium of Inclusive Schooling Practices (CISP), identifies a comprehensive system of professional training in addressing the needs of all learners as one inclusive policy objective.

The professional development opportunities themselves must evolve beyond a top down transmission of knowledge into professional practices that produce lasting change (Greenwood & Abbott, 2001). Specialized training for teachers working in inclusive settings must include a combination of interdisciplinary coursework, standards based, competency seminars and observations, and interdisciplinary internships or practicum settings in inclusive environments (Able-Boone et al., 2002). However, we must also carefully develop and review the curricula designed specifically for unified professional development training.

Researchers also clearly believe that certain areas of college education programs lack sufficient levels of knowledge of the services and supports for students with disabilities and their families for the current professional inclusive educators. Some studies (Russo & Fallon, 2001) clearly demonstrate the need for inclusive educators to better utilize family-centered services within community partnerships, especially in families with younger children with disabilities or families that are more vulnerable to stress events and call for more extensive professional development training in these areas. Effective inclusive educators help families explore practical strategies for working with their child and designing individualized services to overcome them. These professional services must support families rather than enable them and require the professionals contribute resources and expertise. Only with continuing professional development that links families and inclusive educators together can the relationship be truly collaborative and equal (Russo & Fallon, 2001).

Teachers and administrators have a critical need for support to help them understand inclusive educational practices in light of standards-based reform efforts (Roach et al., 2002). As the changing context for policy is developed, self assessment of professional development can be an integral tool for guiding a systemic approach (Russo & Fallon, 2001; Roach et al., 2002). The identification of needs within the larger environment is more likely to produce last change rather than isolated, programmatic changes. State and local partners may provide invaluable technical assistance in identify of needs, structuring communication, and conducting policy audits. Professional performance of all teachers is best determined by repeated measures of teaching performance across time. These repeated measures must clearly evaluate the dispositions, knowledge, and skills of inclusive educators in a meaningful forum. Practices at the district, school, and classroom levels can significantly alter outcomes for students with disabilities. The newly developed policies can bring promised changes and positively affect reform. Conversely, these policies may well increase the requirements for teachers and negatively impact the retention of current inclusive educators.

RECOGNITION OF PROFESSIONAL QUALITY

Of concern to all in the field of special education is the shortened lifetime career spent in the field of special education. Some estimates (Capa et al., 2002; Garnes et al., 2002) suggest that, on average, teachers stay in special education from three to five years, either transferring to other settings or leaving teaching all together. Clearly, we need to retain our best teachers and support their continued growth and development. Some researchers (Boe et al., 1998; Garnes et al., 2002) have studied the reasons why inclusive educators leave the profession at such a high rate and attribute exit attrition to stress, excess paperwork, ability to negotiate better salaries, among other reasons. Clearly the field of special education has to be made more attractive to teachers in the long term and support quality teaching.

One study (Whitaker, 2003) found four generally unmet needs for teachers; the need for learning special education policy, procedures, and paperwork, the need for emotional support, the need for learning system information related to the school, and the need for knowledge of resources and materials to support learning. This researcher concluded that without such general, basic needs being met, beginning inclusive educators will have less satisfaction, more stress, and increase the likelihood of prematurely leaving the field or transferring to general education. Recognizing and building leadership among high quality master teachers as mentors fulfills a dual need to support new teachers and recognize the quality of long term teachers. However, as programs have increased the ways in which teachers are recognized, no study has examined if recognition of professional quality results in retention of high quality educators in the field.

In our context of shifting policy, necessary changes can be enhanced by bringing master teacher practitioners to decision making sessions. A promising approach has been to build communities of practice (Buysse et al., 2003). The framework of communities of practice is built upon the idea to connect what we know with what we do as teachers and to promote dialogue an inquiry. In a community of practice, shared learning and reflection are the benchmarks among teachers who are at varying levels of skills in their careers. Some researchers (Buysse et al., 2003) have found that professional practice schools can have significant outcomes in promoting a common enterprise that learns from the wisdom of high quality teachers using effective teaching methods and integrates it with the energies of those new to the field that require support.

One example of an attempt to recognize professional quality is the updated State Plan to Enhance Teacher Quality developed in 2003 in the state of New York. In this plan, which is to be implemented in late 2003 and early 2004, excellence in teaching is recognized in a variety of ways. New York has state programs such as the Teacher of the Year, the Mathematics Initiative which recognize math experts across the state, the Reading Initiative which does the same for reading experts, the Better Beginnings Program rewards excellence in teaching at the elementary grade levels, and the New York Academy of Teaching and Learning conducts peer reviews of teaching strategies by professionally qualified teachers. It is hoped that such programs will retain high quality teachers in the field of education.

Many states and districts have implemented teacher mentoring programs specifically to support teachers new to the certification area, but also as a means of recognizing the high quality of long time teachers, some of whom have achieved national certification. Many professional organizations, such as the organization for Science Education for Students with Disabilities has an annual Teacher of the Year Award named after Lawrence Scadden, an exemplary inclusive science educator. This type of an award may come with a monetary recognition, but serves primarily to distinguish exemplary practices.

CONCLUSIONS

The issues of selection, training, retention, and support for inclusive educators are highly complex. Among the stakeholders in resolving these complex and critical issues are public schools, colleges, and universities who must forge joint responsibilities among one another to meet and exceed the training needs of pre-service inclusive educators. Often, these groups blame one another for failing to adequately develop the standards, performance criteria, and professional responsibilities of the new inclusive educator to school, district, state, and national standards. Darling-Hammond and Young (2002) believe we must stay the course in teacher preparation using effective research based methods for selection, training, and support. However, to do so may well involve taking a hard look at current practices and focus on new, promising strategies. We must all work together to build partnerships across these differences in viewpoints and agree to meet the needs of the potential candidates using a framework in which changing policies can be carefully evaluated. Linking change in practice to policy increases the likelihood of lasting and meaningful changes within a shifting context of a cohesive "big picture" for inclusive educators.

ACKNOWLEDGMENTS

I would like to acknowledge the research contributions of Dr. Blaine Ackley for his part in the research on admissions decisions in teacher education, those of Dr. Teresa Russo for her part in the worldwide research on military families with children who are disabled, and Dr. Susan Brown for her part in the research on the preparation of teacher educators for the workplace.

REFERENCES

Able-Boone, H., Harrison, M., & West, T. (2002). Interdisciplinary education of social inclusion facilitators in early childhood settings. *Teacher Education & Special Education*, *25*(4), 407–412.
Bennett, D. (2001, Spring). Assessing quality in higher education. *Liberal Education*, 40–45.

Boe, E., Cook, L., Bobbitt, S., & Teranian, G. (1998). The shortage of fully certified teachers in special and general education. *Teacher Education & Special Education, 21*(1), 1–21.

Brouwer, N., Fallon, M., Sanders, P., & Tillema, H. (2003, April). The right teacher in the right spot. *VELON Conference*. Belgium: Louvain.

Buysse, V., Sparkman, K., & Wesley, P. (2003). Communities of practice: Connecting what we know with what we do. *Exceptional Children, 69*(3), 263–277.

Capa, Y., Loadman, W., & Bryant, B. (2002, April). The current status of teacher shortage in the United States. A Paper presented at the Annual Meeting of the American Educational Research Association. New Orleans, LA.

Darling-Hammond, L., & Young, P. (2002, December). Defining highly qualified teachers: What does scientifically based research actually tell us? *Educational Researcher*, 13–25.

Fallon, M., & Brown, S. (2002). Crossing over from student teaching to the first year of teaching. *Curriculum and Teaching Dialogue, 4*(1), 37–46.

Fallon, M., Carroll, J., & Ackley, B., (2001). Admissions decisions and pre-service teachers' classroom performance. A Paper presented at the Annual Meeting of the Oregon Association of Teacher Educators.

Fallon, M., Hammons, J., Brown, S., & Wann, J. (1997). Continuous assessment plans: A model for implementation. *Journal of Excellence in College Teaching, 8*(2), 21–40.

Garnes, L., Menlove, R., & Adams, E. (2002, March). A qualified special educator for every student: Why this isn't happening and what can be done about it? In: *No Child Left Behind: The Vital Role of Rural Schools*. Annual National Conference Proceedings of the American Council on Rural Schools (RC023423). Reno, NV.

Goodnough, A. (2003, June 18). Regents give city more time to have all teachers certified. *New York Times* (Section B, p. 10).

Greenwood, C., & Abbott, M. (2001). The research to practice gap in special education. *Teacher Education & Special Education, 24*(4), 276–289.

Hagedorn, L., & Nora, A. (1996, Winter). Rethinking admission criteria in graduate and professional programs. *New Directions for Institutional Research, 92*, 31–44.

Hammond, B. (2003, November 26). Oregon considers challenging the No Child Left Behind law. *The Oregonian*, Education News Section. Retrieved from http://www.Oregonlive.com.

Haworth, J., & Conrad, C. (1996, Winter). Refocusing quality assessment on student learning. *New Directions for Institutional Research, 92*, 45–60.

Johnson, L., Zorn, D., Tam, B., Lamontagne, M., & Johnson, S. (2003). Stakeholders' views of factors that impact successful interagency collaboration. *Exceptional Children, 69*(2), 195–209.

Kentucky Institute of Educational Research (1997). *The preparation of teachers for Kentucky schools: A survey of new teachers*. Frankfort, KY: Kentucky Institute of Educational Research.

Morrison, T., & Morrison, M. (1995, April). A meta-analysis of the predictive validity of the quantitative and verbal components of the Graduate Record Exam (GRE) with the graduate grade point average representing the criterion of graduate success. *Educational and Psychological Measurement, 55*, 309–316.

Roach, V., Salisbury, C., & McGregor, G. (2002). Applications of a policy framework to evaluate and promote large-scale change. *Exceptional Children, 68*(4), 451–464.

Rosenberg, M., & Sindelar, P. (2001). The proliferation of alternative routes to certification in special education: A critical review of the literature. Developing the Special Education Workforce Series. National Clearinghouse for Professions in Special Education, Arlington, VA: Council for Exceptional Children.

Russo, T., & Fallon, M. (2001). Helping military families who have a child with a disability cope with stress. *Early Childhood Education Journal, 29*(1), 3–8.

Stayton, V., & McCollum, J. (2002). Unifying general and special education: What does the research tell us? *Teacher Education & Special Education, 25*(3), 211–218.

Tillema, H., & Verberg, C. (2002). Recognizing competence: Evaluation of an alternative teacher licensing assessment program. *Studies in Education Evaluation, 28*, 297–313.

Updated State Plan to Enhance Teacher Quality (2003, December). *The University of the State of New York.* Albany, NY: Department of Education, nclbnys@mail.nysed.gov.

Whitaker, S. (2003). Needs of beginning special education teachers: Implications for Teacher Education. *Teacher Education & Special Education, 26*(2), 106–117.